George Hegeman

The Simple Book

Prentice Hall Series in Innovative Technology

Dennis R. Allison, David J. Farber, and Bruce D. Shriver   *Series Advisors*

Kane   *MIPS RISC Architecture*
Rose   *The Open Book: A Practical Perspective on OSI*
Rose   *The Simple Book: An Introduction to Management of TCP/IP-based internets*
Shapiro   *A C++ Toolkit*
Slater   *Microprocessor-Based Design*
Wirfs-Brock, Wilkerson, and Weiner   *Designing Object-Oriented Software*

The Simple Book

An Introduction to Management of
TCP/IP-based Internets

Marshall T. Rose
Performance Systems International, Inc.

Prentice Hall
Englewood Cliffs, New Jersey 07632

Editorial/production supervision: *Jacqueline A. Jeglinski*
Cover design: *Karen Stephens*
Manufacturing buyer: *Kelly Behr/Susan Brunke*
Cover photo: *Imtek Imagineering/Masterfile*

The publisher offers discounts on this book when ordered
in bulk quantities. For more information, write:

Special Sales/College Marketing
Prentice-Hall, Inc.
College Technical and Reference Division
Englewood Cliffs, New Jersey 07632

Printed in the United States of America
10 9 8 7 6 5 4 3 2

ISBN 0-13-812611-9

For information about our audio products, write us at:
Newbridge Book Clubs, 3000 Cindel Drive, Delran, NJ 08370

Prentice-Hall International (UK) Limited, *London*
Prentice-Hall of Australia Pty. Limited, *Sydney*
Prentice-Hall Canada Inc., *Toronto*
Prentice-Hall Hispanoamericana, S.A., *Mexico*
Prentice-Hall of India Private Limited, *New Delhi*
Prentice-Hall of Japan, Inc., *Tokyo*
Simon & Schuster Asia Pte. Ltd., *Singapore*
Editora Prentice-Hall do Brasil, Ltda., *Rio de Janeiro*

for noSauce

Contents

List of Tables

List of Figures

Foreword

It is a pleasure to say a good word about *The Simple Book* and its remarkable author, Marshall Rose.

The book provides a clear, readable, and sometimes entertaining description of perhaps the most important topic in internetworking today, network management and the Simple Network Management Protocol (SNMP).

The author embodies a single large and brilliant individual probably the two most important philosophies of the Internet community pertaining to standards development: the importance of implementation experience, and the importance of lean design with an absence of extraneous features and mis-features. His role in internet management has been to *marshal* the resources necessary to allow others to produce a workable solution to practical problems of internet management. This text is as simple, elegant, concise and unambiguous as the technology and "oral history" that it describes.

As regards the minimalist approach, Marshall expresses it in specific terms related to network management of internets:

> *The impact of adding network management to managed nodes must be minimal, reflecting a lowest common denominator.*

This philosophy focused Marshall's chairmanship of the SNMP Working Group, which gave the Internet-standard Network Management Framework the fundamental "simple and implementable" flavor that guaranteed its widespread adoption and deployment.

Marshall's colorful writing style makes for an interesting and fun read. He skewers both OSI and Internet camps (and even himself on occasion) whenever due. I don't agree with all of his opinions (which he clearly labels) — I dare say no reader could possibly agree with all of them! — but I do recognize the perspicuity of observation which led to those opinions. As an implementor of both OSI and Internet protocols, he is well-versed in both technologies and (rightfully) has a unique perspective on the strengths and weaknesses of both.

Although he is critical of OSI's efforts in network management, it should be noted that OSI recognized the importance of both global "electropolitics" and "infinite" scalability in the global network architecture. This foreword is not the place to write a treatise on these OSI "philosophies," nor to describe how they should complement — not compete with — the Internet philosophies. This foreword *is* the place to say that Marshall Rose is among the small handful of senior Internet people — and he surely is the youngest in the handful! — who understand the philosophical strengths of both the Internet and OSI protocol suites, and who see the networking "big picture." This picture, which is coming to everyone's neighborhood in the next ten years, describes how the OSI, Internet, and proprietary architectures fit together in the future global-Internet that is now coming about due to the efforts of many good standards people and fine engineers in the global networking community. This book — in fact, Marshall's work as a whole — is a fundamental contribution to the development of that global Internet.

Dick desJardins
Past Chair, ISO Subcommittee 21 on OSI
Interop, Inc.
Mountain View, California

Preface

This book is about network management of internets. In particular, this book focuses on the concepts and mechanisms used to manage networks built with the Internet suite of protocols (commonly known as "TCP/IP").

A *protocol* is simply a set of rules used by computers to communicate with each other, and a *protocol suite* is a group of these protocols all related to a common framework. The Internet suite of protocols, started over a decade ago as a high-risk, high-payoff research project, has magnificently blossomed into a dominant force in the computer-communications industry. This unprecedented success, has lead to the construction of large communications infrastructures, termed *internets*. These are composed of wide and local area networks and consist of *end-systems*, such as hosts, terminal servers, and printers; *intermediate-systems*, such as routers; and, *media devices*, such as bridges, hubs, and multiplexors. As the Internet suite of protocols is the first (and as yet only) success of open (non-proprietary) systems, it should not be surprising that these internets are, by their very nature, heterogeneous, multi-vendor environments.

However, the rapid growth of the number and size of internets has made management of these internets problematic:

- equipment additions and changes often lead to configuration errors;

- increased scale makes former, ad hoc, tools impractical;

- increased heterogeneity makes proprietary tools unusable; and,

- wider range of staff expertise requires more sophisticated tools which are easier to use.

In addition to the need to keep today's networks running, there is also a need for traffic and utilization data, so as to design, plan, and justify new extensions.

This book focuses on the concepts, mechanisms, and policies used to meet these needs. Because network management is such a large topic, it is necessary to focus the problem. Thus, *only* management of internets using the TCP/IP protocol suite is considered. Further, the emphasis is on managing the end-to-end portions of those internets rather than the application or media-specific portions.

This book is about the *Internet-standard Network Management Framework*: it focuses on how management information is structured; the "standard" objects which are currently defined; and, the protocol used to convey management information. In addition, the book attempts to capture a great deal of the "oral tradition" of management in the Internet. In particular, this book identifies and discusses the myriad of details and conventions, which are in common use, but, which for one reason or another, never got written down in the standards.

History of Internet Management

The earlier research of the Internet suite produced stellar work in regards to the end-to-end (data transfer) protocols. Unfortunately, this work did not foresee the impact on management that would occur if use of the protocols became wide-spread. This is understandable considering the focus of the researchers and program managers involved. To further obscure this need, the early networks built using these protocols were connected by gateways from a single vendor. Management of the backbone was the responsibility of this vendor, which developed appropriate, proprietary techniques. Thus, the need for multi-vendor, interoperable management techniques was "quite clearly hidden!"

In the mid-80s, the number of networks connected to the Internet (a large collection of networks, derived from the original ARPANET built by the researchers), began to double in size roughly every year. Further, there were now several organizations with the responsibility for managing parts of the network at the backbone-level, the regional-level, and the campus-level, all using equipment from different vendors, and these organizations were struggling. The early model of network management had to evolve to meet this crisis.

In March, 1987, over a *fine dinner* in Monterey, California, a small group of network gurus, from both research and industry, decided that something had to be done. It turns out that this resulted in three "things" heading towards a common collision.

One effort was started by a group of four engineers. Within two months of the *fine dinner*, they had produced a straight-forward protocol termed the *Simple Gateway Monitoring Protocol* (SGMP). Over the next few months, SGMP was implemented on a few different platforms. By August of that year, SGMP was receiving modest, but ever-increasing use outside of the original development networks.

A second effort had begun some time before the *fine dinner*, as a research project. The work in progress was termed the *High-level Entity Management System* (HEMS). HEMS had some novel concepts, but never saw the light of day outside of its development sites. Although this is an entirely reasonable perspective for ongoing research, this lack of use ultimately led to the demise of HEMS.

The third effort had begun about the same time as the *fine dinner*, in response to network management becoming a "hot" topic in OSI. As OSI network management documents began creeping their way through the international standards process, another group, consisting primarily of professionals from the fringe of the Internet community, proposed using the OSI network management protocol and framework to manage networks based on the Internet suite of protocols. This was termed *CMIP over TCP* (CMOT). (CMIP is the OSI *Common Management Information Protocol*, and TCP is the *Transmission Control Protocol* which provides reliable end-to-end transmission of data in the Internet suite of protocols.)

Throughout the remainder of 1987, there was a lot of controversy concerning the three approaches. In February, 1988, the *Internet Activities Board* (IAB), the body concerned with the technical development of the Internet suite of protocols, convened an *ad hoc* committee of interested parties to resolve the issue.

A Digression

`soap...` Before continuing, it is time to introduce a typographical convention used in this book. The author strives to present a balanced set of perspectives. When discussing technical matters, this is usually straightforward. Unfortunately, a lot of the issues involved are inherently non-technical in nature. From time to time, this book will express non-technical perspectives, but will label them as such, namely as *soapboxes*. Look for text bracketed between the symbols `soap...` and `...soap`, which appear in the margin.

I became involved in the Internet network management *shibboleth* in January, 1988. At the time, I was Principal Software Engineer at the Wollongong Group, in Palo Alto, California. Dave Crocker, then Vice President of Software Engineering, asked that I attend some CMOT meetings with Keith McCloghrie, a network management guru and then a Director of Engineering at Wollongong. Since my interest was (and is) OSI, this seemed appropriate. I knew nothing about network management, but had a solid grounding in both the Internet and OSI suite of protocols (having implemented and used large portions of both).

At the first meeting, I experienced severe culture-shock. I have never been at the right places to be on the "inside track" of the Internet, but I'm familiar with the players, and most importantly, the "young turks" who implement most of the things which get used. At my first CMOT meeting, the only person I recognized was Keith! Furthermore, it wasn't until after the meeting when I interrogated Keith as to who was who, it appeared that most of the people in the room from various companies were from marketing and not engineering! (So, you can see that the earlier statement about most of the CMOT players coming "from the fringe of the Internet" is all too accurate.)

The problem which they had been stuck on for some time was how to map the OSI application layer (where CMIP resides) onto TCP. They needed a way for using the OSI application layer on top of the transport service offered in TCP/IP-based internets. So, I designed a *lightweight presentation protocol*: it offered a minimal OSI presentation service, by implementing a few simple mechanisms layered directly on top of TCP.

After making this modest contribution, I began to withdraw from the CMOT process. Partly because I believed (and still do) that they lacked the technical wherewithal to get things done, but mostly because at every CMOT meeting I attended, I would get a debilitating headache: at the first meeting, it took four hours, at the second, two hours, at the third, one hour, and so on. When I got the headache I would excuse myself and go home to rest. (Readers are free to draw their own conclusions.)

So, it was fresh from making the LPP contribution, that I was asked to attend the IAB's ad hoc meeting on network management. `...soap`

The First Ad Hoc Meeting

When the First Ad Hoc Network Management Review group met, it quickly became clear that all three camps were entrenched, and convinced that *each* had the "right" solution.

After much discussion, the technical debate subsided, and it was observed that HEMS was at a significant disadvantage: it did not have the widespread deployment of SGMP (which was then being used in virtually all of the regional-level networks), nor did it have the inevitability of OSI behind it (which the CMOT camp claimed was imminent). Although neither of these weaknesses are *technical* in nature, the lead researcher on the HEMS project withdrew, and a *modus vivendi* emerged:

- SGMP would be slightly upgraded to reflect (then) recently gained experience. The resulting protocol would become the short-term solution for network management in the Internet community.

- The OSI-based approach was to receive extensive scrutiny and experimentation, in the hopes of one day becoming the long-term solution.

To harmonize the two approaches, a common framework for network management, suitable for both the SGMP-successor and CMOT, was to be developed. A new working group was formed to produce this framework. In addition, a working group was formed to produce the follow-on protocol to SGMP, termed the *Simple Network Management Protocol* (SNMP).

The author was selected as the chair of this latter working group, in the hope that having an "OSI person" brokering the negotiations would produce a system more likely to be harmonized with the CMOT approach. In this regard, my role was simply to aim for some OSI-like extensibility and functionality to be placed in SNMP. Of course, there was a very tight loop between Keith and myself in engineering the common framework.

In August of 1988, a scant six months after the first meeting of the IAB's ad hoc committee, the initial specifications of what is now known as the *Internet-standard Network Management Framework* were completed, independently implemented, and declared to be draft standards by the IAB. Further, several implementations appeared in vendor products by the end of that month.

In April of 1989, SNMP was elevated to "recommended" status, and became the *de facto* operational standard for network management of TCP/IP-based internets, as evidenced by widespread vendor support and (more importantly) the number of deployed systems. For example, more than thirty vendors demonstrated SNMP products at the INTEROP® trade-show in October of 1989. (In fact, most of the vendors represented in the original CMOT group had quietly "jumped ship" and were among these thirty.)

Further, some traditionally non-network vendors (e.g., builders of terminal concentrators and PBXs), added a minimal implementation of the Internet suite of protocols to their products, just so they could use SNMP for management! Clearly these vendors have seen the value of interoperable, multi-vendor network management technology.

Unfortunately, work on the CMOT approach had failed to produce any workable implementations in the same time-frame. This left SMNP as the only solution for the management of multi-vendor internets.

The Second Round

After the first round of network management technology, which produced SNMP, had stabilized, work began on the first set of revisions to the management framework. Unfortunately, the SNMP and CMOT camps could not reach agreement on this work. Another meeting of the IAB's ad hoc committee was called in June, 1989. The outcome was that the two camps would be allowed to use different management frameworks, and that the working group that had produced the common framework was to be disbanded!

Thus, the working group that had produced SNMP was reconstituted to produce the next set of revisions. Work began on a draft in August, 1989, and consensus was reached in December, 1989.

And that brings us to the present: in May of 1990, the SMI, MIB-I, and SNMP were elevated as "Standard Protocols" with "Recommended" Status by the IAB. As of this writing, some four months after the SNMP working group went quiescent, vendors are busy in preparation for the annual industry event INTEROP®. Once again, they are preparing new management products and manageable products for demonstration and deployment. And once again, they are using the Internet-standard Network Management Framework as the technical basis for their work.

How to Use this Book

This book is intended to serve both as a graduate-level text and also as a professional reference. It is expected that the reader has a modest background in networking.

The first part of the book, Chapters 1 and 2, presents a brief history of networking and the need for network management. Following this, the Internet suite of protocols is examined. Since this is a book about managing TCP/IP-based internets, many of the management details can make sense only in the presence of a discussion of the protocols and systems being managed. The text tries to present a "detailed introduction". That is, the level of information must be deep enough so that management issues can be explored later on, but not too detailed so as to dwell on the nuances of each protocol.

The second part of the book, Chapters 3 through 5, details the Internet-standard Network Management Framework. In particular, the *Structure of Management Information* (SMI) and the *Management Information Base* (MIB) are thoroughly explored, followed by the mechanism used to manage internets, the *Simple Network Management Protocol* (SNMP).

The third part of the book, Chapter 6, briefly introduces the policies used to manage internets. The actual policies (as opposed to mechanical aspects) of network management are currently poorly understood, so only a basic coverage can be presented at this time.

The fourth part of the book, Chapter 7, gives an overview of an actual implementation, the *4BSD/ISODE SNMP* package. Both an agent and manager implementation will be examined, along with a common *Applications Programmer's Interface* (API).

Finally, as the book concludes, future trends are identified in Chapter 8. In the appendices, the book contains a chapter on Internet management "lore" (commonly asked questions and answers), various lists of object assignments and definitions, and so on. In addition, ordering information for ISODE is given.

Acknowledgments

I would never have taken this Kafka-esque excursion into network management unless David H. Crocker, now of Digital Equipment Corporation, hadn't tricked me into attending a CMOT meeting. So I suppose I should thank Dave for the frustration. Dave is also the *Area Director for Network Management* in the *Internet Engineering Steering Group*, so I suppose he should thank me for the frustration I've caused him!

Fortunately, Keith McCloghrie, now of Hughes LAN Systems, was (and continues to be) instructive in the area of network management. Keith was responsible for much of the writing of two of the documents which define the Internet-standard Network Management Framework. Although both of our names appear on these two documents, Keith really should get most of the credit.

The four authors of SGMP and SNMP, Professor Jeffrey D. Case of the University of Tennessee, Martin L. Schoffstall and Mark S. Fedor of Performance Systems International, and last, but certainly not least, James (Chuck) R. Davin of the M.I.T. Laboratory for Computer Science, have all left their mark on the Internet-standard Network Management Framework. These four have provided the direction and continuity throughout the entire process of design, implementation, and standardization of the framework. Many, if not all, of the design aspects can be traced back to either their original work or their continued work in this area. In addition, most of the future trends identified in Chapter 8 come from discussions I have had with Professor Case. Finally, Mark, Chuck, and Keith were kind enough to contribute many of the questions to the appendix on Internet management lore.

The 4BSD/ISODE SNMP package is a part of the openly available ISODE implementation. This work, which started at the Northrop Research and Technology Center, and then moved with me to Wollongong, NYSERNet, and now Performance Systems International, provided the tools necessary to automate much of the construction of the software. When at NYSERNet, and now at Performance Systems International, the ISODE work was partially supported by the U.S. Defense Advanced Research Projects Agency and the Rome Air

Development Center of the U.S. Air Force Systems Command under contract number F30602–88–C–0016.

It should be noted that before the 4BSD/ISODE SNMP package was written, NYSERNet/PSI had developed a commercial implementation of SNMP. These two packages are entirely independent and separate: the PSI SNMP software is a supported, commercial package available under license, with support for agents and network operation centers (NOCs); the 4BSD/ISODE SNMP package is an openly-available, unsupported package, containing an agent and a prototyping kit for building NOC tools. Nonetheless, I should thank Martin L. Schoffstall, Vice President and Chief Operating Officer of PSI, for having enough foresight to appreciate that the two packages were not in competition with each other. The reproduction of the displays shown in Chapter 6 are provided courtesy of PSI, as they are part of PSI's commercially-available implementation.

Joyce K. Reynolds (the *Internet Assigned Numbers Authority*) and Jon B. Postel (the *RFC Editor*) , both of the USC/Information Sciences Institute , were very helpful in providing official information regarding the most current status of several of the standards described in *The Simple Book.*

Finally, there have been several reviewers which have provided many useful comments on my manuscripts: Geoffrey Baehr of Sun Microsystems, Jeffrey D. Case, David H. Crocker, Geoffrey S. Goodfellow of Anterior Technology, Keith McCloghrie, Craig Partridge of BBN Systems and Technology Corporation, Dave Perkins of 3COM, Einar A. Stefferud of Network Management Associates, and Joseph Touch of the University of Pennsylvania.

Ole J. Jacobsen, editor and publisher of *ConneXions—The Interoperability Report* was kind enough to perform the copy-editing on *The Simple Book.* His efforts brought this work to print in time for the INTEROP® trade-show of 1990.

Although my cat, Cheetah, did not tirelessly wake me each morning at 5:00 am during the writing of this book, he was nonetheless as obtrusive and attention-demanding as ever!

Finally, Adrianne ("noSauce") Glappa brought many wild adventures into my life over the last year. Let's see, she was responsible for: the time I was stranded on a mountain top, the time I was on *rollerblades* and took a bad spill on some railroad tracks with a train coming, the time ... You get the idea, we had a lot of fun together! noSauce also contributed the idea for the title of *The Simple Book*.

/mtr

Mountain View, California

The Simple Book

Chapter 1

Introduction

In earliest days of computer-communications, it was quite a chore
to reliably move bits from a mainframe to an applications terminal.
As technology advanced into the late-70s, terminal networks evolved
into host networks: hosts were attached to a single "packet-switched"
network when they were supposed to communicate. In the mid-80s,
various economic and technological factors made *internetworking* fea-
sible.

In an *internet*, several networks are connected together through
the use of gateways and an *internetworking protocol*. The gateways
(often called routers), using the protocol, hide the underlying details
of the actual networks, in order to provide a uniform service across
networks.

For example, a site-level network might consist of a local area network based on **Ethernet** technology. This network, along with several
other nearby site-level networks, might be attached to a regional network, consisting of a several routers and point-to-point connections.
In turn, this regional network, along with several other regional networks, might be attached to a national backbone, consisting of another
set of routers. Finally, this national network, might be connected to
several other backbone networks, and have international connections.

Going in the other direction, although a site-level network might
appear as a single logical network to its regional network, the site-
level network might actually be composed internally of several media
segments, each connected together with either repeaters, bridges, or

1

other routers! Although the use of repeaters at the physical layer, and bridges at the data-link layer make multiple segments appear as a single "wire," it may still be desirable to divide the site-level network into several internal networks for traffic isolation. (In fact, some sites might be so large as to make infeasible the use of physical or data-link connections.)

Although each "network" might consist of an entirely different underlying technology (Ethernet, proprietary point-to-point, X.25, and so on), each having their own specific rules for transmission, all hosts attached to those networks have a common view of "the network." This is the power of the *internetworking abstraction*. By use of a common protocol and algorithms, even the most byzantine network topology consisting of myriad technologies can be made to look like a simple point-to-point connection over a homogenous physical network!

The premiere internetworking technology is the *Internet suite of protocols*, commonly referred to as TCP/IP (after the two core protocols in the suite). Initial work on the Internet suite of protocols was principally funded by the *Defense Advanced Research Projects Agency* (DARPA). The work on the Internet suite of protocols has paid off so handsomely, that the premiere global network, the *Internet*, uses this technology. As a consequence, the term *internet* (lowercase-I) is used when making a generic reference to a network built using internetworking technology, whilst the term *Internet* (capital-I) is used when specifically referring to this network.

1.1 The Need for Network Management

Of course, the internetworking abstraction does not come without its price. There are several problems, of which only two will be illustrated in modest detail.

1.1.1 Different Devices

Because internetworking allows several different kinds of devices to participate in the internet, these components (the hosts, routers, and media devices) will usually be multi-vendor and heterogeneous in nature, as has long been the case with the Internet.

As of this writing, there are devices from hundreds of vendors and several models from each vendor's product line, which implement TCP/IP. For example, each year, vendors of products using the Internet suite of protocols are invited to contribute to a document[1], which is an informal list of some of the TCP/IP products available (both commercial and non-proprietary). In November, 1989, this guide listed more than 300 products and product lines.

It should be clear that a network management technology specific to a particular vendor is unusable in such environments. Thus, just as using an "open" (non-proprietary) internetworking technology has made multi-vendor internets a reality, an "open" network management technology must be used to manage these internets.

1.1.2 Different Administrations

Because internetworking allows several networks of different size and purpose to be interconnected, these networks will almost certainly be under different administrations, as is now the case with the Internet!

As of this writing, in the United States alone, there are at least four national backbones along with a dozen or so regional (sometimes termed "mid-level") networks, and, according to one source, at least 1500 connected networks with perhaps as many as one to two million daily users.[1] Each of these national, regional, and site-level networks are all owned and operated by different organizations. Further, these organizations receive funding (and direction) from different sources, and only a small number of these are under common coordination. To further intensify matters, there is interest in "policy-based" usage of portions of the Internet, for accountability purposes. And, to achieve an even higher-level of unmanageability, there are now at least three commercial vendors offering (or having announced that they will offer) commercial internet service, with connections to the Internet.

To appreciate the full breadth of networking available on an international scale, the reader might consult [2]. Although this work is not specific to internetworking technology, it does provide excellent coverage of many internets.

---

[1]Note that it is clearly impractical to even consider determining the number of connected hosts or users. The scale of the Internet is such that this problem is easily shown to be unsolvable!

1.1.3 Scope of the Book

The *comprehensive* solution should allow management of all aspects of an internet. However, *The Simple Book* does not attempt to cover all the aspects of the comprehensive solution. Two limiting assumptions are made:

- first, management is done in the context of the Internet suite of protocols;

- second, management is focused on managing the end-to-end portions of those internets, rather than the application or media-specific portions.

The reader should appreciate that other topics pertaining to the comprehensive solution are beyond the scope of *The Simple Book*. In particular, the following topics are quite intentionally **not** covered:

name to address resolution: in the Internet suite of protocols, this is handled by the *Domain Name System* (DNS) [3]; and,

software loading and distribution: in the Internet suite of protocols, this is handled by protocols such as BOOTP [4,5].

1.2   Introduction to Open Systems Interconnection

This is a book about network management of TCP/IP-based protocols. Nonetheless, in any "modern" work, it is foolhardy to ignore the impact (at least the political impact, if not the technical impact), of *Open Systems Interconnection* (OSI).

The need for non-proprietary networking technology has long been recognized by several organizations, including the *International Organization for Standardization/International Electrotechnical Committee* (ISO/IEC). In 1979, ISO in joint activity with the *International Telephone and Telegraph Consultative Committee* (CCITT), developed a reference model for Open Systems Interconnection. Over the last decade, the international and national standards arena has seen intense work in developing the OSI protocol suite.

soap...

Although many see OSI as "the final solution," the author has long argued for *coexistence between* the two protocol suites, rather than *transition from* the Internet suite to the OSI suite. The whole controversy between "open" protocol suites provides great fodder for tremendous political fighting. Of course, neither side is hardly perfect, see the chapter entitled *The Politics of Open Systems* in *The Open Book*[6] for the grisly details.

...soap

Outside of the soapbox, it should be noted that whilst work on both protocol suites began at roughly the same time, the Internet suite of protocols, by focusing on specific technical objectives, has by-and-large achieved the promise of Open Systems, and is rapidly becoming a commodity market. In contrast, by 1990, over ten years after official "birth" of the OSI suite, there were only OSI pilot projects, nothing more.

Regardless of the short- or long-term success of OSI, it has a profound impact on networking terminology. Thus, it is necessary to introduce some basic OSI notation which will prove useful throughout *The Simple Book*. The remainder of this section is condensed from *The Open Book*.

1.2.1 Models, Conventions, and Notation

A model is simply a way of organizing knowledge to explain the way things work.

In OSI, a reference model is used to describe computer communications. The Model is inherently abstract. It does not specify:

- programming language bindings,

- operating system bindings,

- application interface issues, or

- user interface issues.

The Model is intended solely to describe the external behavior of systems, independent of their internal constructions. From a communications standpoint, OSI says what goes on the wire and when, but not how computers are built to exhibit the mandated behavior.

OSI standards are grouped into pairs: one defines the *service* offered by some entity, and the other specifies the *protocol* used by that entity to offer that service. This is a well understood concept of abstraction. It allows individual entities to be constructed with little knowledge of other entities. There are two advantages to an architecture that localizes knowledge:

- undesirable interactions caused by side-effects are avoided, because the external behavior of an entity is well defined; and

- the internal construction of a entity may vary without affecting other entities — providing the former maintains its same external behavior.

The discussion now proceeds to consider how OSI services are described.

1.2.2 Services

An ISO/IEC technical report, [7], defines the conventions used when describing OSI services.

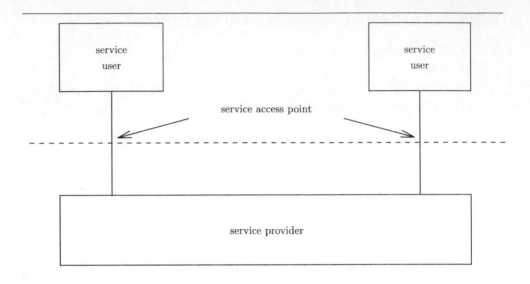

Figure 1.1: Service Users and Provider

A *service* represents a set of functions offered to a user by a provider. As shown here in Figure 1.1, the service is made available through *service access points* (SAPs). From the user perspective, all of the qualities of the service are completely defined by the interface at the SAP. Thus, the provider may be viewed entirely as an abstract entity.

This particular example shows a two-user service. Although this is by far the most common kind of service in OSI, there are other possible services. For example, a multicast service involves multiple receivers for data sent by one user.

It is not hard to imagine that the service provider itself might be composed of smaller entities, which in turn use the service immediately below as shown in Figure 1.2. In addition to introducing a new underlying service provider, this figure also explains how two entities combine to offer a new service: they use the services from below and they communicate using a protocol.

This is the fundamental concept known as *layering*: a relatively simple service may be augmented to offer more powerful services at the layer immediately above. This process may continue indefinitely, until the desired level of abstraction and power is reached.

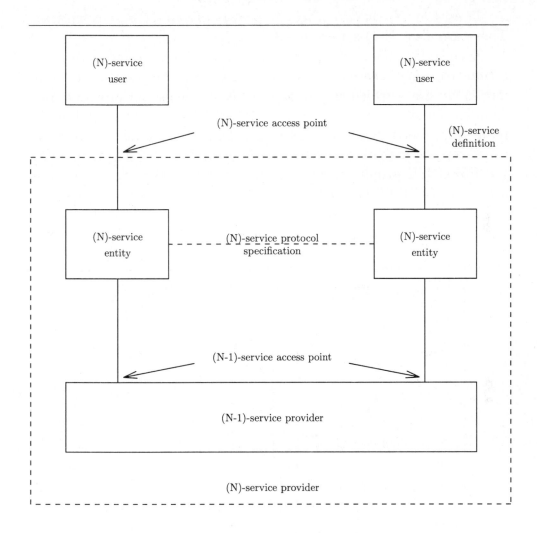

Figure 1.2: Service Layering

In OSI, layers are numbered from the bottom up.

The term "layer-(N)" is used to refer to a generic layer. Similarly, "layer-(N-1)" refers to the layer immediately below, and "layer-(N+1)" refers to the layer immediately above.

Thus, the (N)-service provider consists of two (N)-service entities. These are also (N-1)-service users.

Each service offered by a provider can be characterized in terms of a *time sequence diagram.* In the diagram, a service consists of one or more *primitives* which are invoked by either the user or provider. In a confirmed service, for example, the .REQUEST primitive is used by the requesting user to initiate the service. This is ultimately delivered to the accepting user as an .INDICATION primitive, which in turn issues a .RESPONSE primitive, which is finally returned to the requesting user as a .CONFIRMATION:

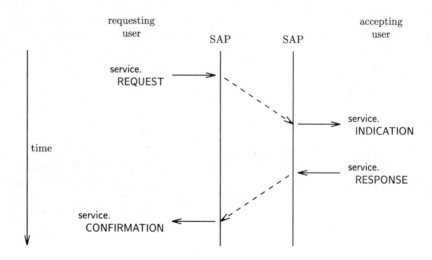

In OSI, time sequence diagrams are used to denote the relationship between the primitives which form a service and the order in which they occur.

1.2.3   Interfaces

Next, the discussion considers the OSI formalism used to describe the interaction occurring when a service primitive causes information to pass from one layer to the next.

Suppose a service provider is asked to transfer some data to the remote service user. This user-data is termed a *service data unit* (SDU). The service provider attaches a small header to the user-data, termed the *protocol control information* (PCI). The PCI identifies the data that is to be transferred.

The resulting object is termed a *protocol data unit* (PDU). This is the unit of information that is exchanged by peers, implementing a protocol to offer a service.

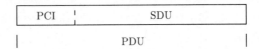

Next, it is necessary to invoke the (N-1)-service provider to cause the data to be transmitted. To do this, *interface control information* (ICI) is (conceptually) attached to the PDU. The ICI identifies the service primitive that is to be invoked from the (N-1)-service.

The resulting object is termed an *interface data unit* (IDU). The (N)-service provider now passes the IDU through the (N-1)-SAP.

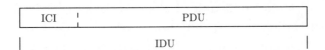

The (N-1)-service provider receives the IDU and breaks it apart into the ICI and an (N-1)-SDU. It then invokes the desired primitive based on the ICI. Note that from the perspective of the (N-1)-service provider, an (N)-PDU is precisely an (N-1)-SDU. All of these relationships are summarized here:

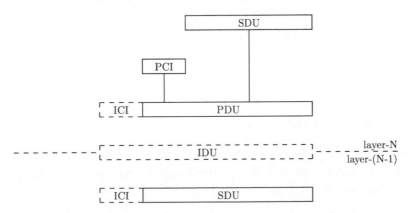

Once the data is transferred, the remote (N-1)-service provider generates an ICI and combines it with the received SDU to form an IDU, and then passes IDU up to the remote (N)-service provider. This is broken into the ICI and PDU, which in turn is broken into the PCI and SDU. Finally, the SDU is delivered to the (N)-service user.

Of course, this is an excruciatingly abstract way to describe how a user and provider interact through service boundaries. The distinction between protocol control information and user-data in a PDU is a well-known technique called *encapsulation*. This allows user-data to be transparently transmitted. More familiar terms from other protocol suites might be:

$$\begin{aligned} \text{SDU} &= \text{data} \\ \text{PCI} &= \text{header} \\ \text{PDU} &= \text{packet} \end{aligned}$$

The introductions of ICI and IDU are used simply to make the notion of the SAP work; they are formalisms that permit a service provider to offer multiple services and still have a single point of interaction. Indeed, many do not particularly care for the notion of an IDU. They prefer to think of the interface information existing in parallel with the data unit, but not attached. That is, they prefer to keep the control and data aspects of the model separated.

It must be stressed that these service conventions are not intended to have any impact on implementations. For example, the IDU mechanism for layer communication is essentially a message passing scheme. Each message (the IDU) carries with it typing information (the ICI) and data (the PDU).

It is important to understand that OSI, per se, never specifies the notion of programmatic conformance to a service. That is, it is always the responsibility (and freedom) of a designer to implement a service faithfully.

OSI makes no constraints as to how that service is implemented.

1.2.4 Protocols

OSI service providers are described as *finite state machines* (FSMs).

The protocol machine for a particular service starts in an initial state. Events, which are service primitives received from the user above or the provider below, as they occur, trigger activity on the part of the FSM. As a part of this activity, actions may be required (service primitives issued to the user and/or the underlying provider), and possibly a new state is entered. Eventually the SAP becomes inactive and the FSM returns to the initial state.

Thus, when examining any OSI protocol, there are three things to be discussed:

- how the underlying service is used;

- the elements of procedure for the protocol, which define the behavior of the FSM; and,

- how PDUs are encoded.

Each OSI protocol specification defines these activities. In addition, each usually contains an annex that contains a state table to describe formally the FSM composing the protocol machine.

1.2.5   The 7 Layers

Finally, with the necessary notational conventions out of the way, the discussion looks at the OSI Reference Model as defined in [8]. The Model divides the task of computer communications into seven functional layers.

There is no mystique to the choice of the number seven. Other protocol architectures have numbers of similar magnitude. The reader is strongly encouraged to read [9] for an insightful discussion on why the actual number of layers is not fixed and is largely unimportant.

The first four OSI layers form the lower-layer infrastructure of the OSI model. These provide the end-to-end services responsible for data transfer. The remaining three OSI layers form the upper-layer infrastructure of the OSI model. These provide the application services responsible for information transfer. The relation between these is shown in Figure 1.3.

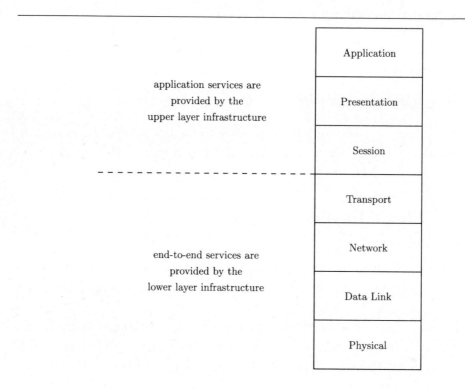

Figure 1.3: The OSI Reference Model

The discussion now considers the individual layers that compose the reference model. The descriptions will be brief.

Physical Layer (Ph): responsible for the electro-mechanical interface to the communications media.

Data Link Layer (Dl): responsible for transmission, framing, and error control over a single communications link.

Network Layer (N): responsible for data transfer across the network, independent of both the media comprising the underlying subnetworks and the topology of those subnetworks.

Transport Layer (T): responsible for reliability and multiplexing of data transfer across the network (over and above that provided by the network layer) to the level required by the application.

Session Layer (S): responsible for adding control mechanisms to the data exchange.

Presentation Layer (P): responsible for adding structure to the units of data that are exchanged.

Application Layer (A): responsible for managing the communications between applications.

1.2.6 Services Revisited

In OSI, the service offered by a layer is either *connection-oriented* or *connectionless*.

A connection-oriented mode (CO-mode) service has three distinct phases:

connection establishment: in which the service users and the service provider negotiate the way in which the service will be used. If successful, this results in a *connection* being established. Once a connection is established, this is an explicit binding between the two service users. All other service primitives occur in the context of this binding.

data transfer: in which the service users exchange data.

connection release: in which the binding between users is discarded.

In contrast, a connectionless mode (CL-mode) service has one phase: data transfer. Any and all options must be supplied for each and every primitive as there is no explicit ongoing relationship established between service users. Typically, each OSI layer provides a single CL-mode service using the verb UNITDATA. This is an unconfirmed service.

The OSI model is inherently connection-oriented. However, the first Addendum to the International Standard, [10], augments the model for connectionless-mode (CL-mode) transmission.

For historical reasons, OSI has been primarily interested only in connection-oriented services and protocols. Originally, only CO-mode versions of the services and protocols were defined. Then, the CL-mode lower-layers were defined. Finally, as of the end of 1988, CL-mode versions of the presentation, session, and transport services existed, but no OSI applications made use of them.

In contrast, both CO-mode and CL-mode versions of the data link and network service exist. The transport service may use either the CO-mode network service or the CL-mode network service in order to provide a connection-oriented transport service. Furthermore, either network service may use either data link service. The gist of this is simply stated: OSI application services are connection-oriented. The underlying end-to-end services presently offer a connection-oriented service, but may be internally composed of connectionless-mode protocols.

1.3 The OSI View of Network Management

In OSI, network management has been the last "major" service to reach solidity. It is largely because of this fluidity, that OSI network management has received much attention but has seen little implementation and even less confidence. This is unfortunate, since lack of a workable network management system will severely hinder the deployment of large OSI networks.

In fact, most network management gurus in the Internet have long decided that it is too resource-intensive to *even* keep track of correspondent efforts in OSI. The usual catch-phrase has become:

soap...

> *Sure, we're for OSI network management... whatever that is this week!*

...soap

Fortunately, the basic model for OSI network management is relatively stable, so it can be discussed here. The functional approach to OSI network management is to view the problem as five sub-problems:

- *configuration management*, which is responsible for detecting and controlling the state of the network (for both logical and physical configurations);

- *performance management*, which is responsible for controlling and analyzing the throughput and error rate of the network (including historical information);

- *fault management*, which is responsible for detecting, isolating, and controlling abnormal network behavior, such as excessive line outages;

- *accounting management*, which is responsible for collecting and processing data related to resource consumption in the network; and,

- *security management*, which is responsible for controlling access to network resources through the use of authentication techniques and authorization policies.

To support these different views, a *Common Mangement Informa-tion Service* (CMIS) and associated protocol (CMIP) have progressed through the standardization process.

Orthogonal to the functional decomposition, the management service provides three types of usage:

- *monitoring*, in which management information is retrieved;

- *control*, in which devices are manipulated; and,

- *reporting*, in which devices report abnormal events.

Hence, one might view applications, which are concerned with one of the five management functions, as using the (common) management service in different ways in order to achieve their goals.

Unfortunately, at this point, the terminology becomes somewhat counter-intuitive: in OSI parlance, *system management* consists of managing the OSI portion of a system, i.e., what most people term *network management*. In OSI, each layer consists of a *layer manage-ment entity* (LME), which "knows about" the protocol(s) operating at that layer. The LMEs communicate with a *system management application-entity* (SMAE) using a local mechanism, which in turn uses CMIP to communicate with other SMAEs. By this process of abstraction, OSI layer management is accomplished.

SMAE				SMAE
LME	A	- - - - - - - - -	A	LME
LME	P	- - - - - - - - -	P	LME
LME	S	- - - - - - - - -	S	LME
LME	T	- - - - - - - - -	T	LME
LME	N	- - - - - - - - -	N	LME
LME	Dl	- - - - - - - - -	Dl	LME
LME	Ph		Ph	LME

As depicted in the figure above, the SMAE has access (via local mechanisms) to the LME at each layer. Further, the SMAE is a user of the OSI application layer in order to access CMIP. The reader should appreciate that this architecture is quite general in that the same protocols and mechanisms used for "normal" data transfer at the application layer can be used for network management.

The OSI Common Management Information Service is based on a connection-oriented model: before management activity occurs, an application association (application layer connection) is formed between the two management entities. Following this, there are several services which might be invoked:

- `get`, which is used to retrieve specific management information;

- `set`, which is used to manipulate management information;

- `action`, which is used to perform some imperative command (e.g., reboot the device);

- `create`, which is used to create a new instance of a management object (e.g., an entry in the routing table);

- `delete`, which is used to delete an instance of a management object; and,

- `event-report`, which is used to report extraordinary events.

All of these services may be performed in a confirmed fashion: after initiating the service, a response is returned by the accepting management entity. In addition, the set, action, and event-reporting services also exist in non-confirmed form.

In order to specify the management objects of interest, the service employs two concepts: *scoping* and *filtering*. In brief: management information is organized in a hierarhical structure. Scoping occurs by identifying a particular node in the tree along with a depth. This marks a subtree rooted at that node and of the specified depth. Next, an arbitrary boolean expression is applied to the attributes of the management information held within that subtree. This is called filtering. Once the management information has been scoped and filtered, the desired management activity occurs.

Beyond this basic model, it is difficult (at least for the author) to identify the stable points of OSI network management technology. Although the service and protocol (CMIS and CMIP) have achieved the final rung in the standards ladder, The key issues of how management information is structured and defined remains, at least by mid-1990, rather fluid. Without stability in these crucial areas, implementation, and more importantly, workability and interoperability of OSI network management is problematic.

Section 5.11 on page 185 compares the Internet-standard Network Management Framework to the OSI view of network management. The reader is urged not to skip ahead, but rather read the intervening text to have a better appreciating of the discussion presented in that section.

Inasmuch as this is a book on management of TCP/IP-based internets, we now turn away from the OSI perspective on network management to concentrate on the Internet suite of protocols and how management occurs in that framework.

Chapter 2

The Internet Suite
of Protocols

The Internet suite of protocols grew out of early research into surviv-able multi-media packet networking sponsored by the U.S. Defense Advanced Research Projects Agency (DARPA). In the beginning, there was only one network, called the ARPANET, which connected a few dozen computer systems around the country. With the advent of different networking technologies, such as Ethernet, Packet Radio, and Satellite, a method was needed for reliable transmission of infor-mation over media that do not guarantee reliable, error free delivery. (Information transmitted using these technologies can be lost or cor-rupted as the result, e.g., of radio propagation or collision). Thus, the Internet suite of protocols was born.

Although, the Internet suite might be thought of as the property of the U.S. military, this is an entirely pedantic view. The protocol suite is administered not by the U.S. military, but by researchers sponsored by many areas of the U.S. government. All computer users, regardless of nationality or profession, have benefited tremendously from the Internet suite.

2.1   A Brief Overview

The best term to use when describing the Internet suite of protocols is *focused*. There was a problem to solve, that of allowing a collection of heterogeneous computers and networks to communicate. Solving the internetworking communications gap required a good deal of cutting edge research. The Internet researchers made open systems a reality by limiting the problem, gauging the technology, and, by and large, making a set of well thought out engineering decisions. In the discussion that follows, the term *Internet Community* refers to all parties, world-wide, that use the Internet suite of protocols, regardless of whether they are connected to the Internet.

The current generation of protocols is *primarily* based on:

- a connection-oriented transport service, provided by the Transmission Control Protocol (TCP); and,

- a connectionless-mode network service, provided by the Internet Protocol (IP).

The major emphasis of the Internet suite is on the connection of diverse network technologies. To this day, excellent research continues on these issues.

There are several application protocols available for production use in the Internet suite:

- the Simple Mail Transfer Protocol (SMTP) [11,12], which provides store-and-forward service for textual electronic mail messages, and RFC822 [13], which defines the format of those messages;

- the File Transfer Protocol (FTP)[14], which provides file transfer services;

- TELNET[15], which provides virtual terminal services; and,

- the Domain Name System (DNS) [3], which primarily provides mappings between host names and network addresses.

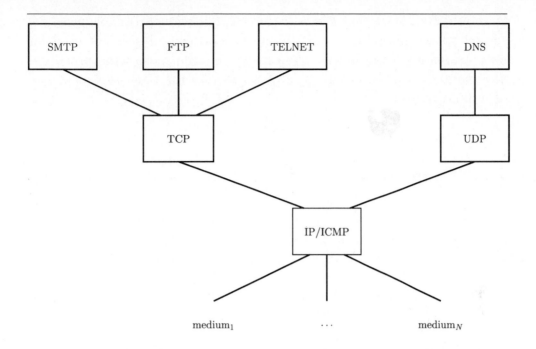

Figure 2.1: Brief Overview of Internet Protocols

The relationship between the application protocols and the end-to-end services is shown in Figure 2.1. This figure, which emphasizes simplicity over detail, also shows a protocol called the User Datagram Protocol (UDP), which is a connectionless-mode transport protocol that is little more than a simple pass-through to IP, and a protocol called the Internet Control Message Protocol (ICMP) which is used to report on the "health" of the internet layer.

There are actually many more services, supporting everything from cross-network debugging, to network management, to voice protocols, and so on. As of this writing, perhaps the two with the most impact have been:

- NFS, a distributed file-system developed by Sun Microsystems [16]; and,

- the X Window System developed by Project Athena at the Massachusetts Institute of Technology [17].

It should be noted that both of these application protocols were designed to be independent of the actual end-to-end services used for data transfer. Nonetheless, they have seen the most widespread deployment on the Internet suite of protocols, for both technical and economic reasons.

2.2 Standardization Process

The technical body that oversees the development of the Internet suite of protocols is termed the *Internet Activities Board* (IAB). The IAB is composed of senior researchers who, for the most part, are the designers and original implementors of the Internet suite. There are also two subsidiary bodies of the IAB: the *Internet Engineering Task Force* (IETF), which is responsible for short-term engineering; and, the *Internet Research Task Force* (IRTF), which is responsible for longer-term research. Each task force is managed by steering groups, namely the Internet Research Steering Group (IRSG), and the Internet Engineering Steering Group (IESG), respectively. The IAB, per se, produces very few documents. Any member of the Internet community can design, document, implement, and test a protocol for use in the Internet suite. The IAB requires that protocols be documented in the *Request for Comments* (RFCs) series. The RFC document series is a convenient place for the dissemination of ideas. Protocol authors are encouraged to use the RFC mechanism regardless of whether they expect their protocol to become an Internet standard.

It is problematic to list or even categorize all of the RFCs which have been published. However, in Appendix A starting on page 253, the RFCs relevant to the topics discussed in *The Simple Book* are listed. This appendix also discusses how RFCs may be retrieved.

Each RFC is assigned a number by the *RFC Editor* (a member of the IAB). If the text of the RFC is revised, a new number is assigned (in contrast to the ISO/IEC scheme of retaining the same number). In order to prevent confusion, if an RFC supercedes any previous RFCs, this is clearly stated on the cover of the newer RFC. In addition to the RFC Editor, there is an *Internet Assigned Numbers Authority* (IANA), which is responsible for keeping the authoritative list of values used in the Internet suite of protocols (e.g., protocol numbers).

In addition to RFCs, there is a second set of documents, the *Internet Draft* series. These are produced by working groups in the IETF, and have no standardization status whatsoever, being viewed only as work in progress. At some point, if an Internet Draft matures (usually after some revision), it may be considered for standardization. It should be noted that vendor product and user procurement literature should cite only RFCs and *not* Internet Drafts. It has been reported that the *Executive Director* of the IAB goes *non-linear* whenever the oxymoronic phrase "adherence to an Internet Draft" is used.

As of this writing, the Internet standards process is undergoing substantive change. At the risk of being topical, the process is roughly as follows: all documents attempting standardization are assigned a working group in the IETF, and the standardization process is managed by the IESG, which in turn makes recommendations to the IAB. The IAB decides the actual standardization status of each RFC.

So, when a working group is satisfied with a document, a decision is made as to whether the document is to be placed "in the standards track." If not, then the document is marked as *experimental* or *informational* and is then given to the RFC Editor. Of course, any document may be directly submitted to the RFC Editor if it is not to be standardized. In this case, at the discretion of the RFC Editor, the document might be immediately published as an RFC or it may undergo review. For example, working groups of both the IETF and IRTF might have their documents published for informational purposes.

Otherwise, if standardization is to be attempted, usually after a suitable constituency has developed which believes the document is credible, then, in the best case, the document progresses through three stages:

- *Proposed Standard* status, during which considerable implementation, experimentation, and interoperability is expected to occur;

- *Draft Standard* status, during which considerable field testing is expected to occur; and, finally

- *Internet Standard* status.

Orthogonal to the standardization status of the document, is the document's *requirement level*, which indicates the level of support the Internet community must accord the document:

- *Historical* or obsolete;

- *Experimental*;

- *Elective*;

- *Recommended*; or,

- *Required*.

The meanings of these terms are hazy at best. A good rule of thumb is that for a particular function, there is usually only a single protocol marked required or recommended. If that protocol is marked recommended then there may be one or more other documents marked elective.

Finally, there are four key RFCs that define the status of documents in the RFC series. These are:

Assigned Numbers: lists the assigned values used for the parameters in the Internet suite of protocols [18];

Official Protocols: lists all official protocols [19];

Gateway Requirements: lists all protocols and practices that relate to router nodes [20]; and,

Host Requirements: lists all protocols and practices that relate to host nodes [21,22].

These RFCs are periodically updated. As with the rest of the RFC series, the most recent document always takes precedence. The key document that relates these RFCs is the IAB Official Standards RFC. This RFC is issued quarterly by the IAB with a strong warning to retrieve the next version when the current document reaches its expiration date. As of this writing, the latest version was [23]. As of this reading, that version is obsolete.

Having described the process by which Internet standards are produced, we now turn to examine some of the key protocols. This is necessary in order to understand how management of these protocols is accomplished. Although the remainder of this chapter is not a thorough exposition of the Internet suite protocols, the author hopes that it is suitably detailed so as to provide the reader with the knowledge necessary to appreciate the management techniques in the chapters which follow.

Like the OSI suite of protocols, there is an architectural model for the Internet suite of protocols, defined in [24]. For our purposes, it is useful to view the Internet suite of protocols as having four layers:

- the *interface* layer, which describes physical and data-link technologies used to realize transmission at the hardware (media) level;

- the *internet* layer, which describes the internetworking technologies used to realize the internetworking abstraction;

- the *transport* layer, which describes the end-to-end technologies used to realize reliable communications between hosts; and,

- the *application* layer, which describes the technologies used to provide end-user services.

It should be noted that other descriptions of the Internet suite of protocols use similar (or slightly different) terminology to describe the architecture. The author feels that this organization strikes a useful balance between historical perspective (from the original Internet research) and "modern" terminology (from the OSI Reference Model).

To briefly remind the reader about layering, when referring to a particular layer, one usually refers to the *entities* residing at that layer. For example, at the internet layer, one refers to the IP entity. This entity provides the internet service to the entities at the layer above. Similarly, the entity uses the interface service provided by the entities at the layer below.

Each of the four layers is now examined in turn.

2.3 Interface Layer

The interface layer is responsible for the transmission on a single physical network, termed a medium. Examples include Ethernet, token ring, fiber optics, X.25, and so on. Thus, the interface layer corresponds to the two lowest layers of the OSI model, the physical and data-link layers. The purist will observe that this also covers part of OSI's network layer, but that distinction is ignored in this text. The technologies that implement these layers vary too widely and change too quickly to be considered here. Instead, consult [25] for an excellent exploration of these topics.

Note that an internet usually consists of several different kinds of media. As such, the interface layer is really composed of several different parts, each responsible for providing a uniform service to the layer above.

For our purposes, there is only one topic of interest:

> *How is data from the Internet suite of protocols sent over a particular medium?*

In order to answer this question, we have to jump ahead a little bit to look at part of the layer above, and in particular the internetworking protocol used, IP.

IP is termed a connectionless-mode (CL-mode) network protocol. This means that it is *datagram-oriented*. When something wishes to send data using IP, it sends that data as a series of datagrams. Each datagram consists of one or more octets (simply termed "bytes") of *user-data*. Associated with each datagram is an address indicating where the datagram should be delivered. This address consists of an *IP address*, and an *upper-layer protocol number* (ULP). The syntax and semantics of IP addresses are considered later on. For now, simply think of IP as delivering datagrams to arbitrary addresses.

Of course, the first thing to be observed is that IP has no "wires" associated with it. Instead, IP must rely on the services of the interface layer below in order to deliver the datagram. So, IP takes the user-data and encapsulates it in an IP datagram, which should contain all the information necessary to deliver the datagram to the IP entity at the destination. The remote IP entity will examine the

IP datagrams it receives, and then strip out the data and pass that up to the appropriate upper-layer protocol.

The second thing to be observed is that because IP is independent of the "wires," it must therefore use addresses which are independent of any physical hardware addressing. That is, although an IP address might indicate where a network device resides in an internet, the IP address need not (and preferably should not) have any relationship to the corresponding media address of the wire where the device is physically attached. This indirection is important for two reasons:

- Media addresses are normally assigned administratively by the manufacturer, so there can be no correlation between geographic location and media address;

- Media addresses can change when interface hardware changes (e.g., to replace a broken board), this should not result in a change in the IP address.

2.3.1   Transmission of IP Datagrams

Given this rather simplistic, but particularly elegant, design, it appears that the interface layer must provide two services:

- mapping from IP addresses to interface-specific addresses; and,

- encapsulation of IP datagrams for transmission over a specific medium.

For each medium which can be used to transmit IP datagrams, there is a document which specifies how these services are provided.

In Section A.3 on page 258, a list of defined mappings is presented. In general, the mechanisms used by these documents fall into one of two categories:

- if the underlying technology is connectionless-mode, then the mechanism is straight-forward: IP datagrams are encapsulated in media frames; otherwise,

- if the underlying technology is connection-oriented, then the interface layer must perform connection management in order to

find an underlying connection over which to send the IP datagram. In this case, it is usually advantageous to manage multiple
connections simultaneously, both to support multiple IP desti-
nations (downwards-multiplexing) and to increase throughput
to a single IP destination (upwards-multiplexing).

In either case, address translation occurs through one of three mechanisms:

- *algorithmically*, if there is a deterministic method for achieving a
  one-to-one mapping between IP addresses and media addresses;

- *statically*, if a table is built during system configuration; or,

- *dynamically*, if a protocol is run to determine the mappings.

Of the three approaches, the dynamic mechanism is clearly the best
as it determines the address mappings in a decentralized fashion.

IP datagrams over Ethernet

To conclude this section on the interface layer, we now examine how
IP packets are encapsulated on Ethernet networks[26].

IP datagrams over Ethernet – Frame Format

Each IP datagram is encapsulated in the data field of an Ethernet
packet. Since the maximum size of this data field is 1500 octets, if
the IP datagram is larger, the IP datagram must be fragmented prior
to transmission. (This topic is discussed in greater detail in the next
section.)

Since the minimum size of the data field is 46 octets, if the IP datagram is smaller, then the sending process inserts null (zero-valued)
octets after the IP datagram to pad the data field to the minimum
length. Note that this padding is transparent to IP. When the data
field is extracted on the remote system, the IP entity will consult a
count in the IP datagram indicating how long the datagram actually
is. Thus, the octets used for padding will be ignored. The frame
format is shown in Figure 2.2.

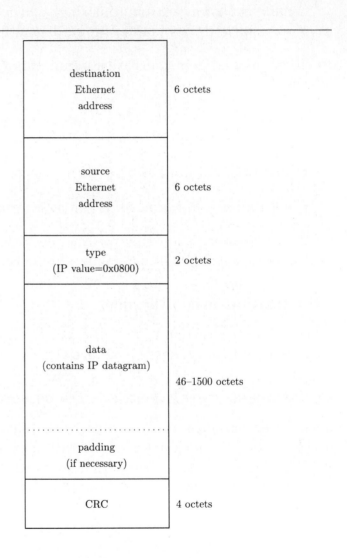

Figure 2.2: IP datagrams over Ethernet

Some implementations optionally use a different encapsulation technique to improve network performance on a particular hardware architecture. This is commonly termed "trailer encapsulation" or just "trailers." This format, the use of which is entirely elective, is described in [27].

IP datagrams over Ethernet – Address Mappings

Because IP addresses are 32 bits in length and Ethernet addresses are 48 bits in length, an algorithmic mechanism can not achieve a one-to-one mapping between them. This leaves either a static approach or the use of a protocol to achieve a dynamic mapping.

In the case of Ethernet, the *Address Resolution Protocol* (ARP), defined in [28], is the dynamic mechanism used in virtually all implementations. ARP makes use of the *broadcasting* facilities of Ethernet technology. When the local IP determines that it must send a packet to an device on an attached Ethernet, the interface layer consults its ARP cache to see if the address mapping from the remote IP address to an Ethernet address is already known. If so, the IP datagram can be sent in an Ethernet packet to the corresponding media address.

If not, the interface layer constructs an ARP request packet, The format of an ARP packet is shown in Figure 2.3. Note that the format of ARP packets is actually media-independent.[1] The "media type" field indicates what kind of hardware is being used. The value 1 is used for Ethernet. Similarly, the "network type" field indicates, in the context of the specified media, what networking protocol is being translated. Since IP datagrams are transmitted using the value 0x0800 over Ethernet, this value is used. As can be seen from the packet format, ARP assumes that both media and network addresses are of fixed length for both source and destination. (A good assumption for both Ethernet and IP, a poor assumption for the OSI connectionless-mode network protocol, CLNP.)

An ARP request uses a value of 1 for the operation code. All fields in the packet, except for the target media address (obviously)

---

[1] The ARP specification uses the term "hardware address" when refering to media addresses, In striving for consistency with the previous discussion, the author has chosen to use the term "media" instead.

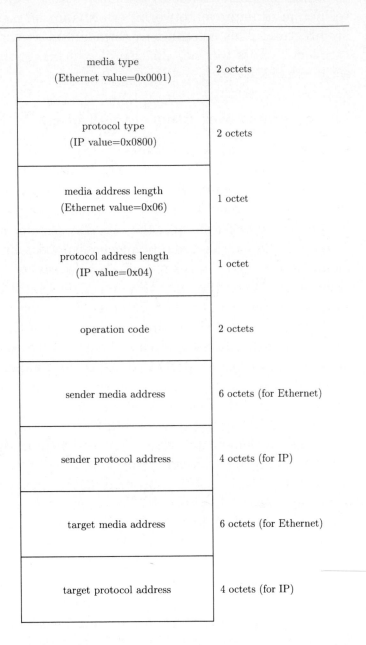

Figure 2.3: Format of ARP packets

are filled-in by the sender. The ARP packet is placed in the data field of an Ethernet packet, and is then sent to the Ethernet *broadcast* address. (Since the length of an ARP packet for Ethernet/IP mapping is 28 octets, and this is less than the minimum size for the data field of an Ethernet packet, the remainder of the Ethernet data field will be padded accordingly.)

Upon receiving an ARP packet, the interface layer verifies that it supports the media type and protocol types described. If not, the packet is discarded. Otherwise:

1. A check is first made to see if the sender's protocol address is already in the local ARP cache, and if so, the correspondent media address is updated.

2. A check is then made to see if the target's protocol address corresponds to the local IP address. If not, the packet is discarded.

3. Otherwise:

   (a) If the sender's protocol address was not already in the local ARP cache (the first check), then media/protocol address mapping for the sender is now added to the cache.

   (b) If the operation code of the ARP packet indicated "ARP request," then an "ARP response" packet is formed (usually by reusing the incoming ARP packet), with all of the fields filled-in. This response packet is then sent on the same physical interface as the original request packet to the Ethernet address of the original sender (i.e., not broadcast).

Note that one of the very last things checked for in the algorithm is whether the ARP packet is a request or a reply. The rationale for this is quite clever: when the local interface layer consults its ARP cache and does not find the desired information, in addition to generating and sending an ARP request, it may simply discard the IP datagram it was going to send. As will be discussed in the next section, inherent to the internet layer is the notion of unreliability. Thus, if the IP datagram is gratuitously discarded, a protocol somewhere above IP is responsible for retransmitting it at a later time. Usually, this will be TCP at the transport layer, but this needn't be the case (e.g., if the application uses UDP at the transport layer, then the application protocol is responsible for retransmission). Regardless of whether the IP datagram was discarded or not, when an ARP packet containing the desired mapping arrives, the ARP cache is updated. Thus, when the next IP datagram (e.g., a retransmission) is to be sent to that remote device, the ARP cache should have the desired information. Since holding onto the IP datagram while waiting for an ARP reply has resource implications (i.e., buffering), the ARP algorithm allows for a simpler, buffer-free implementation.

Although this behavior is permitted, the *Host Requirements* document discourages its use.

2.4 Internet Layer

The internet layer is responsible for providing transparency over both the topology of the internet and the transmission media used in each physical network comprising the internet. To achieve this the network service must provide:

- a common level of *delivery service* which is independent of the capabilities of the underlying media;

- an global *addressing* mechanism; and,

- a *routing* scheme to transfer data through the concatenation of physical networks.

All of these are fundamental if the internetworking abstraction is to be realized. This allows network devices to view an internet as homogeneous in nature.

2.4.1 Delivery Service

At the internet layer, the delivery service is connectionless in nature. User-data is sent as packets containing an integral number of octets termed *datagrams*. Further, from the perspective of the internet layer, there is no explicit relationship between the datagrams. That is, the internet layer is inherently *stateless*. As a consequence, the service is said to be unreliable, because the internet layer doesn't keep track of the datagrams it has previously sent. It is up to the upper-layer protocols to implement the desired level of reliability.

It should be observed that all media technologies can easily support such a delivery paradigm. Clearly, it is easy to map a CL-mode service at the internet layer onto a CL-mode service at the interface layer. Further, given modest connection management algorithms, it is also straight-forward to map a CL-mode internet service onto a CO-mode interface service. Of course, the inverse mapping (constructing a CO-mode internet service over a media which is inherently CL-mode) can be quite complicated. (But it has been done; there are research groups in Europe running X.25 over Ethernet!)

Naturally, a stateless model implies that datagrams may be corrupted, lost, re-ordered, or (even) duplicated. It is the responsibility of other portions of the protocol suite (at some higher layer) to deal with these conditions.

It is important to appreciate that the extremely modest demands made by the internet layer is one of the primary strengths of the protocol suite. By minimizing expectations of the interface layer, the largest number of different media may be easily accommodated. Further, by placing reliability concerns at a layer above, these functions may be centralized at one layer for both efficiency and robustness. However, this argument, usually termed the *end-to-end* argument [29], must be qualified: there are several kinds of reliability. One is data integrity, the other is recovery from lost, duplicated, or mis-ordered datagrams. The philosophy of the Internet suite of protocols is that data integrity is best performed at the interface layer where there are usually powerful checksum algorithms implemented in hardware. In contrast, reliability above the packet level is best achieved at the transport or application layer. (Of course, both the internet and transport layers include a modest checksum, efficiently implementable in software, to provide a simple "sanity check" against potential misbehavior at the layers below.)

2.4.2   Addressing

As foreshadowed above, an IP address is a 32–bit quantity, divided into two fields: a *network-identifier*, and a *host-identifier*. The network-identifier refers to a particular physical network in an internet, and the host-identifier refers to a particular device attached to that physical network. Because of this, an IP address precisely identifies where a network device is attached to an internet. Thus, a network device with multiple attachments will have multiple IP addresses associated with it (usually one IP address per attachment). Such a device is termed a *multi-homed* device. Finally, note that unlike media addresses, an IP address is said to be a *logical* artifact. It bears no relation to hardware, media, or any other physical conundrum.

The choice for 32 bits is both clever and problematic. The clever part is that it allows for extremely efficient implementation of software at the internet layer. The problematic part is that a 32–bit address space, whilst sufficient for the needs of the 8os, may find itself too small for all the devices attached to the Internet by the end of the 9os!

The problem is made harder by the fact that the 32 bits must be divided between network- and host-identifiers. Fortunately, the designers of the IP address developed a flexible scheme for allocating the 32 bits: IP addresses are divided into 5 *classes*, of which only three are germane to the topic at hand:

	bits for identifying	
class	**network**	**host**
A	7	24
B	14	16
C	21	8

Thus, there are potentially 128 class A networks, each containing up to $2^{24}-2$ hosts; potentially 16384 class B networks, each containing up to 65534 hosts; and, potentially 2^{21} class C networks, each containing up to 254 hosts. As one might expect, due to the small amount of class A network numbers possible, it is quite difficult to successfully petition the IANA for such a number.

In each address class, there are two special values for the host-identifier. If all the bits are zero, then the resulting 32–bit quantity refers precisely to the network identified in the IP address, and not to any host attached to the network. Similarly, if all the bits in the host-identifier are one, then the resulting IP address refers to *all* hosts attached to the network (the IP broadcast address for that network).[2] Finally, by convention an IP address with all bits set to one refers to all hosts on the local network (another form of the IP broadcast address).

---

[2]Some early versions of Internet software used all zeroes for the broadcast address. As long as all the devices on an IP network honor the same convention, few problems ensue. If different values are used on the same network, disastrous anomalies, termed *broadcast storms*, occur. However, because of the multi-vendor, heterogeneous nature of IP networks, a single convention (all ones) was chosen.

Address Encodings

As one might expect, choice of a fixed length address, allows for an efficient encoding at the hardware level:

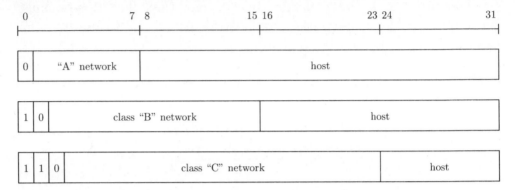

These 32–bit quantities appear in many packets: it is crucial that the ordering of the octets is consistent amongst implementations. In the Internet suite of protocols, the term *network byte order* is used to refer to octet ordering which is used by *all* implementations. When an IP address is transmitted, a "big endian" scheme is used. The most significant byte (the one with bit 0 in the figure above) is sent first, then the next significant byte, and so on.

The implications of this should be well-understood: if a network device treats IP addresses as unsigned, 32–bit integer quantities, and if it represents integers in a different format, then, prior to transmission it must perform the appropriate conversion when stuffing IP addresses into packets. Similarly, upon receipt of a packet, the device must perform the appropriate conversion from the network byte order to the local format, prior to performing any manipulations.

Finally, when describing addresses as printable strings (e.g., for use by humans), the *dotted quad* notation is used: each octet is expressed as a decimal number, separate by a dot, e.g.,

        192.33.4.21

At the application layer, when referring to a host whose name is unknown, a similar notation, the *domain literal* notation is used, e.g.,

        [192.33.4.21]

2.4.3 Routing

Given that IP addresses allow globally unique addresses to be assigned to each network device in an internet, the next question is, how is data transferred between two devices? That is, how is routing accomplished?

To begin, the local IP entity must decide the "next hop." If the destination is on the same IP network (determined by comparing the network-identifier portion of the relevant IP addresses), then choosing the next hop is simple: it is the destination IP address. This is termed *direct* routing.

Otherwise, the next hop must be to a *gateway* (usually termed a *router* in general usage, or an *intermediate-system* in OSI parlance), on the same IP network as the local device, which is somehow "closer" to the destination device. This is termed *indirect* routing.

In the interest of clarity, the discussion will use the term *host* when referring to either the source or destination device, and the term *gateway* when referring to an intermediary device. The term *network device* will continue to refer to any device attached to the network.

First, note that the routing responsibilities of hosts and gateways differ considerably: a host needs routing information only to make a simple determination as to whether the destination host shares a common IP network. The gateways need much more routing information, as they do not originate traffic, they *forward* it.

Each network device maintains a *routing table* containing, among other things, a list of addresses reachable via gateways on an attached IP network. It is often convenient to think of the routing table as being an associative array keyed by destination IP network address.[3] The other columns in a row in the array contain the IP address of the gateway and various routing metrics.

Given this terse discussion, two questions present themselves:

- How does a host find out about the gateways on its IP network?

- How do gateways find out about one another?

---

[3]By routing based on IP network numbers, rather than IP addresses, the size of the routing table is dramatically reduced.

Usually both hosts and gateways start with some initial configuration information on stable storage (e.g., a local disk). Then, they dynamically learn about the network topology through protocol interactions. In addition, there is also the notion of a *default route*, which can be used to reach a destination if its IP network is not in the routing table.

It is beyond the scope of *The Simple Book* to discuss routing protocols, other than to note that routing has been the subject of intense investigation for over a decade, with each new advance leading to a re-occurrence of the "horizon effect" (i.e., every time one problem is solved, another more complicated one arises.)

However, there are a few terms which are used so often in the context of internet routing that they are briefly defined now. These definitions are taken almost verbatim from [30]:

count to infinity: a problem occurring when routing information about an path is bounced back and forth between two routers. When the path becomes unavailable, rather than it immediately being marked unavailable by the two routers, several routing interactions must occur before the real state of the path is realized. (Each round-trip interaction results in the routing metric being incremented by two until it latches at the value used by the routing protocol to denote unreachable.)

hold down: once a path is marked unavailable, a routing policy whereby a router asserts that the path is unavailable for a minimum fixed time, even if the path becomes operational. By doing so, the exchange of information between routers concerning that path has time to become synchronized before it is re-used.

split horizon: a routing policy whereby a router does not use information from a particular router in generating information it sends back to that same router.

Two-level internets

In the mid-8os, when the Internet was beginning to enter a period of fantastic growth, it was based on a two-level connection scheme:

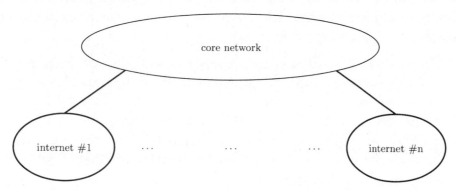

In this scheme, internets are connected to the Internet through a collection of *core gateways*, and the core network is used for *all* traffic between these internets (i.e., the resulting topology was an acyclic graph). As a consequence, the core gateways are required to have routing information on all networks available in the entire topology.

Each internet connected to the core is termed an *Autonomous System*, which underscores the notion that each is under a single administrative control and using the same routing procedures.

In such a scheme, the gateways in each Autonomous System need different kinds of information about a network. If the network is inside the same Autonomous System, then routing information is needed. Otherwise, if the network lies outside the Autonomous System, then only *reachability* information is needed (since the only way to route traffic is through the core).

To exchange reachability information between Autonomous Systems and the core, A special protocol, the *Exterior Gateway Protocol* (EGP) [31] was developed. Although the needs of the Internet have long outgrown the capabilities of EGP, it provided a much-needed service for several years. The successor to EGP is the *Border Gateway Protocol* (BGP) [32].

2.4.4   Addressing Revisited: Subnetting

Although the two-level addressing hierarchy seems reasonable at first glance, in practice many sites have found a need to have multiple physical networks. Earlier we noted that the network-identifier corresponds to precisely one physical network. A logical conclusion (no pun intended) is that if a site was running several physical networks, then it would need several IP network-identifiers, one for each physical network.

Unfortunately, this solution is not scalable since it increases the size of the routing tables with semantically redundant information. A better solution is to introduce a three-level addressing hierarchy which allows each site to partition the host-identifier portion of their IP network address. A network so sub-partitioned is termed a *subnet*, and the mechanisms used to achieve subnetting are described in [33], which is now Internet-standard.[4]

The idea behind subnetting is simple: outside of a site using sub-nets, the IP address appears to have two components, the network- and host-identifiers. Inside the site, the host-identifier is further divided into two parts: a *subnet-number*, and a *host-number*. The subnet-number refers to a particular physical network within the site's IP network, and the host-number refers to a particular device on that subnet:

network-identifier	host-identifier	
network-identifier	subnet-number	host-number

As with "ordinary" addresses, the question arises as to how the bits in the host-identifier should be divided between the subnet- and host-numbers. To provide maximum flexibility, a *subnet mask* is used. This is a 32–bit quantity which is logical-ANDed with an IP address in order to derive the actual physical network being identified:

---

[4]This name chosen (*subnet*) for this concept is unfortunate. In OSI parlance, the term *subnetwork* is used to denote a physical network. Needless to say, the similarity of these terms causes endless confusion and consternation.

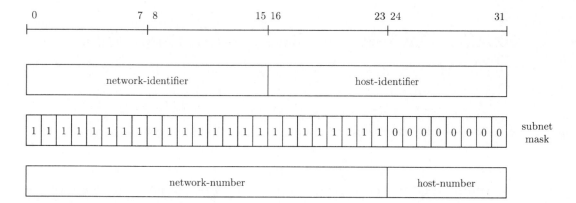

So, a new column is added to the routing table, the subnet mask. As a default condition, if the network device doesn't know if an IP network is subnetted, the subnet mask consists of a 32–bit quantity in which all of the bits in the network-portion of the IP address are set to one.

In such an architecture, the routing table is no longer considered as an associated array. Rather, when the next hop for an address, say A, must be determined, the device scans its routing table: for each entry, it logically-ANDs A with the subnet mask associated with that entry. It then checks to see if the resulting quantity is equal to the destination address of the entry. If so, then it forwards the packet to the corresponding IP gateway.[5]

Note that this approach generalizes quite nicely with the addressing architecture: if the network device is connected to a non-subnetted network, the mask is set to extract just the network-identifier, and this algorithm is equivalent to scanning the routing table sequentially, comparing A to the destination address in each entry. Of course, it is slighly slower since an additional 32-bit logical operation is performed for each entry.

Finally, one might wonder how information about subnet masks is determined. The same mechanisms are used as with the routing table: usually there is some initial configuration from stable storage;

---

[5]As one might imagine, the default route in such a scheme consists of an entry with both the destination address and subnet mask set to all zeros.

following this, there is usually some dynamic learning through protocol interactions.

2.4.5   Devices Revisited: Gateways or Hosts

Earlier it was noted that all gateways and some hosts have multiple network attachments and as such have multiple IP addresses. This leads to the obvious question as to how one distinguishes between a gateway and multi-homed host.

At the highest-level, the distinction is simple: gateways forward packets, whilst hosts originate packets. As such, gateways have additional requirements placed on their internet layer. Of course, a network device might function in both capacities, and the distinction can be made only from context of usage.

Although one might view participating in a routing protocol as the only requirement, the difference is much more fundamental:

> *If a device is not configured to act as a gateway, then it should never forward datagrams.*

Thus, if a host receives a datagram for an remote IP address, it should discard the datagram.[6] This behavior is critical in determing problems at the internet layer. If the failure was due to transient causes a protocol above the IP will cause a retransmission, and communications will resume. Otherwise, the failure will become visible and network management tools can be used to determine the cause of the problem.

In order to heal transient problems, gateways use both ICMP (a protocol discussed momentarily in Section 2.4.7) and routing protocols to synchronize their view of the internet. A host does not employ these mechanisms, and as such, can only *contribute* to the problem by forwarding the IP datagram. In particular, it is difficult to see how any good can result from a host, with only a single network attachment, deciding to forward some of the IP datagrams it receives.

---

[6]There is one exception. An IP datagram can contain an option for source-routing indicating the path that a datagram should take through an internet. So, if an IP datagram with such an option is received, it should be forwarded according to the source route, regardless of whether the IP entity is functioning as a host or a gateway.

2.4.6   The Internet Protocol

We finally come to the actual protocol used in the internet layer, the *Internet Protocol* (IP) [34].   For our purposes, little need be said. Each IP datagram contains a header containing addressing and other information, followed by user-data:

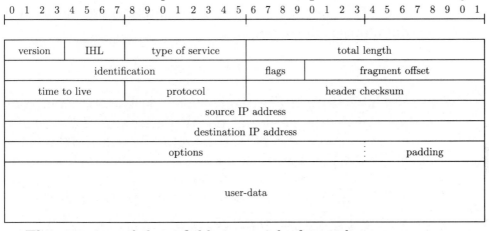

The meaning of these fields is straight-forward:

version: identifies the format used. The current number is 4.

IHL: the length of IP header in 32–bit words (the minimum allowed value is 5).

type of service: indicates the quality of service (precedence, delay, throughput, and reliability) desired for the datagram.

total length: the length of the datagram (both header and user-data), measured in octets. As noted earlier, this is necessary since some media (e.g., Ethernet) require padding if a small amount of data is transferred.

identification: a 16–bit value assigned by the originator of this datagram. It is used during reassembly (discussed momentarily).

flags: control bits determining if this datagram may be fragmented, and if so, whether other later fragments exist.

fragment offset: a 13–bit value indicating the position of this
fragment, in units of 8 octets, in the original datagram.

time to live: the upper bound (in seconds) that the datagram
may be processed within the internet. Each time the datagram passes through the internet layer on any network device, the IP entity must decrement this field by at least
one. If the field reaches zero at an intermediary device, the
datagram is discarded.

protocol: identifies the upper-layer protocol using IP.

header checksum: a one's-complement arithmetic sum, computed over the header of the IP datagram. This value is
re-calculated each time the datagram is sent (originated or
forwarded) by the IP entity on any network device.

source IP address: the IP address of the initial sender.

destination IP address: the IP address of the final recipient.

options: a collection of zero or more options.

padding: zero to three octets used to pad the datagram header
to a 32–bit boundary.

user-data: zero or more octets of data from the upper-layer protocol. (Note that it is an artifact of the convention used in
producing the figure above that this field appears to be a
multiple of 4 octets in length. No such requirement is made
by IP.)

As noted earlier in the interface layer, each medium has a maximum
size for the data field used to encapsulate an IP datagram. This
is termed the *Maximum Transmission Unit* (MTU). The interface
layer communicates this information to the internet layer using a local
mechanism.

When the local IP entity wishes to send a datagram larger than the
interface's MTU, it must *fragment* the datagram prior to transmission.

Here's how it works: each datagram generated by an IP entity is assigned an identification number, which is carried in the datagram. When an IP entity attempts to send the datagram, it checks the MTU of the associated interface. If the MTU is greater than or equal to the size of the datagram, then no further processing is required. Otherwise, the IP entity checks to see if the **flags** field in the datagram permits fragmentation. If not, the datagram is discarded. Otherwise, the IP entity generates two or more fragments. Each fragment contains a portion of the user-data from the original datagram: the user-data portion in each fragment, except the last, is a multiple of 8 octets. The **fragment offset** field contains a number corresponding to where the user-data belongs, in 8–octet increments, in the original datagram. Then, for each fragment, except for the last in the sequence, the *more fragments* bit is set in the **flags** field.

IP fragments are treated just like IP datagrams when they are in transit. When they arrive at the destination IP address, the IP entity must buffer the fragments until it has received all of them.[7] At that point it can reassemble the original datagram. Of course, since fragments may be routed over different paths, the fragments may arrive out of order. Further, some of the fragments may be lost or corrupted. In this case, the datagram can not be reassembled and the fragments which did arrive intact are discarded. Because IP fragmentation has no concept of selective retransmission of fragments (this would be contrary to the stateless behavior described earlier), it is up to the protocols above to retransmit the original datagram.

Although necessary to provide the internetworking abstraction, fragmentation has its drawbacks. Because a richly-connected internet may have several paths between two devices, there is (as yet) no deterministic mechanism to find what value the IP entity should use as the optimal MTU for entire path. Hence, if an IP datagram is to be routed indirectly, the IP entity might "guess" that a lower MTU will be encountered along the path taken by the datagram. If the guess is too high, fragmentation will still result. If the guess is too low, additional overhead will be generated by excessive fragmentation. The current "rule of thumb" is to assume an intervening MTU size of 576

---

[7]Gateways do not reassemble fragments as they may be sent over different paths.

octets, if the first hop is to a gateway. But even then, this may un-realistic. For example, if IP is being run over X.25, a packet size of 128 octets might be optimal for that portion of the path.

Further, note that if repeated fragmentation occurs and if the network experiences only modest congestion, the likelihood of lossage of a single fragment is alarmingly high. Because of this, the entire datagram will be discarded, presumably causing retransmission by the protocols above. Of course, only one small part of the datagram was lost, so this is a rather inefficient use of resources.

2.4.7   The Internet Control Message Protocol

Associated with the IP is another protocol providing low-level feed-back about how the internet layer is operating. This protocol is termed the *Internet Control Message Protocol* (ICMP) [35]. ICMP provides very simple advice within the internet layer as to how it might tailor its behavior. At the end of this chapter, it will be shown how this functionality can be used for ad hoc network management.

For now, it is important to understand that ICMP provides a modest number of basic control messages for error-reporting. Even though both protocols are a part of the internet layer, ICMP uses the delivery services of IP. If the **protocol** field of an IP datagram has the value 1, the user-data contained in the datagram is an ICMP packet. Although the format of ICMP packets varies with each control message, the first 32–bits contains the same three fields:

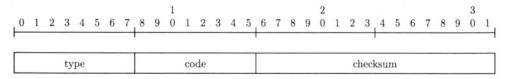

The meaning of these fields is straight-forward:

type: identifies which control message is being sent (and thereby defines the format of the rest of the packet).

code: identifies a basic parameter for the control message (the semantics depends on the value of the **type** field).

header checksum: a one's-complement arithmetic sum, computed over the entire ICMP packet. (Recall that the IP checksum is calculated *only* for the IP header, not the user-data.)

The control messages supported by ICMP include:

destination unreachable: to report that a datagram couldn't be delivered because a network or host was unreachable, a protocol was not running, or fragmentation was necessary but disallowed by the **flags** field.

time exceeded: to report that a datagram was discarded because its **time to live** field reached zero, or a fragment was discarded because it was on the reassembly queue too long.

parameter problem: to report an error in an IP header.

source quench: to report that a network device is discarding datagrams due to lack of resources (e.g., buffers).

redirect: to report a gateway closer to a destination IP address. This is one means whereby a host can learn about gateways: the host starts with a default gateway, and performs all indirect routing through it. If the gateway knows of another gateway on the same IP network which is closer to the desired destination, it can generate an ICMP redirect message to inform the host.

echo/echo reply: to test reachability of an IP address, an echo message is sent. Upon receiving such a message, the local IP entity responds by sending an echo reply message.

timestamp/timestamp reply: to sample the delay in the network between two network devices.

information request/information reply: to determine the address of the local IP network.

address mask request/address mask reply: to determine
the subnet mask associated with the local IP network.
(These two messages are defined in [33].)

It is a fundamental principle that an ICMP message is never sent in
response to an ICMP message (or correspondent IP datagram) which
contains an error.

2.5 Transport Layer

The transport layer is reponsible for providing data transfer between end-systems to the level of reliability desired by the application. That is, the transport layer provides end-to-end service.

In theory, the end-to-end needs of different applications can vary tremendously. In practice however, there are really only two widely-used service paradigms:

reliable: in which the service offered is a "virtual pipeline":

- *stream-oriented*: rather than dealing in packet exchanges, the end-to-end service provides a sequence of octets, termed a *stream*, to the application.

- *full-duplex*: the stream provided by the end-to-end service is full-duplex in nature.

- *connection-oriented*: before the stream can be used, a virtual connection is established between the two applications.

- *application-layer addressing*: an application needs a means of identifying its peer on the remote system to which the stream should be connected.

- *in-sequence delivery*: the end-to-end service guarantees that user-data is delivered in the same order in which it was sent.

- *user-data integrity*: the end-to-end service guarantees that any user-data delivered has not been corrupted during network transmission.

- *graceful release*: because user-data may be buffered both at the hosts and in the network, the end-to-end service will make sure that *all* of the data sent by the user is successfully transmitted before the stream is released.

Note that these are general guidelines, and not fixed. In particular, the OSI CO-mode transport service, whilst offering a reliable transport paradigm, uses a packet-oriented (rather than stream-oriented) user-data paradigm, and has no graceful release mechanism (the functionality of which resides at the layer above). Regardless, the remaining characteristics are core to the concept of a reliable transport service.

unreliable: in which the service offered is virtually identical to that of the internet datagram service. The only added features are:

- *application-layer addressing*; and,
- *user-data integrity.*

It shouldn't be surprising that the reliable service paradigm corresponds closely to a connection-oriented transport service, whilst the unreliable service paradigm is similar to a connectionless-mode transport service.

The Internet suite of protocol provides two different transport protocols to meet these vastly different needs. Since both protocols use identical mechanisms to achieve application-layer addressing and user-data integrity, the simpler protocol is described first.

2.5.1   The User Datagram Protocol

The *User Datagram Protocol* (UDP) [36] is the connectionless-mode transport protocol in the Internet suite.   As UDP is a transport layer protocol, for delivery, it uses the services of IP. If the **protocol** field of an IP datagram has the value 17 (decimal), the user-data contained in the datagram is a UDP packet:

```
                    1                   2                   3
 0 1 2 3 4 5 6 7 8 9 0 1 2 3 4 5 6 7 8 9 0 1 2 3 4 5 6 7 8 9 0 1
+---------------------------------------------------------------+
```

source port	destination port
length	checksum

user-data

The meaning of these fields is straight-forward:

source/destination port: identifies an application running at the correspondent IP address.

length: the length of the UDP packet (header and user-data), measured in octets.

checksum: a 16–bit one's-complement arithmetic sum.

user-data: zero or more octets of data from the upper-layer protocol. (Note that it is an artifact of the convention used in producing the figure above that this field appears to be a multiple of 4 octets in length. No such requirement is made by UDP.)

The uses of these fields are now explained.

Application-layer Addressing

To achieve application-layer addressing, UDP manages 16–bit unsigned integer quantities, termed *ports*. Port numbers less than 512 are assigned by the Internet Assigned Numbers Authority. These are termed *well-known ports*. In those cases when a service might be available over both TCP and UDP, the IANA assigns the same port number to that service for both protocols.

On Berkeley UNIX, port numbers less than 1024 are reserved for privileged processes (an easily spoofed, but still quite useful, security mechanism).

The combination of an IP address and a port number is termed an internet *socket* which uniquely identifies an application entity running in an internet.

Of course, the notion of application-layer addressing is just another example of the multiplexing operation of protocols:

- at the interface layer, each medium usually distinguishes between clients (entities at the internet layer) by using different values in a **type** field (e.g., Ethernet uses a value of 0x0800 to indicate IP);

- at the internet layer, IP distinguishes between clients (entities at the transport layer) by using different values in a **protocol** field (e.g., IP uses a value of 6 to indicate TCP); and,

- at the transport layer, TCP and UDP distinguish between clients (entities at the application layer) by using different values in a **port** field (e.g., UDP uses a value of 161 (decimal) to indicate SNMP).

The Assigned Numbers RFC [18] lists the complete set of protocol numbers used at all layers in the Internet suite of protocols.

User-Data Integrity

To achieve both user-data integrity and modest protection against misbehavior at the layers below, UDP calculates a *pseudo-header* which is conceptually prefixed to the UDP packet. The checksum algorithm is then run over the resulting string of octets:

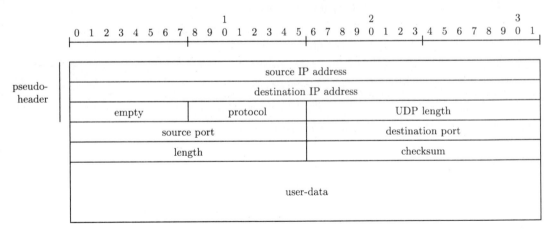

The fields of the pseudo-header are relatively self-explanatory: the **empty** field is simply a zero-valued octet, the **protocol** field is the value used by IP to identify UDP (17 decimal), and the **UDP length** field is the length of the UDP packet.

TCP also uses this 96–bit pseudo-header in its checksum calculation when achieving user-data integrity.

2.5.2   The Transmission Control Protocol

The *Transmission Control Protocol* (TCP) [37] is the connection-oriented transport protocol in the Internet suite. As TCP is a connection-oriented transport protocol, it goes through three distinct phases: connection establishment, data transfer, and connection release. To keep track of a particular connection, each TCP entity maintains a *Transmission Control Block* (TCB). This is created during connection establishment, modified throughout the life of the connection, and then deleted when the connection is released.

TCP is best described as a finite state machine, which starts in the CLOSED state. As *events* occur (either activity from a user of TCP or from the network), the TCP entity performs some *action* and then enters a new state. The TCP state diagram is presented in Figure 2.4 on page 62, which is taken from the RFC which defines TCP. It is suggested that the reader study the intervening text before examining the figure.

Connection Establishment

A connection enters the LISTEN state when an application entity tells TCP that it is willing to accept connections for a particular port number. This is termed a *passive open*.

Sometime later, another application entity tells TCP that it wishes to establish a connection to an IP address and port number which corresponds to the application entity which is listening. This is termed an *active open*.[8]

When two TCP entities communicate, the exchanged units of data are termed *segments*. The format of a segment is presented later on. Segments are interpreted relative to a *connection*. In TCP, a connection is defined as the pairing of the two internet sockets. This 96–bit quantity (source IP address and TCP port, destination IP address and TCP port) uniquely identifies the connection in an internet.

When an active open is attempted, the originating TCP entity computes an *initial sequence number*, which is a "starting number"

---

[8]It is possible for two application entities to simultaneously issue active opens for each other. In this case, a single TCP connection is established.

for this direction of the new connection. The sequence number must be chosen carefully so that segments from older instances of this connection, which might be floating around the network, won't cause confusion with this new connection. A SYN (synchronize) segment is then sent to the destination TCP entity. Upon receiving this segment, the destination TCP entity checks to see that an application entity is listening on the destination TCP port. If not, the connection is aborted by sending a RST (reset) segment.[9] Otherwise, the destination TCP entity computes a sequence number for its direction, and sends this back in a SYN/ACK (synchronize/acknowledge) segment which acknowledges the sequence number for the originating TCP entity.

Upon receiving this segment, the original TCP entity makes sure that its sequence number was acknowledged, and, if all is well, sends an ACK segment back to acknowledge the sequence number for the destination TCP entity.

This protocol interaction is termed a *three-way handshake*. Once the three-way handshake has been successfully concluded, the connection enters the data transfer phase.

Data Transfer

In the data transfer phase, user-data is sent as a sequence of octets, each of which is numbered.

Each segment specifies a window size (in octets) which may be sent in each direction before an acknowledgement is returned. Each segment sent by a TCP entity contains an implicit acknowledgement of all octets contiguously received thus far. Precisely stated, the acknowledgement field indicates the number of the *next* octet that is expected by a TCP entity.

This windowing strategy allows the TCP entities to achieve a *pipelining effect* in the network, while at the same time providing a flow control mechanism. The pipelining effect increases throughput by keeping more data in the network, whilst the flow control mechanism prevents either TCP entity from overrunning the connection resources (such as buffers for user-data) of the other.

---

[9]In the interests of simplicity, Figure 2.4 does not show this transition, or any transition involving a RST segment.

The disadvantage of this approach is that if segments are re-ordered, this information can not be conveyed in an acknowledgement. For example, if two segments are sent, and the first one is delayed, the receiving TCP entity can not acknowledge the second segment until it receives the first one.

Data Transfer – Retransmission

The discussion thus far has not considered loss or corruption of segments. Each time a TCP entity sends a segment, it starts a retransmission timer. At some time in the future, one of two events will happen first: either an acknowledgement for the segment will be received, and the timer can be stopped; or, the timer will expire. In this latter case, the TCP entity *retransmits* the segment and restarts the timer. Retransmission continues some number of times until eventually the TCP entity gives up and declares the transport connection to be aborted. That is, TCP achieves reliability through retransmission. The trick, of course, is knowning *when* to retransmit. If data is lost or corrupted in the network and the sending transport entity retransmits too slowly, then throughput suffers. If data is delayed or discarded due to congestion in the network and the transport entity retransmits too quickly then it merely adds to the congestion and throughput gets even worse!

The reader should appreciate that because of the service offerred by IP, a TCP entity can not distinguish between lossy or congested networks. Hence, TCP uses one of several adaptive algorithms to predict the latency characteristics of the network, which may fluctuate considerably because of other traffic.

The retransmission timeout usually varies for each segment, based on the recent history of latency and loss exhibited by the network. Recent work reported in [38,39] suggests some novel, common sense insights into this problem.

As might be expected, acknowledgements and retransmission interact with the window strategy. Once again suppose two segments are sent, and the first segment is lost. The receiving TCP entity can not acknowledge the second segment. The retransmission timer expires for the sending TCP entity. It must now decide whether to retransmit the first segment or both segments. If it retransmits both the segments, then it is "guessing" that both segments were lost. If this is not the case, then network bandwidth is being wasted. Otherwise if it retransmits the first segment only, it must wait for an acknowldgement to see if the second segment also needs to be retransmitted. If not, it has reduced its sending throughput by waiting for a round-trip transaction in the network.

Data Transfer – Queued Delivery

In addition to trying to optimize network traffic, a TCP entity may try to reduce the overhead of communicating with local application entities. This is usually achieved by buffering user-data in the TCP entity, both as it is received from the local application entity, in order to efficiently use the network, and also as user-data is received from the network, in order to efficiently communicate with the local application entity. Because of this, an application entity might need a mechanism for ensuring that all data it has previously sent has been flushed from wherever it might be bufferred.

This is accomplished using a PSH (push) function. When sending, an application entity may indicate that data previously sent should be pushed. The local TCP entity sets a PSH bit in the next new segment it sends. Upon receiving such a segment, the remote TCP entity knows that it should push user-data up to its own application entity.

Although the push function must be present in each TCP implementation, few implementations of applications actually use this functionality. This is because most TCP entity implementations will periodically push any queued data towards the destination. Further, it should be noted that there are no semantics associated with the push function. It is simply a way of telling TCP to deliver all data previously sent to the remote application entity. On the remote device, the application entity will see only the user-data and will not receive any explicit indications of the push function having been invoked. Experience has shown that the push function is largely an internal matter: application protocols should be designed so that the push function is not used.

Data Transfer – Urgent Data

Finally, TCP supports the concept of *urgent data*. The semantics of urgent data are application-specific. What TCP does is to indicate where urgent data ends in the stream. The receiving application entity, upon being notified that urgent data is present in the stream, can quickly read from the stream until the urgent data is exhausted.

Connection Release

When an application entity indicates that it has finished sending on the connection, the local TCP entity ensures that all the segments it has sent have been acknowledged. Once this is true, the local TCP entity generates a FIN (finish) segment, to indicate that it is finished sending new data.

Upon receiving this segment, the remote TCP entity will send an ACK segment for the FIN, and will indicate this (using a local mechanism) to the application entity. When that process indicates that it too has no more data to send, a FIN is generated in this direction also. When all data in transit and the segments containing the FINs have been acknowledged, the two TCP entities declare the connection released. In order to ensure that old, duplicate packets do not interfere with new connections being established between the two application entities, the TCPs will judiciously increment their segment numbers.

Instead of requesting a graceful release, an application entity may determine that it wishes to immediately abort the connection. In this case, the local TCP entity generates a RST (reset) segment, and the connection is immediately released. Any data in transit is lost.

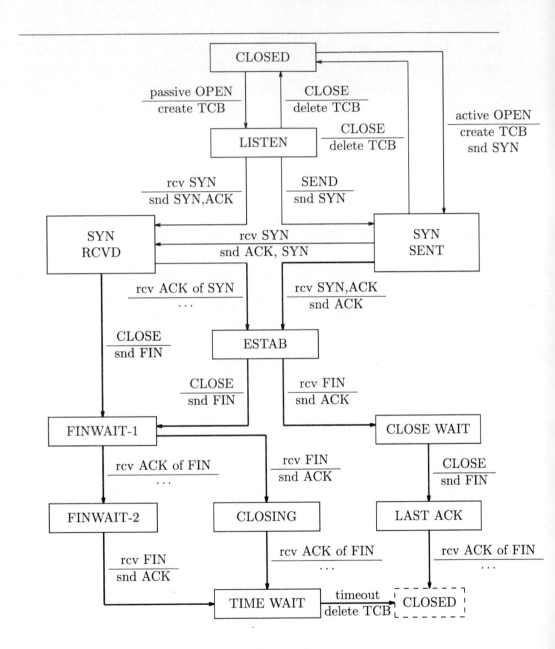

Figure 2.4: TCP State Diagram

...t Format

When TCP wishes to send a segment, it uses the services of IP. If the **protocol** field of an IP datagram has the value 6 (decimal), then the user-data contained in the datagram is a TCP segment:

```
                    1                   2                   3
 0 1 2 3 4 5 6 7 8 9 0 1 2 3 4 5 6 7 8 9 0 1 2 3 4 5 6 7 8 9 0 1
```

source port	destination port
sequence number	
acknowledgement number	

offset	reserved	flags	window

checksum	urgent pointer
options	padding

user-data

The meaning of these fields is straight-forward:

source/destination port: identifies an application running at the correspondent IP address.

sequence number: the number of the first octet of user-data in this segment.

acknowledgement number: if the ACK bit is set in the **flags** field, then this field indicates the next sequence number that the TCP entity is expecting to receive.

offset: the length of the TCP segment in 32–bit words (the minimum allowed value is 5).

flags: control bits indicating special functions for this segment.

window: the number of octets of user-data (starting with the octet indicated in the **acknowledgement** field), which the TCP entity is willing to accept.

checksum: a one's-complement arithmetic sum, computed over a pseudo-header and the entire TCP segment, as discussed earlier.

urgent pointer: if the URG bit is set in the **flags** field, then this field when added to the **sequence number** field indicates the first octet of non-urgent data.

options: a collection of zero or more options.

padding: zero to three octets used to pad the segment header to a 32–bit boundary.

user-data: zero or more octets of data from the upper-layer protocol. (Note that it is an artifact of the convention used in producing the figure above that this field appears to be a multiple of 4 octets in length. No such requirement is made by TCP.)

2.6 Application Layer

Historically, management of the Internet suite of protocols has focused on the lower three layers (interface, internet, and transport) of the architecture. Therefore, there is little to be gained by describing even the core application protocols at this time. Perhaps when management of the application layer is understood and in use, a subsequent revision of *The Simple Book* will describe the correspondent protocols.

2.7   Ad Hoc Management Techniques

Even given the modest functionality provided by ICMP, it is still possible to build two useful tools in trouble-shooting connectivity problems at the internet layer. Historically, these mechanisms are the lowest common denominators available.

2.7.1   Ping

The *packet internet groper* (*ping*) program sends an ICMP echo request packet to an IP address and awaits a reply. Since implementation of ICMP is mandatory for all network devices supporting the Internet suite of protocols, this provides a crude means of seeing if "you can get there from here."

Of course, *ping* is useful only for testing the connectivity from the local network device to a remote one even though typical implementations report the time taken to receive the reply, and by sending multiple requests, they report the percentage of loss. However, *ping* cannot report on the general health of an internet. Nor can it report on the path taken by an IP datagram as it traverses the networks between the local and remote network devices.

The first problem can not be solved in the absence of general network management technology (which is what the next three chapters of *The Simple Book* are devoted to). However, there is a clever means by which the second problem can be solved.

2.7.2   Traceroute

The *traceroute* program sends a series of "probe packets" using UDP to an IP address and awaits, of all things, ICMP replies!

Here's how it works: the IP datagrams carrying the UDP packets are sent with monotonically increasing values in the **time to live** (TTL) field, and the UDP port number used is chosen so as to most likely not be in use. For each TTL value, the *traceroute* program sends a fixed number of packets (usually 3), and reports back the IP addresses of the devices responding. This process continues until an

ICMP port unreachable packet is received or some TTL threshold is reached (usually 30).

If a gateway receives an IP datagram and decrements the TTL to zero, then it returns an ICMP time exceeded packet. If the IP datagram eventually reaches the network device in question, an ICMP port unreachable packet will be returned. Combining the information from all the replies, the *traceroute* program can report on the whole route.

It should be noted that *traceroute* is not entirely fool-proof in its operation: sadly, not all implementations of even IP, ICMP, and UDP operate correctly. If the probes sent by *traceroute* encounter such devices, interesting interactions result.

2.7.3 Passive Management

Both *ping* and *traceroute* work by introducing management traffic onto the network. However, a large number of management problems can be solved simply by examining the traffic generated by the protocol in question. For example, in trying to analyze the problems of a TCP connection (e.g., poor throughput), a lot can be learned by building programs which simply capture and decode the TCP segments being exchanged. These "packet monitors" have been in use since the beginning of networking and are now quite sophisticated.

The passive approach to management relies on *capture* and *analysis*. In order to capture the protocol traffic, the monitor must either be co-resident with, or attached to, the same physical medium as the device being studied. Note that if a device being monitored is multi-homed, then, in order to guarantee complete access to all traffic, the monitor must be attached to all cable segments attached to the device in question.

Indeed, quite a market has been built for devices which do nothing but monitor all traffic on a cable segment, select that traffic which is interesting for the manager, and then provide information about that traffic. Of course, given the amount of traffic that can be generated by a sender and receiver on a high-bandwidth media, the monitor must be able to filter and store traffic at an equally fast rate. This usually argues for use of a special-purpose monitoring device, and one which can perform capture and analysis separately.

Once data has been captured, it must be analyzed. This means that the monitor must have an excellent understanding of the protocol in question, in addition to being able to understand any underlying protocols in use. Further, for connection-oriented protocols such as TCP, it must be able to maintain state for a connection being monitored, so as to be able to understand the actions of the TCP entities involved. In many cases, the difficulty of this cannot be overstated.

Analysis is, of course, dependent on the protocol being monitored. At the simplest level, the monitor can advise the manager of duplicated packets, the timing relationships between packets, and so on.

Chapter 3

Concepts

Having introduced the core portions of the Internet suite of protocols, it is now time to proceed to the main focus of *The Simple Book*: network management of internets which use these protocols.

The framework used for network management in the Internet suite of protocols is markedly different than the corresponding OSI framework. These differences can be primarily attributed to the critical need for operational network management capabilities in the Internet. These immediate needs mandated the development of a system based on proven, well-understood practices, rather than catering to every theoretical requirement.

We term the framework used for network management in the Internet suite of protocols the *Internet-standard Network Mangement Framework*. This is primarily due to historical reasons: prior schemes were ad hoc and proprietary. The current framework is based on three RFCs which, in May, 1990, were elevated as "Standard Protocols" with "Recommended" status by the IAB.

3.1   A Model

A network management system contains three components:

- several *managed nodes*, each containing an *agent*;

- at least one *network management station* (NMS); and,

- a network management *protocol*, which is used by the station and the agents to exchange management information.

These are now considered in turn.

3.1.1   Managed Nodes

A managed node refers to a device of some kind, falling into one of three categories:

- a host system, such as a workstation, terminal server, or printer;

- a gateway system, or,

- a media device, such as a bridge, hub, or multiplexor.

The commonality between these categories is that all devices have some sort of network capability. The first two categories implement the Internet suite of protocols, whilst the primary function of devices in the third category is media-dependent. As can be seen, the potential diversity of managed nodes is quite high, spanning the spectrum from mainframes to modems.

The Fundamental Axiom

A successful network management system must take notice of this dichotomy, and provide an appropriate framework. In the previous chapter, it was noted that the success of IP is largely due to the minimal requirements that it places on the interface layer below. A similar philosophy is taken with the Internet-standard Network Management Framework:

> *The impact of adding network management to managed nodes must be minimal, reflecting a lowest common denominator.*

This *Fundamental Axiom* is mandated by the wide differences between managed nodes, and is argued quite eloquently in [40].

The Commonalities of Managed Nodes

Given the focus of the Fundamental Axiom, what commonalities between managed nodes can we exploit? Basically, any managed node can be conceptualized as containing three components:

```
┌─────────────────────────────────────────────┐
│           MANAGEMENT PROTOCOL                 │
├──────────────────────────────┬──────┬────────┤
│                              │      │   I    │
│                              │      │   N    │
│                              │      │   S    │
│                              │  M   │   T    │
│                              │  A   │   R    │
│                              │  N   │   U    │
│         "USEFUL"             │  A   │   M    │
│                              │  G   │   E    │
│                              │  E   │   N    │
│         PROTOCOLS            │  M   │   T    │
│                              │  E   │   A    │
│                              │  N   │   T    │
│                              │  T   │   I    │
│                              │      │   O    │
│                              │      │   N    │
└──────────────────────────────┴──┬───┴────────┘
                                   │
                          NETWORK
───────────────────────────────────────────────
```

These are:

- *useful protocols*, which perform the function desired by the user;

- a *management protocol*, which permits the monitoring and control of the managed node; and,

- *management instrumentation*, which interacts with the implementation of the managed node in order to achieve monitoring and control.

The interaction between these components is straight-forward: the instrumentation acts as "glue" between the useful protocols and the management protocol. This is usually achieved by an internal communications mechanism in which the data structures for the useful protocols may be accessed and manipulated at the request of the management protocol.

Actually this view is slightly simplistic: exchanges of management information, per se, are insufficient to achieve management functionality of the managed node. The management protocol must also provide an *administrative framework*, which implements authentication and authorization policies. This allows the managed node to determine how it is managed, so that only authorized application processes may perform management.

For example, there may be several administrations responsible for management of an entire internet. Some nodes might be managed by multiple administrations.

3.1.2   Network Management Stations

A network management station refers to a host system which is running:

- the network management protocol; and,

- network management applications.

If the network management protocol is viewed as providing the mechanism for management, then it is the network management applications which determine the policy used for management.

Earlier it was noted that the Fundamental Axiom indicated that "adding network management" should have a minimal impact on the managed nodes. As a consequence, the burden is shifted to the management station. Thus, one should expect that the host systems supporting a management station are relatively powerful in comparison to the managed nodes. How much power is necessary? Experience shows that most workstations are quite capable of providing the resources needed to realize an effective management station.

Note that since there are many more managed nodes that management stations in an internet, scalability favors this approach: it is better to require significant functionality from a small percentage of devices, rather than the vast majority.

As a final rationale consider that because the marketplace for products using the Internet suite of protocols is fast becoming a commodity market, vendors of TCP/IP-based products are highly price-sensitive. If "adding network management" to a gateway implies adding another memory board or a faster processor, the vendor will balk. In contrast, since software for the management station is an unbundled item, it is more attractive, from an economic perspective, to focus development resources there.

The management stations run by the operations staff of a large network is termed a *Network Operations Center* (NOC). There is no fixed relationship between managed nodes and NOCs. For example, there might be many network elements assigned to a single NOC station, but there might also be one or many NOC stations for each network element.

3.1.3   Network Management Protocol

Depending on the paradigm used for network management, there are several forms that a management protocol, supporting a particular paradigm, might take. For example, in a remote execution paradigm, the management protocol is used to exchange "program fragments" which are executed on the managed node.

In the Internet-standard Network Management Framework, a "remote debugging" paradigm is used. Each managed node is viewed as having several "variables." By reading the value of these variables, the managed node is monitored. By changing the value of these variables, the managed node is controlled.[1] The advantage of using this paradigm is that it is straight-forward to build a simple management protocol to meet these goals.

---

[1]Note that this approach obviates the need for so-called *imperative* commands (e.g., "reboot the device") which are found in the OSI management framework: any imperative command can be realized in terms of changing the value of a variable which has been specially defined for this purpose.

In addition to read and write operations, there are two other operations that are required:

- a traversal operation, which allows a management station to determine which variables a managed node supports; and,

- a trap operation, which allows a managed node to report an extraordinary event to a management station.

These both require a bit more explanation.

Traversal

Since managed nodes perform different functions, it shouldn't be surprising that they might contain different management variables. In the Internet-standard Network Management Framework, variables related to a particular functionality are grouped together. For example, each device which implements the internet layer would be expected to provide the variables in the "internet layer" group.

Of course, such an approach also argues for *extensibility*. As network management becomes better understood, things will change. The management framework must take this into account to provide an easy way for the new to interwork with the old.

Given that different managed nodes may support different management variables, there must be an efficient means for a management station to determine which variables are supported. Hence, the protocol must provide a means of traversing the list of variables supported by a managed node.

But, there is even a more basic need for traversal: thus far the discussion has implicitly assumed that these variables are scalar-valued. What about the IP routing table? Clearly this is not a scalar, but a table consisting of zero or more rows (one for each routing entry), and each row containing several columns. The management protocol must now provide two functions:

- if the management station knows which routing entry it is looking for, the management protocol should provide a means for retrieving the desired columns of that entry efficiently.

- if the management station wishes to browse the routing table, the management protocol should provide a means for incrementally examining the contents of the routing table.

Traps

Since the dawn of operating systems, there has been a never-ending debate as to the merits of using either an *interrupt-driven* approach or a *polling* approach in order to keep abreast of extraordinary events. It should not be surprising that the debate has spilled over into the network management arena.

In network management parlance, the arguments are phrased in terms of *traps* and *polling*:

- With the trap-based approach, when an extraordinary event occurs (such as a link going down), the managed node sends a trap to the NOC (assuming that the node has not crashed and that there is a path in the network by which the NOC can be reached). This has the advantage of providing an immediate notification.

  There are also several disadvantages: it requires resources to generate the trap. If the trap must contain a lot of information, the managed node may be spending too much time on the trap and not enough time working on useful things. For example, if traps require some sort of acknowledgement from the manager, this places further requirements on the agent's resources. Of course, when a trap is generated, the agent is assuming that the NOC is ready to receive such information. Careful design must be used in order to achieve a system in which traps can be idempotent!

  Further, if several extraordinary events occur, a lot of network bandwidth is tied up containing traps, which is hardly desirable if the report is about network congestion. So, to refine the trap-based approach, a managed node might use *thresholds* when deciding when to report: traps are generated only when the occurrence of an event exceeds some threshold. Unfortunately, this means that the agent must spent substantive time

determining if an event should generate a trap. As a result, use
of the trap-based approach has a severe impact on the performance of the agent, or the network, or both! And in any event,
the managed node has only a very limited view of the internet,
so it is arguable as to whether it can provide "the big picture"
on the problem by using traps.

- With the polling-based approach, the NOC periodically queries
  the managed node as to how things are going. This has the
  advantage of keeping the NOC in control as it determines what
  "the big picture" really is.

  The disadvantage of course is one of timeliness. How is the NOC
  to know which managed elements to poll and how often? If the
  interval is too small, network bandwidth is wasted; if too large,
  the response to catastrophic events is slow.

In the Internet-standard Network Management Framework, the model
used is one of *trap-directed polling*. When an extraordinary event
occurs, the managed node sends a *single*, simple trap to the NOC.
The NOC is then responsible for initiating further interactions with
the managed node in order to determine the nature and extent of the
problem. This compromise is surprisingly effective: the impact on
managed nodes remains small; the impact on network bandwidth is
minimized; and, problems can be dealt with in a timely fashion. Of
course, since they are sent unreliably, traps serve as an early-warning;
low-frequency polling is needed as a back-up.

3.1.4 Proxy Management

Thus far, the discussion has implicitly focused on managed nodes
which can directly support the management protocol. As a consequence, if the management protocol runs over the Internet suite of
protocols, the discussion has assumed that all managed nodes support (at least a subset) of these protocols. In the cases of media
devices which appear on the network, such as repeaters, bridges, and
(perhaps someday) toasters, this needn't be the case. In addition, if
host or gateway systems, which implement other protocol suites, but

not the Internet suite of protocols, are on the network, then they, too, cannot be managed. For lack of a better term, the media devices and those devices which implement only other protocols from other suites are termed *foreign* devices. How might network management be made universal to all devices in an internet?

In the Internet-standard Network Management Framework, a special agent, termed a *proxy agent*, acts on behalf of the foreign device. When such a device is to be managed, the management station contacts the proxy agent, and indicates (in some fashion) the identity of the foreign device. The proxy agent then translates the protocol interactions it receives from the management station into whatever interactions are supported by the foreign device.

The nature of the actual translation varies:

- If the foreign device supports the mangement protocol, but not the end-to-end service used to transmit the actual management protocol data units (e.g., UDP and IP), the proxy agent need only strip out these protocol data units and then send them to the foreign device using a different transmission service.

  This approach is generally not necessary: experience has shown that it is usually easier to implement the minimal protocols needed for end-to-end service and avoid using a proxy agent. (Of course, this is a direct consequence of the purposefully minimal requirements of the management protocol used.)

- Otherwise, if the foreign device supports a different management protocol, the proxy agent acts as an *application-gateway*.

There is also a very clever use of a proxy agent: caching of management information. In some environments, some management questions get asked frequently. If the answers don't change as frequently, a proxy agent might be placed between the managed node and several management stations so as to minimize the processing burden on the managed node. However, it is difficult to implement an efficient caching scheme to support the browsing capability mentioned earlier.

3.1.5   In Perspective

The Fundamental Axiom of the Internet-standard Network Management Framework is based on the notion of universal deployment:

> *If network management is viewed as an essential aspect of an internet, then it must be universally deployed on the largest possible collection of devices in the network.*

As noted earlier, by taking a minimalist approach, the management framework enjoys significant leverage in terms of economy of scale. There are many more agents than management stations. Thus, minimizing the impact of management on the agents is the most attractive solution to the problem.

A second, though equally important, tenet is that network management is unlike all other applications:

> *When all else fails, network management must continue to function, if at all possible.*

As with the Fundamental Axiom, this tenet is argued quite eloquently in [40].

As noted earlier, this tenet mandates that many of the functions traditionally found in the transport layer (e.g., retransmission) be directly addressed by applications in the management station since it is only the applications themselves that know the reliability requirements of each operation. Therefore, the transport service must not be "helpful." It should be the simplest possible pass-through available to the network.

The chapter now closes with a a terse (but still lengthy), discussion of data representation at the application layer.

3.2 Data Representation

Throughout Chapter 2 there were numerous diagrams showing the bit-wise layout of the packets exchanged by some of the lower-layer protocols of the Internet suite. As might be expected, each implementation of these protocols has an *internal representation* which denotes these structures. The actual layout of each data structure depends on the programming language, language compiler, and machine architecture of each platform.

Because the packets are relatively simple, the only major concern is that of using a network byte ordering scheme (as discussed earlier). At the application layer, the data structures exchanged by protocol entities are potentially much more complex. Therefore, it is necessary to introduce a new formalism for describing these structures.

This new formalism is termed an *abstract syntax,* which is used to define data without regard to machine-oriented structures and restrictions. In the Internet-standard Network Management Framework, an OSI language, termed *Abstract Syntax Notation One* (ASN.1) is used for this purpose.

It must be emphasized that ASN.1 is used for two distinct purposes by the management framework:

- defining the formats of the PDUs exchanged by the management protocol; and,

- as the means for defining the objects which are managed.

That is: abstract syntax is used both to describe the data structures exchanged at the protocol level, along with the management information which is conveyed through those data structures. Note that this second use is at a conceptually higher-level than the first.

Hand in glove with abstract syntax is the notion of a *transfer syntax.* Once data structures can be described in a machine-independent fashion, there must be some way of transmitting those data structures, unambiguously, over the network. This is the job of a transfer syntax notation. Obviously, one could have several transfer syntax notations for a single abstract syntax. But, as of this writing, only a single abstract syntax/transfer syntax pair have been defined in OSI.

ASN.1 is used as the machine-independent language for data structures, and the *Basic Encoding Rules* (BER) is used as the encoding rules.

soap...
The *official* reason for using ASN.1 is to ease the eventual transition to OSI-based network management protocols. The *actual* reason is that the Internet research community got caught napping on this one, having never spent much time dealing with application-layer structuring. This is particularly humorous since ASN.1 can trace its roots back to a decade-earlier research project staffed by some of the Internet researchers! Fortunately, ASN.1 is destined, for better or worse, to become the network programming language of the 90s, just as the *C* programming language is largely seen as having been the systems programming language of the 80s. So, the choice of ASN.1 is
...soap
a good one.

ASN.1 is a *formal* language, which means that it is defined in terms of a *grammar*. The language is defined in [41]. Some extensions to the language were more recently defined in [42].

It is clearly beyond the scope of *The Simple Book* to present a thorough treatment of ASN.1; the reader should consult Chapter 8 of *The Open Book* for a detailed exposition. Thus, the remainder of this chapter will introduce ASN.1 only to the extent that it is used by the mangement framework.

The Internet-standard Network Management Framework uses only a subset of the capabilities of ASN.1. The idea behind this is that whilst the general principles of abstract syntax, as embodied by the ASN.1 language, are good, many of the "bells and whistles" of ASN.1 lead to unnecessary complexity. Referring back to the Fundamental Axiom, prudence dictates that a minimalist approach be taken in order to decrease resource requirements on the managed nodes (in terms of both code size and execution time).

Note that this chapter will not discuss how values are encoded on the network. This is postponed until the actual management protocol is discussed in Section 5.10 on page 167.

3.2.1 Modules

A collection of ASN.1 descriptions, relating to a common theme (e.g., a protocol specification), is termed a *module*. The high-level syntax of a module is simple:

```
<<module>> DEFINITIONS ::= BEGIN

<<linkage>>

<<declarations>>

END
```

The `<<module>>` term names the module, both informally and possibly authoritatively (uniquely) as well. Think of the authoritative designation as allowing several modules to be placed in a library and then unambiguously referenced through the `<<linkage>>` term. Thus, modules can `EXPORT` definitions for use by other modules, which in turn `IMPORT` them. Finally, the `<<declarations>>` term contains the actual ASN.1 definitions.

Three kinds of objects are defined using ASN.1:

- *types*, which define new data structures;

- *values*, which are instances (variables) of a type; and,

- *macros*, which are used to change the actual grammar of the ASN.1 language.

Each of these objects is named using an ASN.1 word; however, ASN.1 uses an alphabetic case convention to indicate the kind of object to which the word refers:

- for a *type*, the word starts with an uppercase letter (e.g., `Gauge`);

- for a *value* (an instance of a type), the word starts with a lowercase letter (e.g., `internet`); and,

- for a *macro*, the word consists entirely of uppercase letters (e.g., `OBJECT-TYPE`).

The keywords of the ASN.1 language appear entirely in uppercase.

The management framework defines only one ASN.1 macro, which is defined in the next chapter. Only ASN.1 types and values need be introduced at this time.

3.2.2   Types and Values

An ASN.1 type is defined using a straight-forward syntax:

```
NameOfType ::=
    TYPE
```

Similarly, a value (more properly an instance of a data type) is defined as:

```
nameOfValue NameOfType ::=
    VALUE
```

That is, first the variable is named (`nameOfValue`), then it is typed (`NameOfType`), and then a value is assigned.

The management framework uses four kinds of ASN.1 types, which are now discussed in turn.

Simple Types

The simple ASN.1 types used in the management framework are now described:

INTEGER: a data type taking a cardinal number as its value. Note that since ASN.1 is describing a conceptual object, there is no limitation to the bit-level precision that may be required to represent the number.

In addition to defining a integer-valued data type, it is often convenient to associate symbolic names for the values that might be taken on by instances of the data type, e.g.,

```
Status ::=
    INTEGER { up(1), down(2), testing(3) }

myStatus Status ::= up      -- or 1
```

According to ASN.1, any integer-valued quantity may be assigned to `myStatus`. By convention, in the mangement framework, if symbolic values for an integer-valued data type are enumerated, then only those values are valid for instances of that data type.

OCTET STRING: a data type taking zero or more octets as its value. Each byte in an octet string may take any value from 0 to 255.

OBJECT IDENTIFIER: a data type referring to an authoritative designation. This data type has such complicated (and important semantics) that it discussed in length at the end of this section, starting on page 86

NULL: a data type acting as a place holder. Although the management framework admits to the existence of this data type, it is currently not used.

Constructed Types

The constructed ASN.1 types used in the management framework are:

SEQUENCE: a data type denoting an ordered list of zero or more *elements*, which are other ASN.1 types. This is similar to a "structure" in most programming languages.

SEQUENCE OF type: a data type denoting an ordered list of zero or more elements of the same ASN.1 type. This is analogous to the dynamic array in many programming languages: the number of elements is not usually known until the array is created, but each element has identical syntax.

Tagged Types

In addition to using constructed types, ASN.1 provides a means for defining new types by "tagging" a previously defined type. The new and old types are distinguishable by having different tags, but they refer to the same conceptualization.

ASN.1 defines four kinds of tags, based on the identification requirements of the applications programmer:

1. The identification must be globally unique. These data types use *universal* tags. Such a tag may be defined only in the ASN.1 document or its addenda. These provide the well-known data types that have been introduced thus far. These data types, and their tags, are shown in Table 3.1.

2. The identification must be unique within a given ASN.1 module. These data types use *application-wide* tags. In any particular ASN.1 module, only one data type may be defined that uses such a tag.

3. The identification must be unique in order to satisfy a constructor type, such as a **SEQUENCE** or a **CHOICE**. In cases such as these, *context-specific* tags are used. These tags have no meaning outside of the ASN.1 type they are defined in.

4. The identification must be unique within an given enterprise, as provided by bilateral agreement. A *private-use* tag is used for these purposes.

All tags consist of a class (one of the four just introduced) and a non-negative integer. Thus, several application-wide tags might be defined in a module, each with a different number. The ASN.1 syntax used to convey the tagging information for cases 1, 2, and 4 is straightforward: when defining a data type, after entering the name and the ::= symbol, the tag is entered using the [...] notation, e.g.,

```
Opaque ::=
    [APPLICATION 4]
        IMPLICIT OCTET STRING
```

(context-specific tags are defined differently, but since they aren't used by the management framework, they won't be described here).

From a conceptual level, tagging a data type results in "wrapping" the existing data type, tag and all, inside a new data type. This is necessary to tell what kind of data type is really being used. If this knowledge can be derived by other means, e.g., hard-wired into

Universal Tag	ASN.1 Type
1	**BOOLEAN**
2	**INTEGER**
3	**BIT STRING**
4	**OCTET STRING**
5	**NULL**
6	**OBJECT IDENTIFIER**
7	**ObjectDescriptor**
8	**EXTERNAL**
9	**REAL**
10	**ENUMERATED**
12–15	Reserved for addenda
16	**SEQUENCE, SEQUENCE OF**
17	**SET, SET OF**
18	**NumericString**
19	**PrintableString**
20	**TeletexString**
21	**VideotexString**
22	**IA5String**
23	**UTCTime**
24	**GeneralizedType**
25	**GraphicsString**
26	**VisibleString**
27	**GeneralString**
28	**CharacterString**
29–...	Reserved for addenda

Table 3.1: ASN.1 Universal Tags

the management framework, then this wrapping is unnecessary. The
IMPLICIT keyword is used to denote this, as shown in the example
above.

Subtypes

In addition to tagging a data type to duplicate the semantics of a data
object, it is also useful to refine the semantics. For example, earlier
it was observed how each octet in an OCTET STRING carried a value
from 0 to 255. It may be useful to create a new data type for strings
for other repertoires, such as ASCII.

A useful extension defined for ASN.1 is that of *subtyping*, which
allows the ASN.1 programmer to make these refinements. The ASN.1
rules for subtyping are long and complex. Fortunately, the management framework makes use of only two, as evidenced in these two
examples:

```
IpAddress ::=              -- in network-byte order
    [APPLICATION 0]
        IMPLICIT OCTET STRING (SIZE (4))


Counter ::=
    [APPLICATION 1]
        IMPLICIT INTEGER (0..4294967295)
```

In the first example, a new data type IpAddress which contains a
string of octets is defined. Although no requirements are made on the
value of each octet, the length of the string is exactly 4. Appearing
with the definition is a comment indicating how an IP address is
represented within the string of octets. In the second example, a new
integer-value data type is defined. Instances of the data type may
take any non-negative value less than 2^{32}.

3.2.3   OBJECT IDENTIFIERs

An OBJECT IDENTIFIER is a data type denoting an authoritatively
named object. OBJECT IDENTIFIERs provide a means for identifying
some object, regardless of the semantics associated with the object
(e.g., a standards document, an ASN.1 module, and so on).

An `OBJECT IDENTIFIER` is a sequence of non-negative integer values that traverse a tree. The tree consists of a *root* connected to a number of labeled *nodes* via edges. Each label consists of a non-negative integer value and possibly a brief textual description. Each node may, in turn, have children nodes of its own, termed *subordinates*, which are also labeled. This process may continue to an arbitrary level of depth. Central to the notion of the `OBJECT IDENTIFIER` is the understanding that administrative control of the meanings assigned to the nodes may be delegated as one traverses the tree.

When describing an `OBJECT IDENTIFIER` there are several formats that may be used. The most concise textual format is to list the integer values found by traversing the tree, starting at the root and proceeding to the object in question. The integer values are separated with a dot.[2] Thus,

```
1.0.8571.5.1
```

identifies the object found by starting at the root, moving to the node with label 1, then moving to the node with label 0, and so on. The node found after traversing this list is the one being identified.

The root node has three subordinates:

- `ccitt(0)`, which is administrated by the International Telegraph and Telephone Consultative Committee (CCITT);

- `iso(1)`, which is administered by the International Organization for Standardization and International Electrotechnical Committee (ISO/IEC); and,

- `joint-iso-ccitt(2)`, which is jointly administered by ISO/IEC and CCITT.

---

[2] The reader should not confuse the `OBJECT IDENTIFIER` notation with the conventions used for writing IP addresses.

Thus, at the first cut, the naming tree looks like this:

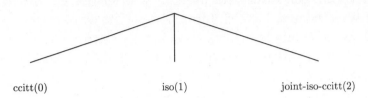

ccitt(0)   iso(1)   joint-iso-ccitt(2)

and, the administrative authority for each node is free to assign further subordinate nodes and optionally to delegate authority to others to name objects under those nodes.

In the context of the management framework, only the iso(1) subtree is of interest. ISO/IEC has defined four subordinates:

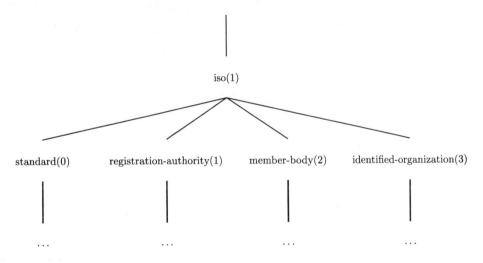

These are:

- **standard(0)**, which has a subordinate assigned to each International Standard. For example, the OSI file service, FTAM, is International Standard 8571. Thus, when FTAM defines objects, these start with the prefix 1.0.8571. Each standard is then responsible for the naming hierarchy used under its assigned prefix.

- **registration-authority(1)**, which is reserved for use by OSI registration authorities, as they are created.

- `member-body(2)`, which has a subordinate assigned to each member body of ISO/IEC. The value of the label assigned to each node is a *decimal country code* (DCC). Each member body is then responsible for further organization of its respective naming space.

- `identified-organization(3)`, which has a subordinate assigned to any organization that ISO/IEC wishes to favor. This permits a way for any organization to name objects (even proprietary objects) without fear of collisions in the naming hierarchy.

Finally, joint committees of ISO/IEC and CCITT delegate naming authority under the `joint-iso-ccitt(2)` tree.

The `OBJECT IDENTIFIER` syntax is straight-forward:

```
Document-Type-Name ::=
    OBJECT IDENTIFIER

fTAM-1 Document-Type-Name ::=
    { 1 0 8571 5 1 }
```

In this example, the value declaration shows only the numeric values of the nodes. The textual values may also be used, providing that those strings are unambiguous:

```
fTAM-1 Document-Type-Name ::=
    { iso standard 8571 5 1 }
```

(An unambiguous string is one that uniquely names an immediate sibling of a node.) In order to promote readability, but not risk ambiguity, these two forms can be combined, as in

```
fTAM-1 Document-Type-Name ::=
    { iso(1) standard(0) 8571 5 1 }
```

or

```
internet OBJECT IDENTIFIER ::= { iso org(3) dod(6) 1 }
directory OBJECT IDENTIFIER ::= { internet 1 }
```

3.2.4   Does Simplicity Cost?

As evidenced throughout this section, only a small subset of the ASN.1 syntax is used in the management framework. For example, a cursory comparison with Table 3.1 on page 85 shows the following data types not allowed by the framework:

```
BOOLEAN
BIT STRING
ObjectDescriptor
EXTERNAL
REAL
ENUMERATED
SET
SET OF
```

along with over 10 refinements to the `OCTET STRING` data type. Aren't these serious restrictions?

In a word: *no*. At the risk of starting a soapbox, consider: one could argue that the basic data structures of computing are numbers, byte strings, and structures. One can easily emulate the semantics of the unsupported ASN.1 data types above using only

```
INTEGER
OCTET STRING
SEQUENCE
SEQUENCE OF
```

For example, a `BOOLEAN` can be represented by an `INTEGER` taking the value zero (for false) and non-zero (for true). Similarly, a `BIT STRING` can be represented by an `OCTET STRING` in which some of the bits in the last octet might be marked as "reserved" if the string of bits is not a multiple of eight in length.

So, what do all these data types buy you? Primarily, they buy completeness in the language. They achieve elegance. But, there is also a cost. Adding support for another two dozen data types, or worse yet, for arbitrary data types, has substantive cost, both in terms of program development, code size, and execution time. Falling back on the Fundamental Axiom, it seems wise to vastly restrict the data types supported by the framework so as to minimize the impact on managed nodes.

Chapter 4

Management Objects: SMI and MIB

It is now time to examine two of the three key documents of the Internet-standard Network Management Framework: the first defines how management information is structured, the second defines the management information which is standard to the core protocols of the Internet suite.

The initial IAB strategy for network management, as reported in [43], was to follow a two-pronged approach:

- in the short-term, an existing management protocol, the *Simple Gateway Monitoring Protocol* (SGMP) would be modified to reflect the experience gained by its use in operational networks and would be called the *Simple Network Management Protocol* (SNMP); and,

- for the long-term, use of the (ever-)emerging OSI network management protocol, the *Common Management Information Protocol* (CMIP) would be investigated.

The disadvantage of a two-pronged approach is, of course, that a transition is needed from the short-term to the long-term solution. In order to provide for an orderly transition between the technologies, it was essential that a framework be developed that was suitable for use with both protocols.

To achieve this independence, a set of rules were developed for defining objects which are managed. The rules were constructed in such a way as to be independent of the actual management protocols being used to convey the management information.

Earlier, the term "variable" was used in regards to management activities. This was for expository convenience. It is now time to clarify the relationship between variables, objects, and object types. The terms *object* and *object-type* are used in the framework as a means of object-oriented expression: that is, a management object has associated with it a syntax and semantics which are entirely abstract. In contrast, a *variable* refers to a particular instance of a particular object. The term more commonly used for this is *object instance*, since this conveys the desired meaning and is not easily confused with programmatic terminology.

4.1 Structure of Management Information

The *Structure of Management Information* (SMI) [44] defines these rules.

If one views the collection of managed objects residing in a virtual store, such as a database, the SMI defines the *schema* for that database. In fact, there is a precise name for this database, it is called the *Management Information Base* (MIB).

The ASN.1 definition of the SMI is found in Figure 4.2 starting on page 106. It is suggested that reader study the intervening text before examining the figure.

4.1.1 Managed Objects

Each managed object is described using an ASN.1 macro defined in the SMI. This is termed the OBJECT-TYPE macro:

```
OBJECT-TYPE MACRO ::=
BEGIN
    TYPE NOTATION ::= "SYNTAX" type (TYPE ObjectSyntax)
                      "ACCESS" Access
                      "STATUS" Status
    VALUE NOTATION ::= value (VALUE ObjectName)

    Access ::= "read-only"
                    | "read-write"
                    | "write-only"
                    | "not-accessible"
    Status ::= "mandatory"
                    | "optional"
                    | "obsolete"
    END
```

This formalism is used to precisely capture the management definition of a managed object.

Before describing how this macro is used, consider a simple example:

```
sysDescr OBJECT-TYPE
      SYNTAX OCTET STRING
      ACCESS read-only
      STATUS mandatory
      ::= { system 1 }
```

which describes a managed object called `sysDescr`. Each "clause" of this macro is now described.

Syntax

The syntax for a managed object defines the data type which models the object. According to the macro, this is taken from the data type `ObjectSyntax`. Rather than delve into the details now, just think of the managed object being taken from the ASN.1 subset described earlier in Section 3.2.2 on page 82.

Access

The proscribed level of access for the managed object is one of:

- *read-only*, instances of the object may be read, but not set;

- *read-write*, instances of the object may be read or set;

- *write-only*, instances of the object may be set, but not read; or,

- *not-accessible*, instances of the object may not be read nor set.

Of course the management profile (authentication/authorization) used by the managed element may place further restrictions on the level of access. This is why the *not-accessible* level of access was defined.

Status

The implementation requirement for the managed object is one of:

- *mandatory*, managed nodes must implement this object;

- *optional*, managed nodes may implement this object;

- *obsolete*, managed nodes need no longer implement this object.

Name (value)

The value of the object `sysDescr` is, according to the macro, of the type `ObjectName`. The SMI defines this type as:

```
ObjectName ::=
    OBJECT IDENTIFIER
```

So, managed objects are named by `OBJECT IDENTIFIER`s. It is now necessary to explore MIB naming and syntax in more detail.

4.1.2 Names

As noted in Section 3.2.3 on page 86, an `OBJECT IDENTIFIER` is an authoritatively assigned name. The prefix used in the Internet is:

```
internet OBJECT IDENTIFIER ::= { iso org(3) dod(6) 1 }
```

which is concisely written as:

```
1.3.6.1
```

As shown in Figure 4.1, underneath this subtree, four nodes have been defined. Three of these are of interest for management purposes.

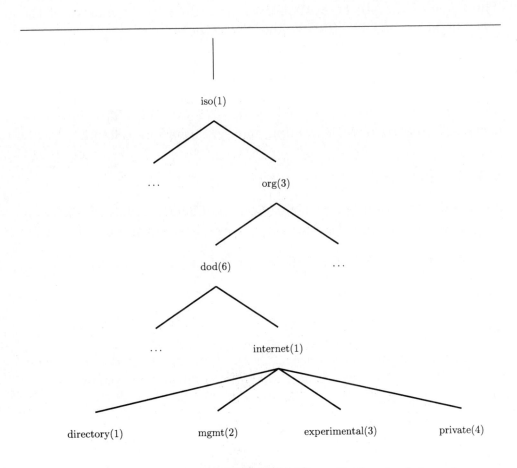

Figure 4.1: OBJECT IDENTIFIER prefix for the Internet

The MGMT subtree

Objects defined under the subtree

```
mgmt OBJECT IDENTIFIER ::= { internet 2 }
```

are registered by the Internet Assigned Numbers Authority:

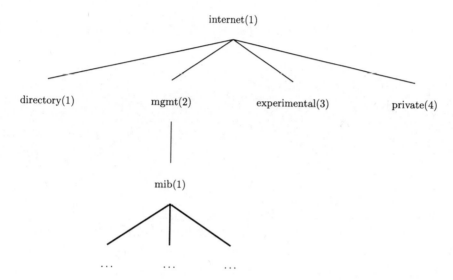

At present, only one subtree is defined, `mib(1)`. This is where objects defined in the Internet-standard MIB, described in Section 4.2 on page 109, reside.

The Experimental subtree

Objects defined under the subtree

```
experimental OBJECT IDENTIFIER ::= { internet 3 }
```

are registered by the Internet Assigned Numbers Authority:

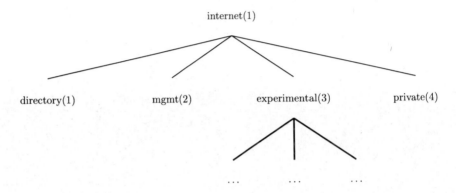

Each management experiment is assigned a new number by the Authority. The impact of these experimental MIBs is discussed on page 112 in Section 4.2.1. The current list of experimental MIBs, as of June, 1990, is given in Appendix A on page 260.

The Private subtree

Objects defined under the subtree

```
private OBJECT IDENTIFIER ::= { internet 4 }
```

are registered by the Internet Assigned Numbers Authority:

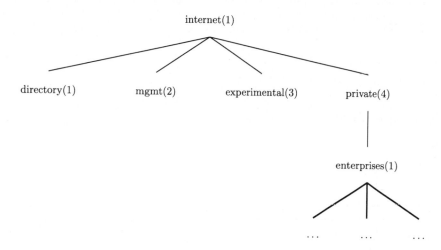

At present, only one subtree is defined, `enterprises(1)`. This is where vendor-specific objects are registered. The current list of enterprise MIBs, as of May, 1990, is given in Appendix A in Table A.1 which starts on page 262.

Still More on Naming

It should be noted that `OBJECT IDENTIFIER`s offer the management framework an extensible name space. Because there is no effective limit to the depth of the tree, nor on the magnitude of non-negative integers assigned to labels, an infinite number of names are available for authoritative use. An important consequence is that once a name is assigned, it must *never* be reused.

4.1.3 Syntax

Earlier it was noted that managed objects have a syntax defined by the ASN.1 data type called `ObjectSyntax`. This is defined as a `CHOICE` in the ASN.1 language, meaning that the actual type can be one of any of the types defined in the `CHOICE`. There are three kinds of choices:

- *simple*, which refer to the four primitive ASN.1 types described earlier in Section 3.2.2 on page 82;

- *application-wide*, which refer to special data types defined by the SMI; or,

- *simply constructed*, which refer to the two constructed ASN.1 types described earlier in Section 3.2.2.

Each are now described in turn

Simple Types

The four simple types are:

```
INTEGER
OCTET STRING
OBJECT IDENTIFIER
NULL
```

In addition, if an `INTEGER` data type lists enumerations, then a label having value zero shall not be present. (This is to catch common encoding errors for integer-valued data types.)

There is also a second convention with `INTEGER`s, which regrettably is not stated in the SMI. If the data type lists enumerations, then instances of objects of that type *must* take only those values listed in the enumeration. MIBs defined under the management framework always provide a label called `other` with the obvious semantics.

Finally, if an `OCTET STRING` is used, the repertoire used for the string must either be binary (an octet can take a value from 0 to 255), or is taken from the NVT ASCII character set defined in pages 10–11 of [15]. Regrettably, this convention is also not stated in the SMI, but it is necessary as in ASN.1 a repertoire need not encode each individual character as a single octet.

Application-Wide

The SMI defines five six new data types for use in the management framework:

IpAddress: a data type representing an IP address:

```
IpAddress ::=           -- in network byte order
    [APPLICATION 0]
        IMPLICIT OCTET STRING (SIZE (4))
```

NetworkAddress: a data type representing an address from one of possibly several protocol families. At present, only one CHOICE is present.

```
NetworkAddress ::=
    CHOICE {
        internet
            IpAddress
    }
```

Thus, whenever NetworkAddress occurs, simply think of IpAddress.

Counter: a data type representing a non-negative integer, which monotonically increases until it reaches a maximum value, when it wraps back to zero.

```
Counter ::=
    [APPLICATION 1]
        IMPLICIT INTEGER (0..4294967295)
```

The maximum value is $2^{32} - 1$.

Gauge: a data type representing a non-negative integer, which may increase or decrease, but which latches at a maximum value.

```
Gauge ::=
    [APPLICATION 2]
        IMPLICIT INTEGER (0..4294967295)
```

The maximum value is $2^{32} - 1$.

TimeTicks: a data type representing a non-negative integer, which counts the time in hundredths of a second since some epoch, not exceeding $2^{32} - 1$.

```
TimeTicks ::=
    [APPLICATION 3]
        IMPLICIT INTEGER (0..4294967295)
```

The definition of each object with a syntax of `TimeTicks` must identify the correspondent epoch.

Opaque: a data type representing an arbitrary encoding.

```
Opaque ::=               -- arbitrary ASN.1 value,
    [APPLICATION 4]   -- "double-wrapped"
        IMPLICIT OCTET STRING
```

This data type is used as an escape mechanism, to bypass the limitations of the restrictive data typing used by the SMI. An instance of an arbitrary ASN.1 data type is encoded using the *Basic Encoding Rules* (described in Section 5.10 on page 167). The resultant string of octets forms the value for the `Opaque` type.

It is important to appreciate that such a scheme works only with bilateral agreement between the managed node and the management station, as the only requirement placed on either device is the ability to recognize and accept opaquely-encoded data. A device need not be able to unwrap the data and interpret the contents.

Simply Constructed

The SMI defines two kinds of constructed types. Both are purposely limited in scope.

list: a data type of the form

```
<list> ::=
    SEQUENCE {
        <type1>,
        ...
        <typeN>
    }
```

in which each `<type>` resolves to a primitive type (simple or application-wide). These are used to form a column in a table. Whilst ASN.1 allows some or all of the elements in a `SEQUENCE` to be `OPTIONAL`, this is not allowed by the SMI.

table: a data type of the form

```
<table> ::=
    SEQUENCE OF
        <list>
```

It should be clear from examination that all tables defined in the management framework are two-dimensional in nature: a table, when instantiated, consists of zero or more rows, each row having the same number of columns. Once again, this seemingly strange restriction is motivated by the fundamental axiom.

4.1.4 Instance Identification

It should also be noted that more than just the name of an object is needed in order to access that object on a manged node. Objects, per se, are only templates. It is the *instances* of objects which are manipulated by a management protocol. Hence, in addition to knowing the object name, the *instance identifier* must also be specified.

Selection of instance-identifiers is a matter which is dependent on the management protocol being used. The SMI does not define how instance-identifiers are selected. It is the responsibility of each management protocol operating in the Framework to define instance-identifier information, for both tabular and non-tabular objects.

4.1.5   Changes to the SMI

Since its original publication in August of 1988, the SMI has proven to be a solid document. In all honesty, it does contain a few "modest" errors:

- the version numbering scheme is completely wrong; subsequent work ignores this section altogether. The text contains a lot of *mumbo-jumbo* about "head-space" and "tail-space," which was never clearly understood and unnecessary as well![1]

- the SMI specifies that instances of object types are encoded for transmission using the *Basic Encoding Rules*. This is clearly outside the bounds of the SMI. The choice of encoding rules is dependent on the management protocol in use.

  Since the management protocol in the framework uses the Basic Encoding Rules, no harm is done by this lapse in layering.

- use of the write-only level of access is problematic.

As of this writing, it is unlikely that the technical content of the SMI will change.

However, when a second MIB was completed at the end of 1989, a few refinements were made:

- a new implementation requirement has been added, the *deprecated* status, which is used to prepare implementors for future changes in the MIB. A deprecated object is one which must be supported, but one which will most likely be removed from the next version of the Internet-standard MIB.

  Objects are usually marked deprecated when new objects, with equal or superior functionality, are defined.

---

[1]As the person who wrote this section of the SMI, I have to take my lumps on this one. A number of IAB members expressed disbelief that such a scheme was usable, but their fears were calmed by my sophistry. They were right!

- a new textual convention,

```
DisplayString ::=
    OCTET STRING
```

is introduced. The octets in a `DisplayString` are restricted to the "NVT ASCII" repertoire. Note that this is entirely a presentational artifact, it does not require a change in the encoding of objects which previously took their syntax from `OCTET STRING`.

For the remainder of *The Simple Book*, the discussion assumes that these refinements are in effect. Since they are fully compatible with the Internet-standard SMI, no loss of generality occurs.

4.1.6   Extensions to the MIB

The SMI defines three extensibility mechanisms: addition of new standard objects through the definitions of new versions of the Internet-standard MIB; addition of widely-available, but non-standard, objects through the experimental subtree; and, addition of private objects through the enterprises subtree. Such additional objects can not only by used for vendor-specific elements, but also for experimental as required to further the knowledge of which other objects are essential.

There are three rules to be used when defining new versions of a MIB module:

1. New object types may be defined with new names.

2. Existing tables may be augmented by appending non-aggregate types to the object types in the list. and,

3. Previously defined object types may be marked as obsolete, but their names may not be reused.

The critical aspect is to not reuse previously assigned object names — new things are always added "down and to the right."

RFC1155–SMI **DEFINITIONS** ::= **BEGIN**

EXPORTS –– *EVERYTHING*
      internet, directory, mgmt, experimental, private, enterprises,
      OBJECT–TYPE, ObjectName, ObjectSyntax, SimpleSyntax,
      ApplicationSyntax, NetworkAddress, IpAddress,
      Counter, Gauge, TimeTicks, Opaque;

–– *the path to the root*

                                                                                               10

internet   **OBJECT IDENTIFIER** ::= { iso identified–organization(3) dod(6) 1 }

directory   **OBJECT IDENTIFIER** ::= { internet 1 }

mgmt   **OBJECT IDENTIFIER** ::= { internet 2 }

experimental **OBJECT IDENTIFIER** ::= { internet 3 }

private   **OBJECT IDENTIFIER** ::= { internet 4 }
enterprises **OBJECT IDENTIFIER** ::= { private 1 }   20

–– *definition of object types*

OBJECT–TYPE MACRO ::=
BEGIN

    TYPE NOTATION ::= "SYNTAX" type (**TYPE** ObjectSyntax)
                            "ACCESS" Access
                            "STATUS" Status   30

    VALUE NOTATION ::= value (**VALUE** ObjectName)

    Access ::= "read-only"
               | "read-write"
               | "write-only"
               | "not-accessible"
    Status ::= "mandatory"
              | "optional"
              | "obsolete"   40

END

Figure 4.2: Structure of Management Information

```
-- names of objects in the MIB

ObjectName ::=
    OBJECT IDENTIFIER

-- syntax of objects in the MIB

ObjectSyntax ::=
    CHOICE {
        simple                                                    10
            SimpleSyntax,

-- note that simple SEQUENCEs are not directly mentioned here to keep things simple
-- (i.e., prevent mis-use).   However, application-wide types which are IMPLICITly
-- encoded simple SEQUENCEs may appear in the following CHOICE

        application-wide
            ApplicationSyntax
    }
                                                                 20
SimpleSyntax ::=
    CHOICE {
        number
            INTEGER,

        string
            OCTET STRING,

        object
            OBJECT IDENTIFIER,                                    30

        empty
            NULL
    }

ApplicationSyntax ::=
    CHOICE {
        address
            NetworkAddress,
                                                                 40
        counter
            Counter,

        gauge
            Gauge,

        ticks
            TimeTicks,

        arbitrary                                                50
            Opaque

-- other application-wide types, as they are defined, will be added here
    }
```

Figure 4.2: Structure of Management Information (cont.)

-- *application-wide types*

NetworkAddress ::=
  CHOICE {
        internet
            IpAddress
  }

IpAddress ::=
  [**APPLICATION** 0]   -- *in network-byte order*   10
        IMPLICIT OCTET STRING (**SIZE** (4))

Counter ::=
  [**APPLICATION** 1]
        IMPLICIT INTEGER (0..4294967295)

Gauge ::=
  [**APPLICATION** 2]
        IMPLICIT INTEGER (0..4294967295)
                                                                          20
TimeTicks ::=
  [**APPLICATION** 3]
        IMPLICIT INTEGER (0..4294967295)

Opaque ::=
  [**APPLICATION** 4]   -- *arbitrary ASN.1 value,*
        IMPLICIT OCTET STRING -- *"double-wrapped"*

END

Figure 4.2: Structure of Management Information (cont.)

4.2   Management Information Base

The Internet-standard *Management Information Base* (MIB), as defined in [45], describes those objects which are expected to be implemented by managed nodes running the Internet suite of protocols.

4.2.1   Evolution of the MIB

The first Internet-standard MIB, referred to as *MIB-I*, was designed to include the minimal number of managed objects thought to be useful for internet management. For an object to be included, it had to meet these criteria:

- The object must be essential for either fault or configuration analysis.

- Due to lack of a secure authentication framework, any control objects must have weak (limited) properties.

- The object must have evidenced utility.

- To make the first MIB more attractive to vendors, a limit was set at approximately 100 objects. (114 objects were defined initially.)

- The object must not be (easily) derivable from other objects (e.g., by arithmetic means).

- The object must be sufficiently general in nature as to be found on many different platforms.

- Only one counter-like object per critical loop was allowed. (This goal was not fully realized.)

Observant readers will note that only some of these rules are of a technical nature. However, *all* are of a practical nature.

All devices claiming to be managed nodes are required to implement the Internet-standard MIB. However, not all functions in the protocol suite are present on all nodes. For example, one would not normally expect a gateway to support management objects for electronic mail.

To allow for this, MIB-I divided the objects into eight groups. If a managed node contained functions of that group, it must implement all of the managed objects in that group:

group	no.	objects for
system	3	the managed node itself
interfaces	22	network attachments
at	3	IP address translation
ip	33	the Internet Protocol
icmp	26	the Internet Control Message Protocol
tcp	17	the Transmission Control Protocol
udp	4	the User Datagram Protocol
egp	6	the Exterior Gateway Protocol
total	114	

These are described in greater detail in Section 4.2.3 starting on page 116.

MIB-II

Initially, there were grand plans for MIB-II. Unfortunately, there were so many competing agendas that little work was completed, and the effort was sadly disbanded. After the IAB revised its strategy for network management, as reported in [46], the *SNMP Working Group* took responsibility for the Internet-standard MIB and began work on MIB-II. Work on MIB-II was completed at the end of 1989. This is currently a *proposed* Internet-standard, and is specified in [47].

The primary emphasis of MIB-II was to create new objects whilst maintaining compatibility with the SMI and MIB-I. Keeping this in mind, there were three areas to be addressed:

- incremental additions to reflect new operational requirements;

- improved support for multi-protocol devices; and,

- textual clean-up to improve clarity.

The SMI refinements described in Section 4.1.5 on page 104 were made in MIB-II.

To briefly compare MIB-II to its predecessor:

group	no.	comments
system	7	was 3
interfaces	23	was 22
at	3	will be 0
ip	38	was 33
icmp	26	unchanged
tcp	19	was 17
udp	7	new table
egp	18	expanded table
transmission	0	new
snmp	30	new
total	171	50% larger

There were three substantive changes:

address translation: MIB-I provided for one-way mapping of protocol addresses to physical addresses, but components of other network protocols, such as the OSI *End-System to Intermediate-System* (ES-IS) protocol, require inverse mappings. Unfortunately, indexing a single table to provide mappings in both directions is too difficult for some implementations. The address translation table was *deprecated*, and each protocol family now introduces one or two tables for mappings in the appropriate direction. (Of course, as with all tables in the MIB, these are virtual tables — many implementations may choose to physically realize this as a single data structure internally.)

transmission: MIB-II defines a new group containing objects for each specific type of interface (token-ring, loopback, etc.). These definitions are introduced in the experimental or vendor space of the MIB and eventually transfer to the Internet-standard space as consensus and experience dictates.

snmp: MIB-II defines a new group containing objects about SNMP. This allows the NMS to manipulate the SNMP portion of the entities that it manages.

MIB-II uses the same naming scheme as MIB-I. Since MIB-II is a superset of MIB-I, each object in common has an identical name in the two MIBs.

Relation to the Experimental Subtree

A key administrative policy of the approach taken by the SNMP Working Group, is that virtually all new activities result in MIBs being defined in the experimental space. The advantage of this approach is that ideas must be proven as experiments before they are considered for standardization. If an experiment is successful, the correspondent MIB has credibility when its proponents argue for its inclusion in the Internet-standard MIB.

Relation to the Enterprises Subtree

It should be noted that the Internet-standard MIB represents the core management objects which are common across the widest range of network devices which implement the Internet suite of protocols. Individual vendors are strongly encourarged to develop their own private MIBs which are specific to their product line. The current list of enterprise-specific MIBs, as of May, 1990, is given in Appendix A in Table A.1 which starts on page 262. Further, some of these are available for public inspection, and the appendix contains information as to how those MIB modules might be retrieved.

A Common Misconception

Because the Internet-standard MIB was first used with SNMP, which had (at that time) recently evolved from SGMP, a common misconception was that it was a MIB for gateway management.

In examining the table above, it can be observed that 55% of the objects are related to the management of both hosts and gateways, 25% are host-specific, and 20% are gateway-specific. Clearly, the Internet-standard MIB is not gateway-centric.

4.2.2 Format of Entries

In MIB-I and MIB-II, each object is defined with the `OBJECT-TYPE` macro. In addition, each object has an accompanying textual explanation. In addition to containing the information in the macro invocation (e.g., syntax), the textual explanation contains a paragraph-long description of the object.

Naming Conventions

By convention, no object is defined in the Internet-standard MIB with a name that ends with a sub-identifier of zero. This value is reserved for use with future extensions. Thus, the first variable in the system group

```
system OBJECT IDENTIFIER ::= { mib 1 }
```

has the name

```
{ system 1 }
```

or

```
1.3.6.1.2.1.1.1
```

A second convention is that the symbolic descriptors of objects, e.g., `sysDescr` in

```
sysDescr OBJECT-TYPE
    SYNTAX OCTET STRING
    ACCESS read-only
    STATUS mandatory
    ::= { system 1 }
```

should be short, mnemonic strings. Furthermore, they should be unique within the MIB module.

A final convention, which regrettably is not stated in the MIB documents, is that if the syntax of an object is `Counter`, then the symbolic descriptor should end with the letter "s." (Of course, non-counter objects can also have textual descriptors which end in this letter.)

Access Conventions

It is a convention of the Internet-standard MIB that no object may have an **STATUS** field of *optional*. All objects are considered to be *mandatory*.

Experimental MIBs may define *optional* objects. However, if the objects contained therein are to be placed in the Internet-standard MIB, then either:

- the implementation requirement must be changed to *mandatory*;

- or, a new group in the MIB module must be formed to partition the object from the others. Support of the group is said to be optional, although the implementation requirement of the object is again marked as *mandatory*.

Case Diagrams

It is often useful to pictorially represent the relationship between MIB objects in a protocol entity. A useful tool, the *Case Diagram*, was developed for this purpose[48].[2]

Recall that one of the criteria for an object to be included in MIB-I was it must not be derivable from other objects. In the case of objects with a **Counter** syntax, this means that the objects must not be (easily) related arithmetically. Case Diagrams are used to visualize the flow of management information in a layer and thereby mark where counters are incremented. This helps to decide if an object meets this arithmetic-derivability criterion.

Consider an example of a Case diagram shown in Figure 4.3. According to this diagram, two invariants hold:

- the number of packets received from the layer below is equal to:

$$inErrors + forwPackets + inDelivers$$

---

[2]The term Case Diagram, is named after the eminent Professor Case. The term was coined by Craig Partridge, then chair of the working group which produced MIB-I.

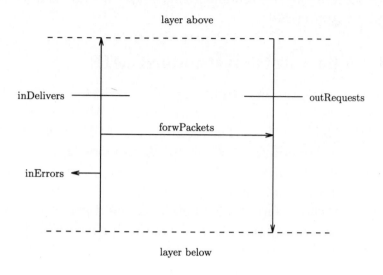

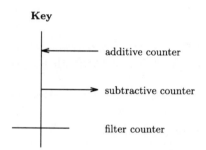

Figure 4.3: Example of a Case Diagram

- the number of packets sent to the layer below is equal to:

$$\text{outRequests} + \text{forwPackets}$$

The limitation of Case Diagrams is that they imply a sequential flow. Many error counting objects can be incremented from anywhere inside a protocol entity. From a visual perspective however, the error counter is incremented only in one place. Of course, since they are meant to be pictorially simple, they cannot convey any complex semantics. Thus, a Case Diagram is an aid to, not a substitute for, a textual MIB description.

Throughout the remainder of this chapter, Case Diagrams will be used where appropriate.

4.2.3   The Internet-standard MIB

It is now time to present a summary of the objects in MIB-I and MIB-II. Since MIB-II is upwards compatible with MIB-I, objects from both can be listed without loss of generality. The ASN.1 definition of MIB-II is found in Appendix C, which starts on page 283.

In the definitions which follow, a check ($\sqrt{}$) in the margin next to the descriptor name indicates that the object was introduced in MIB-II. The reader should also note that the description given of the objects is purposefully terse. For the authoritative definition, the MIB document should be consulted.

System Group

The system group must be implemented by all managed nodes, and contains generic configuration information:

```
system OBJECT IDENTIFIER ::= { mib 1 }
```

sysDescr: description of device

sysObjectID: identity of the agent software

sysUpTime: how long ago the agent started

$\sqrt{}$ **sysContact:** name of contact person

$\sqrt{}$ **sysName:** device name

$\sqrt{}$ **sysLocation:** device physical's location

$\sqrt{}$ **sysServices:** services offered by device

Of these, it is perhaps instructive to consider the description of the last object in greater detail.

The `sysServices` object is a concise means of determining the set of services which the device potentially offers. It is an integer-value, initially zero. Then for each layer, L, in the range 1 through 7, that the device performs transaction for, the number 2^{L-1} is added to the value. For example, a device which only performs routing functions would have a value of $2^{3-1} = 4$. The layers are:

layer	functionality
1	physical (e.g., repeaters)
2	data-link (e.g., bridges)
3	internet (e.g., supports IP)
4	end-to-end (e.g., supports TCP)
7	application (e.g., supports SMTP)

A "dump" of the object-instances in the MIB-II system group might look like this:

```
sysDescr       "4BSD/ISODE SNMP"
sysObjectID    1.3.6.1.4.1.4.1.2.1
sysUpTime      45366736
               (5 days, 6 hours, 1 minutes, 7.36 seconds)
sysContact     "Marshall Rose <mrose@psi.com>"
sysName        wp.psi.com
sysLocation    "Troy machine room"
sysServices    0x48 (transport, application)
```

The `sysLocation` object is read-only. If it were not, then in response to a new value, the managed node would most likely mail itself to the new location! (The preceeding is a joke ...).

Interfaces Group

The interfaces group must be implemented by all managed nodes, and contains generic information on the entities at the interface layer. This group contains two top-level objects: the number of interface attachments on the node, and a single table containing information on those interfaces:

```
interfaces OBJECT IDENTIFIER ::= { mib 2 }

ifNumber OBJECT-TYPE
    SYNTAX INTEGER
```

```
          ACCESS read-only
          STATUS mandatory
          ::= { interfaces 1 }

  ifTable OBJECT IDENTIFIER ::= { interfaces 2 }
  ifEntry OBJECT IDENTIFIER ::= { ifTable 1 }
```

Each row of the table contains several columns:

ifIndex: interface number

ifDescr: description of the interface

ifType: type of interface

ifMtu: MTU size

ifSpeed: transmission rate in bits/second

ifPhysAddress: media-specific address

ifAdminStatus: desired interface state

ifOperStatus: current interface state

ifLastChange: how long ago interface changed state

ifInOctets: total octets received from the media

ifInUcastPkts: unicast packets delivered above

ifInNUcastPkts: broadcast/multicast packets delivered above

ifInDiscards: packets discarded due to resource limitations

ifInErrors: packets discarded due to format error

ifInUnknownProtos: packets destined for unknown protocols

ifOutOctets: total octets sent on the media

ifOutUcastPkts: unicast packets from above

ifOutNUcastPkts: broadcast/multicast packets from above

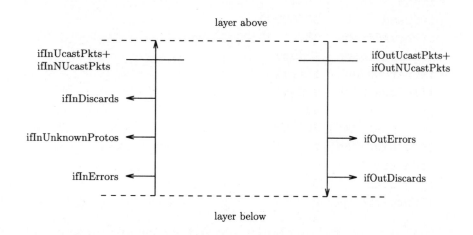

Figure 4.4: Case Diagram for the Interfaces Group

ifOutDiscards: packets discarded due to resource limitations

ifOutErrors: packets discarded due to error

ifOutQlen: packet size of output queue

ifSpecific: MIB-specific pointer ✓

Figure 4.4 shows a Case Diagram relating many of these objects.

All of these objects are generic in that they apply to all interfaces regardless of the interface type. Support for interface type-specific objects is possible by using the `ifSpecific` object as a "pointer" to some interface-specific MIB.

The `ifAdminStatus` object is a means for conveying to the agent an imperative action. For example, if the value is changed from **down** to **up**, the agent understands this to mean that the interface should be initialized and brought into the ready state, if possible.

A "dump" of the object-instances in the row corresponding to the first interface on the managed node might look like this:

```
ifIndex      1
ifDescr      "le0"
ifType       6 (ethernet-csmacd)
```

```
ifMtu           1500
ifSpeed         10000000
ifPhysAddress   08:00:20:00:38:ba
ifAdminStatus   1 (up)
ifOperStatus    1 (up)
ifInUcastPkts   986357
ifInErrors      94
ifOutUcastPkts  887098
ifOutDiscards   0
ifOutErrors     0
ifOutQLen       0
ifSpecific      0.0
```

Note that not all of the columns defined earlier are present. This is because it is simply not possible for some implementations to support those objects. In this case, the correct behavior is for the managed node to consider those variables as having a *not-accessible* level of access.

Address Translation Group

The address translation group must be implemented by all managed nodes, and contains address resolution information. In fact, the group contains a single table used for mapping IP addresses into media-specific addresses:

```
at OBJECT IDENTIFIER ::= { mib 3 }

atTable OBJECT IDENTIFIER ::= { at 1 }
atEntry OBJECT IDENTIFIER ::= { atTable 1 }
```

Each row of the table contains three columns:

atIfIndex: interface number

atPhysAddress: media address of mapping

atNetAddress: IP address of mapping

A "dump" of the object-instances in the address translation table might look like this:

atIfIndex	atPhysAddress	atNetAddress
1	08:00:20:00:38:ba	192.33.4.20
1	00:00:c0:d5:8f:13	192.33.4.3
1	00:00:22:08:2a:c3	192.33.4.4

In MIB-II, the address translation group was marked *deprecated*, as information on address resolution was moved to the each network protocol group (i.e., the IP group).

IP Group

The IP group must be implemented by all managed nodes. The group contains several scalars and four tables.

```
ip OBJECT IDENTIFIER ::= { mib 4 }
```

The scalars are:

ipForwarding: acting as a gateway or a host

ipDefaultTTL: default TTL for IP packets

ipInReceives: total datagrams from below

ipInHdrErrors: datagrams discarded due to format error

ipInAddrErrors: datagrams discarded due to misdelivery

ipForwDatagrams: datagrams forwarded

ipInUnknownProtos: datagrams destined for unknown protocols

ipInDiscards: datagrams discarded due to resource limitations

ipInDelivers: datagrams delivered above

ipOutRequests: datagrams from above

ipOutNoRoutes: datagrams discarded due to no route

ipReasmTimeout: timeout value for reassembly queue

ipReasmReqds: fragments received needing reassembly

ipReasmOKs: datagrams successfully reassembled

ipReasmFails: reassembly failures

ipFragOKs: datagrams succesfully fragmented

ipFragFails: datagrams needing fragmentation but the IP **flags** fields said not to

ipFragCreates: fragments created

Figure 4.5 shows a Case Diagram relating many of these objects.

The IP address table keeps track of the IP addresses associated with the managed node:

```
ipAddrTable OBJECT IDENTIFIER ::= { ip 20 }
ipAddrEntry OBJECT IDENTIFIER ::= { ipAddrTable 1 }
```

Each row of the table contains several columns:

ipAdEntAddr: the IP address of this entry

ipAdEntIfIndex: interface number

ipAdEntNetMask: subnet-mask for IP address

ipAdEntBcastAddr: LSB of IP broadcast address

√ **ipAdEntReasmMaxSize:** the largest IP datagram able to be reassembled

A "dump" of the object-instances in a row of this table might look like this:

```
ipAdEntAddr         192.33.4.20
ipAdEntIfIndex      1
ipAdEntNetMask      255.255.255.0
ipAdEntBcastAddr    1
ipAdEntReasmMaxSize 65535
```

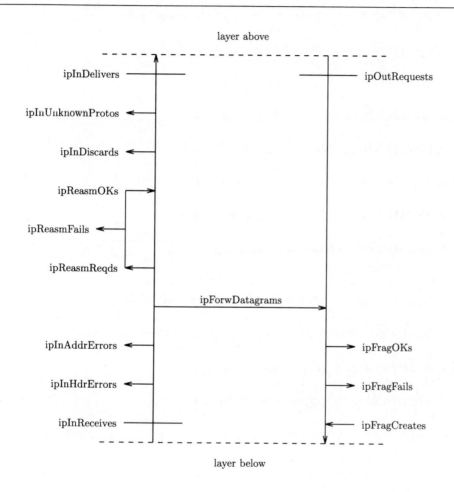

Figure 4.5: Case Diagram for the IP Group

The IP routing table keeps track of the IP routes associated with the managed node:

```
ipRoutingTable OBJECT IDENTIFIER ::= { ip 21 }
ipRouteEntry OBJECT IDENTIFIER ::= { ipRoutingTable 1 }
```

Each row of the table contains several columns:

ipRouteDest: destination IP address

ipRouteIfIndex: interface number

ipRouteMetric1: routing metric #1

ipRouteMetric2: routing metric #2

ipRouteMetric3: routing metric #3

ipRouteMetric4: routing metric #4

ipRouteNextHop: next hop (gateway IP address for indirect routing)

ipRouteType: type (direct, remote, valid, invalid)

ipRouteProto: mechanism used to determine route

ipRouteAge: age of route in seconds

ipRouteMask: subnet-mask for route

If the value of the `ipRouteType` is invalid, then the correspondent row is invalidated.

A "dump" of the object-instances in this table might look like this:

```
   Dest         IfIndex      NextHop        Type          Mask
0.0.0.0           1        192.44.33.3    4 (remote)   0.0.0.0
192.44.33.0       1        192.44.33.20   3 (direct)   255.255.255.0
```

(The routing metrics, protocol, and age fields have been omitted.) The first entry is the default route used by the managed node.

The IP address translation table, added in MIB-II, keeps track of the mapping between IP and media-specific addresses:

```
iNetToMediaTable OBJECT IDENTIFIER ::= { ip 22 }
ipNetToMediaEntry OBJECT IDENTIFIER ::= { ipNetToMediaTable 1 }
```

Each row of the table contains four columns:

ipNetToMediaIfIndex: interface number

ipNetToMediaPhysAddress: media address of mapping

ipNetToMediaNetAddress: IP address of mapping

ipNetToMediaType: how mapping was determined

If the value of the `ipNetToMediaType` is invalid, then the correspondent row is invalidated.

A "dump" of the object-instances in this table might look like this:

```
                         ipNetToMedia
   IfIndex         PhysAddress        NetAddress        Type
      1         08:00:20:00:38:ba     192.33.4.20    3 (dynamic)
      1         00:00:c0:d5:8f:13     192.33.4.3     3 (dynamic)
      1         00:00:22:08:2a:c3     192.33.4.4     3 (dynamic)
```

ICMP Group

The ICMP group must be implemented by all managed nodes. The group consists of 26 counters. In the interests of brevity, this group can be summarized as:

- for each ICMP message type, two counters exist, one counting the number of times this message type was generated by the local IP entity, the other counting the number of times this message type was received by the local IP entity.

- there are four additional counters which keep track of the total number of ICMP messages received, sent, received in error, or not sent due to error.

```
icmp OBJECT IDENTIFIER ::= { mib 5 }
```

Figure 4.6 shows a Case Diagram relating these objects.

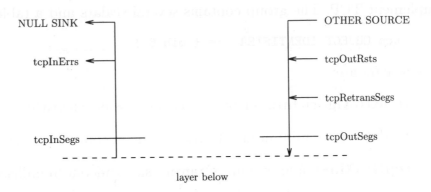

Figure 4.7: Case Diagram for the TCP Group

Each row of the table contains five columns:

tcpConnState: state of connection

tcpConnLocalAddress: local IP address

tcpConnLocalPort: local TCP port

tcpConnRemAddress: remote IP address

tcpConnRemPort: remote TCP port

The distinguished value 0.0.0.0 is used for IP addresses when this information is not yet bound for the connection.

A "dump" of the object-instances in this table might look like this:

	tcpConnLocal		tcpConnRemote	
tcpConnState	Address	Port	Address	Port
2 (listen)	0.0.0.0	21	0.0.0.0	0
11 (timewait)	127.0.0.1	4459	127.0.0.1	111
5 (estab)	192.33.4.20	23	192.33.4.4	1803
. . .				

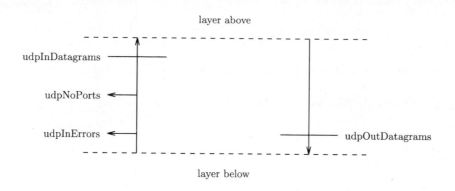

Figure 4.8: Case Diagram for the UDP Group

UDP Group

The UDP group must be implemented by all managed nodes which implement UDP. This group contains four counters and a table.

```
udp OBJECT IDENTIFIER ::= { udp 7 }
```

The scalars are:

udpInDatagrams: datagrams delivered above

udpNoPorts: datagrams destined for unknown ports

udpInErrors: datagrams discarded due to format errors

udpOutDatagrams: datagrams sent from above

Figure 4.8 shows a Case Diagram relating these objects.

The table, added in MIB-II, is used to keep track of the application entities which are using UDP:

```
udpTable OBJECT IDENTIFIER ::= { udp 5 }
udpEntry OBJECT IDENTIFIER ::= { udpTable 1 }
```

Each row of the table contains two columns:

udpLocalAddress: local IP address

udpLocalPort: local UDP port

The distinguished value 0.0.0.0 is used for IP addresses when this information is not yet bound.

A "dump" of the object-instances in this table might look like this:

```
udpLocalAddress     udpLocalPort
    0.0.0.0              42
    0.0.0.0              53
    0.0.0.0             111

...

  127.0.0.1             53
 192.33.4.20            53
 192.33.4.20           1024
```

EGP Group

The EGP group is mandatory for those managed nodes which implement the *Exterior Gateway Protocol*, which as described earlier, is a reachability protocol used between Autonomous Systems. Space limitations prevent this group from being described here.

Transmission Group

The transmission group is defined in MIB-II as a place-holder for media-specific MIBs. These MIBs start out in the experimental space and may ultimately be placed in the Internet-standard MIB, as described on page 4.2.1 in Section 109.

SNMP Group

The SNMP group is defined in MIB-II. It doesn't make a lot of sense to discuss it without first describing SNMP. This treatment is postponed until Section 5.7 on page 163.

Chapter 5

Mechanism: SNMP

It is now time to examine the last of the three key documents of the Internet-standard Network Management Framework: the document which defines the network management protocol.

Before the IAB postulated its initial strategy for network management, a group of four engineers produced a protocol called the *Simple Gateway Monitoring Protocol* (SGMP) [49], in order to meet the crushing requirements of their line-management responsibilities. As reported in [43], the initial IAB strategy for network management, SGMP was modified:

- to reflect the experience gained by its use in operational networks; and,

- to achieve conformance with the SMI and MIB described in the previous chapter.

The resulting protocol is termed the *Simple Network Management Protocol* (SNMP) [50].[1]

---

[1]The original RFC number for the SNMP was 1067. In April of 1989, the SNMP was elevated to "Recommended" status, and a new RFC, number 1098, was issued indicating the change in status. Otherwise, there are neither technical nor editorial changes between the documents.

Hence, SNMP is a second-generation protocol. Because of the pressing need for *workable* network management in the Internet, this protocol has enjoyed unprecedented success in rapid deployment. Although not every device in the Internet is network manageable, SNMP is implemented on a wide range on hardware and software platforms across numerous vendor product lines.

5.1 Philosophy

It would be pleasing to declare that the philosophy of SNMP was influenced by the concepts of the Internet-standard Network Management Framework. In point of fact, both SNMP and the management framework are largely derived from SGMP.[2] Briefly, SNMP is aligned with the fundamental axiom in that it is a purposefully simple protocol, requiring few resources to implement efficiently.

5.1.1 Operations

Only four operations are available in the protocol:

- `get`, which is used to retrieve specific management information;

- the powerful `get-next`, which is used to retrieve, via traversal, management information;

- `set`, which is used to manipulate management information; and,

- `trap`, which is used to report extraordinary events.

It should be noted that only a small number of traps are pre-defined, to support the trap-directed polling model of the management framework.

5.1.2 Use of the Transport Service

The transport requirements of SNMP are modest. Although superficially, this is consistent with the fundamental axiom, there is a deeper reason. Network management functions usually occur in a trouble-shooting or "fire-fighting" mode. The management application entity is in the best position to decide what the reliability constraints are for management traffic. The lowest common denominator is a connectionless-mode transport service, so this is what SNMP prefers to use. This choice allows the management station to determine the

---

[2]Although earlier work had impact on the management framework, SGMP has clearly had the greatest influence.

appropriate level of retransmission in order to accommodate lossy or congested networks.

In Section 5.6 on page 159, the full range of transport mappings for SNMP is explored. This includes both direct media-access along with mappings onto the CO-mode and CL-mode OSI transport services.

5.2 Administrative Framework

Before discussing the actual protocol, it is necessary to describe the administrative framework used by SNMP. It is this framework that determines the authentication and authorization policies used between SNMP application entities.

SNMP defines a *community* to be a relationship between an SNMP agent and one or more SNMP managers. The semantics of a community are complex, however the syntax is simple. An SNMP community is written as a string of uninterpreted octets. This string of octets is called a *community name*. Each octet may take a value from 0 to 255, although the octets in most community names use only printable ASCII characters.

When SNMP messages are exchanged, they contain two parts:

- a community name, along with any additional information required to validate that the sending SNMP entity is a member of the identified community; and,

- data, containing an SNMP operation and associated operands.

Note that because the community name is a handle for the administration relationship, it defines the authentication mechanism employed to validate use of the community by the sending SNMP entity.

5.2.1 Authentication

At present, only *trivial* authentication mechanisms are available with SNMP.[3] This means that the community name is placed, in the clear, in an SNMP message. If the community name corresponds to a community known to the receiving SNMP entity, the sending SNMP entity is considered to be authenticated as a member of that community.

5.2.2 Authorization

Once the sending SNMP entity is authenticated as a member of a community, the managed node must determine what level of access is

---

[3]A separate working group in the IETF is developing authentication mechanisms based on crytographic technologies.

allowed. At the first cut, an arbitrary subset of the objects visible to
a particular community is called a *view*.[4]

For each object in the view, the community defines an *access mode*,
which is one of:

- *read-only*; or,

- *read-write*.

By intersecting the community view with the access modes defined by
the community, the *community profile* for each object in the view is
defined. For each object, the community profile defines the operations
which are permitted on the object:

access mode	object access according to MIB			
	read-only	read-write	write-only	not-accessible
read-only	3	3	1	1
read-write	3	2	4	1

where:

class	operations allowed
1	none
2	get, get-next, set, trap
3	get, get-next, trap
4	get, get-next, set, trap

Note that for class 4, if the get or trap operations are used, then the
value of the associated instance is implementation-specific.

---

[4]Note that as a simple consequence of this definition, objects which are *manda-tory* for implementation (according to the MIB definition), but which cannot be realized due to platform deficiencies, are simply considered to be outside any of the views recognized by the agent.

A more intuitive way of thinking about a view is as follows: Consider all of the managed objects known to an agent to reside in a two-dimensional plane divided into four quadrants:

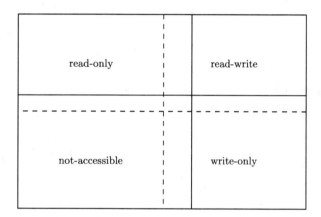

Associated with each community is a view which translates the axes accordingly:

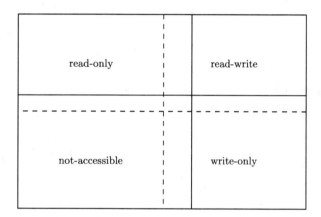

This model, which is not in the official SNMP document, is a more concise description.

5.2.3 Proxy

It should be noted that the proxy mechanism introduced in Section 3.1.4 on page 76, can be simply realized using SNMP communities. A proxy agent has a view of managed objects corresponding to its foreign devices. Since all of the objects contained by an agent needn't be visible to a community, a proxy community has a view containing exactly those objects corresponding to a particular foreign device. From this point on, the community access mode is applied and the permissible proxy operations are defined.

Again it must be stressed that the community name is an arbitrary string of octets. It need not (and probably should not) explicitly contain addressing information for the foreign device.

5.3 Instance Identification and Retrieval

In order to provide an efficient means for traversing the management information, SNMP employs a rather clever method for identifying instances: an `OBJECT IDENTIFIER`, formed by concatenating the name of the object type with a suffix, is used. The form of the suffix depends on the object type, and is calculated according to these rules:

1. Only instances of *leaf* objects may be identified. Thus, table and row objects are not manipulated, as aggregates, using SNMP.

2. If the object is not a column in a table, the suffix is simply 0.

   Thus, the identity of an instance of `sysDescr` is simply

   ```
   sysDescr.0
   ```

   or

   ```
   1.3.6.1.2.1.1.1.0
   ```

3. Otherwise, the object is a column in a table. The textual description of that table in the correspondent MIB defines how the suffix is formed, by selecting those columns necessary to make the suffix unique for that column.

   For example, instances of the columns of the `ifTable` are identified by using the value of the `ifIndex` column. So, the instance of `ifDescr` associated with the first interface is simply:

   ```
   ifDescr.1
   ```

   or

   ```
   1.3.6.1.2.1.2.2.1.2.1
   ```

By naming instances using `OBJECT IDENTIFIER`s, a *lexicographic ordering* is enforced over all object instances. This means, that for instance names a and b, one of three conditions consistently holds: either $a < b$, $a = b$, or $a > b$.

5.3.1   The Powerful Get-Next Operator

Note that the community profile determines which objects, and therefore which object instances, are visible to a manager through use of that community. As a consequence, the community profile should be thought of as a (potentially) sparse tree, with lexicographic ordering providing a means for visiting each and every readable object instance in a defined fashion. This allows SNMP to provide a powerful `get-next` operator, which moves from one object instance to the next.

The call

```
get-next (sysDescr.0)
```

returns the name and value of the next instance in the tree, which in a conformant system, we would expect to be

```
sysObjectID.0
```

Refer to the MIB-II definition in Appendix C on page 283 to check that the name of the `sysObjectID` object immediately follows that of the `sysDescr` object.

Of course, the operand needn't identify an instance, it can be *any* `OBJECT IDENTIFIER`. Hence, the call

```
get-next (sysDescr)
```

returns the name and value of the next instance in the tree, which in a conformant system, we would expect to be

```
sysDescr.0
```

This illustrates an important concept: the powerful `get-next` operator can be used to see if an object is supported by an agent, simply by specifying the name of the object rather than naming the desired instance of that object.[5]

Similarly, one could imagine that the call

---

[5]See the discussion comparing the `get` and the powerful `get-next` operators on page 154 to gain an important insight as to why this is more useful than might seem at first glance.

```
get-next (0.0)
```

would return the name and value of the very first instance in the community profile. A traversal is achieved by using the result of the first call to the powerful **get-next** operator as the operand of the second, and so on, until an error is returned.

Further, because of the naming architecture used in the MIB, tables are traversed in column-row order. When traversing a table, each instance of the first column is "walked," then each instance of the second column is "walked," and so on, until the end of the table is reached. At this point, the next object instance, which is arbitrarily distant from the table, lexicographically speaking, is returned. An error is returned *only* if an operand given to the powerful **get-next** operator is lexicographically greater than or equal to the instance identifier in the community profile with the lexicographically largest value. Again, using the tree analogy, the only time the powerful **get-next** operator returns an error is when the operand is either the rightmost instance in the tree, or to the right of that instance.

Because the powerful **get-next** operator can be given multiple operands, it is possible to efficiently traverse an entire table. Hence, the call

```
get-next (ipRouteDest, ipRouteIfIndex, ipRouteNextHop)
```

returns the name and value of these three columns in the first row of the IP routing table. If there was a default route installed in the routing table, we might expect these names to be:

```
ipRouteDest.0.0.0.0
ipRouteifIndex.0.0.0.0
ipRouteNextHop.0.0.0.0
```

To find the next row in the table, these names are used as operands to another call to the powerful **get-next** operator:

```
get-next (ipRouteDest.0.0.0.0,
          ipRouteifIndex.0.0.0.0,
          ipRouteNextHop.0.0.0.0)
```

This process may be continued until the entire table is traversed. The manager knows that it has reached the end of the table when a name is returned which no longer shares the same prefix as the desired object type. Consider this example, in which only the routing destination field is of interest:

```
get-next (ipRouteDest)            -> ipRouteDest.0.0.0.0
get-next (ipRouteDest.0.0.0.0)    -> ipRouteDest.192.33.4.0
get-next (ipRouteDest.192.33.4.0) -> ipRouteIfIndex.0.0.0.0
```

The third call to the powerful **get-next** operator returned an instance with a different prefix than the supplied operator. Thus, the manager knows it has reached the end of that column in the table.

Of course, if one wanted to start the traversal in the middle of the routing table, only a partial instance identifier need be used, e.g.,

```
get-next (ipRouteDest.192,
          ipRouteIfIndex.192,
          ipRouteNextHop.192)
```

which will retrieve the first entry in the routing table after the indicating starting point, e.g., for destination IP address 192.33.4.20.

soap... It should be obvious to the reader why this operator is termed the *powerful* **get-next**. There is however a more subtle meaning. Other management protocols, most notably in OSI, have extremely complicated mechanisms for traversing management information. Usually these involve subtree scoping and attribute filtering. By using a simple-minded naming scheme, SNMP is able to provide an extremely functional traversal mechanism with little or no additional overhead. Proponents of the Internet-standard Network Management Framework always say "the powerful get-next" to remind proponents of other systems that true power in a well-designed system comes from simplicity in design not over-wrought complexity. It should not be surprising that this fact is lost on many proponents of the OSI

...soap network management framework.

It should be noted that there is one interesting interaction which when the powerful **get-next** operator is used with a large number of operands to sweep an empty table, and the variable following is a large string. It is possible that a **tooBig** error response might be returned, instead of returning multiple instances of that next variable. This is a correct protocol interaction!

5.3.2 Problems with Naming

The drawback to this scheme is that it assumes that each row in a table is uniquely identified by some combination of columns. Further, one must be able to translate the values of these columns into a (often multi-valued) suffix. In the TCP connection table, for example, four columns are needed to uniquely identify a connection and thereby a particular row in the table. Hence, to determine the state of the TCP connection for

tcpConnLocalAddress	89.1.1.42
tcpConnLocalPort	21
tcpConnRemAddress	10.0.0.51
tcpConnRemPort	2059

the name

    tcpConnState.89.1.1.42.21.10.0.0.51.2059

or

    1.3.6.1.2.1.6.13.1.1.89.1.1.42.21.10.0.0.51.2059

is used.

Of course, it might be possible that there is no way to uniquely identify a particular entry in the table. For example, the IP routing table has its rows identified by destination IP address. Suppose there are two routes to the same destination?

A special "hack" can be used in this case. If multiple rows in a table have the same key, the agent marks one of these rows as the primary. The other rows with the same key are marked as secondary (tertiary, and so on) and assigned an implementation-dependent, small, unique non-negative integer. To identify an instance of a secondary row, this integer is appended onto the instance identifier of the primary row.

This special hack is also used for the `ipAddrTable` in MIB-II.

5.4 Table Access

It is the responsibility of each management protocol operating in the management framework to define how tabular objects are manipulated. The discussion has already described how the columnar objects (leaves) within tables are directly manipulated. The remaining consideration is how rows, as a whole, are indirectly manipulated. There are two operations to consider, namely the addition and deletion of entire rows. These are described in turn.

5.4.1 Row Addition

Using SNMP, a new row is added to a table by using a single set operation. Each variable in the operation corresponds to a column in the new row, along with the new instance identifier. Thus, for a table containing five objects in a row, the set operation will have five variables, one for each object, and each with the same instance identifier.

5.4.2 Row Deletion

Using SNMP, a row is removed from a table by a single set operation which changes the value of one of the columns in that row to invalid. The textual definition of the table indicates which column this is. For example, to remove an entry from the routing table, one sets the instance of the ipRouteType object corresponding to that entry to invalid.

The *only* exception to this rule is unfortunate: the address translation group in the Internet-standard MIB contains a table which does not have a field defining the status of the entry. (This table has subsequently been deprecated by a new, more capable table.) So the convention used when removing an entry from the address translation table is to set the atPhysAddress object corresponding to that entry to an empty string (zero length).

Using either strategy, one nuance must be exposed:

> *It is an implementation-specific matter as to whether the agent removes an invalidated entry from the table.*

Accordingly, management stations must be prepared to receive tabular information from agents that corresponds to entries not currently in use. The station can check the validity of the information by examining the appropriate field (i.e., the same field used to delete an entry).

5.5   The Protocol

SNMP is an asynchronous request/response protocol. This means
that an SNMP entity needn't wait for a response after sending a
message. It can send other messages or do other activities. Further,
since the request or response might be lost by the underlying transport
service, it is up to the sending SNMP entity to implement the desired
level of reliability.There are four primitive protocol interactions:

The manager retrieves management information from the agent:

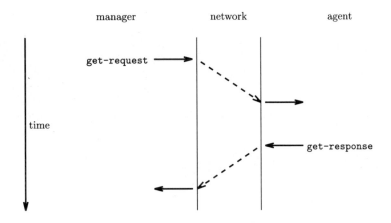

The manager traverses a portion of the agent's view:

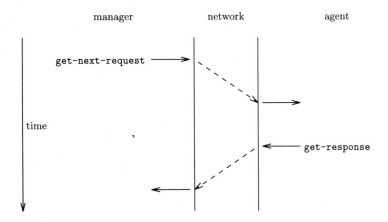

The manager stores management information with the agent:

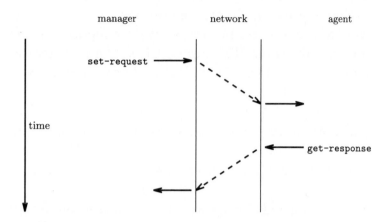

The agent reports an extraordinary event:

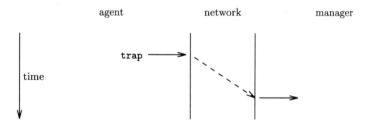

Of course, all of these operations are subject to the community profile used by the sending SNMP entity.

It is important to understand that SNMP is a *symmetric* protocol. Instrumentation in the agent or the applications in a manager, which is layered on top of an implementation of the SNMP finite state machine, makes asymmetric use of the protocol, as described in the examples above. In particular, if the SNMP FSM is properly implemented, it can invoke and perform all operations, and thus be used by both an agent and a manager, all within the same system.

5.5.1 Messages

The ASN.1 definition of SNMP is found in Figure 5.1 starting on page 149. The influence of the fundamental axiom can be seen in these definitions. For example, neither of the **error-status** and `error-index` fields are used in the `GetRequest-PDU` data type. But, by including them, a single ASN.1 data type can be used for the messages exchanged by all SNMP operations, but one. This means that only two routines need be written to encode and decode these messages for transmission. This approach is contrary to the ASN.1 philosophy of defining specialized, highly-descriptive data types for each message type.

At the top-level, an SNMP `Message` consists of version information followed by a community name and some data. Unlike most protocols, there is no version negotiation in SNMP. If an SNMP entity receives an SNMP `Message` containing an unknown version number, it simply discards it.

Note that a response is returned using the same community as the correspondent request.

RFC1157−SNMP **DEFINITIONS** ::= **BEGIN**

IMPORTS
    ObjectName, ObjectSyntax, NetworkAddress, IpAddress, TimeTicks
        FROM RFC1155−SMI;

−− *top−level message*

Message ::=   10
        SEQUENCE {
            version   −− *version−1 for this RFC*
                INTEGER {
                    version−1(0)
                },

            community   −− *community name*
                OCTET STRING,

            data   −− *e.g., PDUs if trivial*   20
                ANY   −− *authentication is being used*
        }

−− *protocol data units*

PDUs ::=
        CHOICE {
            get−request
                GetRequest−PDU,   30

            get−next−request
                GetNextRequest−PDU,

            get−response
                GetResponse−PDU,

            set−request
                SetRequest−PDU,
                                  40

            trap
                Trap−PDU
        }

Figure 5.1: Simple Network Management Protocol

GetRequest−PDU ::=
    [0]
            IMPLICIT PDU

GetNextRequest−PDU ::=
    [1]
            IMPLICIT PDU

GetResponse−PDU ::=
    [2]   10
            IMPLICIT PDU

SetRequest−PDU ::=
    [3]
            IMPLICIT PDU

PDU ::=
            SEQUENCE {
                request−id
                        INTEGER,   20

                error−status   −− *sometimes ignored*
                        INTEGER {
                            noError(0),
                            tooBig(1),
                            noSuchName(2),
                            badValue(3),
                            readOnly(4),
                            genErr(5)
                        },   30

                error−index   −− *sometimes ignored*
                        INTEGER,

                variable−bindings   −− *values are sometimes ignored*
                        VarBindList
            }

Figure 5.1: Simple Network Management Protocol (cont.)

```
Trap−PDU ::=
     [4]
          IMPLICIT SEQUENCE {
               enterprise                    −− type of object generating
                    OBJECT IDENTIFIER,       −− trap, see sysObjectID

               agent−addr                    −− address of object generating trap
                    NetworkAddress,

               generic−trap                  −− generic trap type                    10
                    INTEGER {
                         coldStart(0),
                         warmStart(1),
                         linkDown(2),
                         linkUp(3),
                         authenticationFailure(4),
                         egpNeighborLoss(5),
                         enterpriseSpecific(6)
                    },
                                                                                      20
               specific−trap                 −− specific code, present even
                    INTEGER,                  −− if generic−trap is not
                                              −− enterpriseSpecific

               time−stamp                    −− time elapsed between the last
                    TimeTicks,                −− (re)initalization of the network
                                              −− entity and the generation of the
                                              −− trap

               variable−bindings             −− "interesting" information           30
                    VarBindList
          }

VarBind ::=
     SEQUENCE {
          name
               ObjectName,

          value
               ObjectSyntax                                                          40
     }

VarBindList ::=
     SEQUENCE OF
          VarBind

END
```

Figure 5.1: Simple Network Management Protocol (cont.)

Use of Authentication

As noted earlier, since the community name identifies an authentication scheme, it indicates how the data is to be interpreted. The receiving SNMP entity passes three things to an *authentication entity*:

- the community name;

- the data; and,

- the (claimed) transport address of the sending SNMP entity.

The authentication entity, which is cognizant of the authentication scheme used by the community, returns one of two things, either:

- an instance of the SNMP `PDUs` data type, along with authoritative identification of the sending SNMP entity; or,

- an exception.

In the former case, the sending SNMP entity is said to be authenticated as a member of the community, and the receiving SNMP entity processes the request. Otherwise, an authentication failure has occurred, and the receiving SNMP entity may, depending on its configuration, generate an `authenticationFailure` trap.

At present, only one authentication scheme is used, namely *trivial*. In the trivial scheme, the data field in the SNMP `Message` is exactly the `PDUs` data type. The authentication entity simply checks the list of communities known by the receiving SNMP entity. If a match isn't found, an exception is returned. Otherwise, if a list of authorized transport addresses is associated with the community, the transport address of the sending SNMP entity must be listed there, or an exception is returned. If no list is present, or if the transport address is present in the list, then the data field is returned unaltered.

There are two things to observe: first, trivial authentication is inherently *insecure*; but, second, by using other schemes this approach to authentication is sufficiently general to support both private (unreadable) and signed (verified) exchanges.

5.5.2 PDUs

The PDUs data type is actually one of two other ASN.1 types: a PDU which is used for the majority of operations, and the Trap-PDU which is used for traps.

The fields of the PDU data type are now described. Note that by convention, the term *variable-binding* refers to the name and value of an instance of an object.

request-id: an integer-value used by a manager to distinguish among outstanding requests. This allows a management application, if it so desires, to rapidly send several SNMP messages. The incoming replies can then be correlated to the correspondent operations.

Further, this provides a simple, but effective, means for identifying messages duplicated by the network (or operations duplicated by retransmissions).

error-status: if non-zero, this indicates an exception occurred when processing the request. The values are:

- tooBig, the agent could not fit the results of an operation into a single SNMP message;

- noSuchName, the requested operation identified a unknown variable name (according to the community profile);

- badValue, the requested operation specified an incorrect syntax or value when trying to modify a variable;

- readOnly, the requested operation tried to modify a variable that, according to the community profile, may not be written; and,

- genErr, otherwise.

error-index: if non-zero, this indicates which variable in the request was in error. This field is non-zero only for the errors noSuchName, badValue, and readOnly. In this case, it is the positive offset into the variable-bindings field (the first variable is said to be at offset 1).

variable-bindings: a list of variables, each containing a name and value. The value portion of a variable is not meaningful for `GetRequest-PDU` and `GetNextRequest-PDU` data types; by convention, the value is always an instance of the ASN.1 data type `NULL`. However, the receiving SNMP eneity should simply ignore whatever value is supplied by the sending SNMP entity.

After performing the authentication step and retrieving the associated community profile, an SNMP entity performs the following actions upon receipt of a given PDU:

Get

For each variable in the request, the named instance is retrieved, in the context of the community profile. If the instance does not exist, a `get-response` is returned with error `noSuchName`.

Otherwise, a `get-response` is returned identical to the request but with the value portions of the variables filled-in accordingly.

The Powerful Get-Next

For each variable in the request, the instance lexicographically following the named instance, in the context of the community profile, is retrieved. If the end of the lexicographic space is reached, a `get-response` is returned with error `noSuchName`.

Otherwise, a `get-response` is returned identical to the request but with the name and value portions of the variables filled-in accordingly.

Get versus The Powerful Get-Next

Both the `get` and the powerful `get-next` operators work sequentially. For example, if an error occurs while processing the first variable in a request, the remainder of the operands are not processed.

In cases in which errors are not likely to occur, this allows the manager to reduce network traffic by coallescing several requests for the same operation into one. However, if a `get-response` indicates

an error, then all variable value instances contained therein are unde-
fined. This puts the manager in somewhat of a dilemma, if it asks for
a lot of variables in a `get` operation, referencing a single invalid instance will result in no useful information being returned; otherwise,
if it asks for only a single variable, it must make several independent
requests, adding to network traffic.

One solution might be to change the definition of a variable so it
is really a triple:

- *name*, of the object instance;

- *value*, of the object instance; and,

- *validity*, of the object instance and value.

This would allow an agent to indicate which of the variables in a
response were valid, and if so, had valid values associated with them.
In the original design of SGMP, this option was considered. However,
such a definition probably fails the fundamental axiom, as there is
a simpler solution that doesn't require additional complexity in the
agent: rather than using the `get` operator to retrieve the values of
the instance associated with a leaf object, why not use the powerful
`get-next` operator instead? After all, the powerful `get-next` operator
works on any object, not just those found in tables!

Suppose a manager is interested in the value of two variables:

```
sysDescr.0
sysName.0
```

The former is defined in the Internet-standard MIB, and the latter is
defined in MIB-II. Therefore it is possible that the call

```
get (sysDescr.0, sysName.0)
```

might fail because the agent does not support the object type associated with the second operand. The solution is to issue

```
get-next (sysDescr, sysName)
```

instead. If the agent supports MIB-II, then the names and values of

```
sysDescr.0
sysName.0
```

will be returned. Otherwise, the names and values of

```
sysDescr.0
ifNumber.0
```

will be returned. Since the name of the `sysName` and `ifNumber` are
different, the manager can easily determine that the `sysName` object
is not available.

Set

For each variable in the request, the named instance is identified, in
the context of the community profile. If the instance does not exist,
a `get-response` is returned with error `noSuchName`. If the instance
does exist but does not permit writing, a `get-response` is returned
with error `readOnly`. If the instance exists and permits writing, but
the value supplied in the request is poorly-formed (wrong syntax) or
poorly-valued (range error), a `get-response` is returned with error
`badValue`.

Otherwise, all of the variables are updated simultaneously, and a
`get-response` is returned identical to the request. Note that *simultaneously* is all very well in theory, but may be impossible in some
implementations. Regardless, either all variables must be updated or
none of them.

Get-Response

The manager checks its list of previously sent requests to locate the
one which matches this response. If no record is found, the response
is discarded.

Otherwise, the manager handles the response in an appropriate
fashion.

5.5.3 Traps

The fields of a `Trap-PDU` are now described:

enterprise: the value of the agent's `sysObjectID`.

agent-addr: the value of the agent's `NetworkAddress`.

generic-trap: one of a few extraordinary events:

- `coldStart`, the agent is (re-)initializing itself, and objects in its view may be altered (e.g., the protocol entities on the managed node are starting);

- `warmStart`, the agent is re-initializing itself, but the objects in its view will not be altered;

- `linkDown`, an attached interface has changed from the `up` to the `down` state (the first variable identifies the interface);

- `linkUp`, an attached interface has changed to the `up` state (the first variable identifies the interface);

- `authenticationFailure`, an SNMP message has been received from an SNMP entity which falsely claimed to be in a particular community;

- `egpNeighborLoss`, an EGP peer has transitioned to state `down` (the first variable identifies the IP address of the EGP peer); and,

- `enterpriseSpecific`, some other extraordinary event has occurred, identified in the `specific-trap` field (using an enterprise-specific, e.g., private, value).

specific-trap: identifies the `enterpriseSpecific` trap which occurred, otherwise this value is zero.

time-stamp: the value of the agent's `sysUpTime` MIB object when the event occurred.

variable-bindings: a list of variables containing information about the trap.

Sending a Trap-PDU

When an exception event occurs, the agent identifies those managers which it sends traps to, if any. For each manager, it selects an appropriate community and sends a `Trap-PDU` to that manager.

Receiving a Trap-PDU

Upon receiving a `Trap-PDU`, the manager handles the message in an appropriate fashion.

5.6   Transport Mappings

SNMP is meant to be transport protocol-independent. There are currently several mappings defined.

All of the mappings have one thing in common. Instances of the SNMP `Message` data type are transmitted on the network through a process termed *serialization*. This allows an arbitrary data structure to be encoded as a sequence of octets for sending. When the octets are received, they may be converted back to a data structure with *identical* semantics. Section 5.10 on page 167 describes how this is performed. For now, the reader should understand that there is an unambiguous one-to-one mapping between the ASN.1 data structures defined thus far and a string of bytes.

All implementations of SNMP are required to accept messages which are serialized in 484 octets or less. There is no requirement on sending SNMP entities.

5.6.1   Mapping onto UDP

This is the preferred mapping, and is specified directly in the RFC which specifies SNMP. A sending SNMP entity serializes an SNMP `Message` and sends it as a single UDP datagram to the transport address of the receiving SNMP entity. The UDP packet format is:

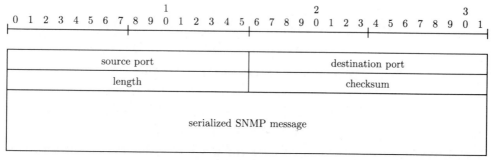

The transport address consists of an IP address and a UDP port. All SNMP agents listen on UDP port 161. If the `Message` contains a trap, the receiving SNMP process listens on UDP port 162. By convention, all responses are sent with the source/destination ports swapped from the corresponding request. Thus, a `get-request` sent

from port 1094 will have the corresponding `get-response` sent back
to port 1094 from port 161.

5.6.2   Mapping directly onto Ethernet

This mapping is defined in [51]. A sending SNMP entity serializes an
SNMP `Message` and sends it as a single `Ethernet` frame to the transport address of the receiving SNMP entity. The transport address
consists of an `Ethernet` address and type 0x814c. If the serialized data
is less than 46 octets, then enough zero-valued octets are appended
to bring the data field to 46 octets in length. The frame format is
shown in figure 5.2.

`soap...` As noted earlier, usage of this mapping is to be discouraged as it
hinders interoperability. The amount of incremental work necessary
to realize UDP and IP is quite small. By doing so, management
requests can be fielded across an internet, instead of restricting them
to the local LAN.

Remote LAN management can be achieved using the same applications and techniques that are used locally. This yields tremendous
leverage!

The author found it tempting to simply ignore the mapping onto
`Ethernet`, but acquiesced in the interests of completeness. However, in
case it's not clear: defining mappings of SNMP onto anything other
`...soap` than a transport service is **pointless**.

5.6.3   Mapping onto the OSI CLTS

This mapping is defined in [52]. A sending SNMP entity serializes an
SNMP `Message` and uses a single T-UNIT-DATA.REQUEST with the
transport address of the receiving SNMP entity as the called address.

The transport address consists of an OSI network address and a
transport selector. By convention, all SNMP agents using CLTS reside
at selector "snmp" (a selector consisting of four ASCII characters), and
SNMP entities listening for traps reside at selector "snmp-trap" (a
selector consisting of nine ASCII characters).

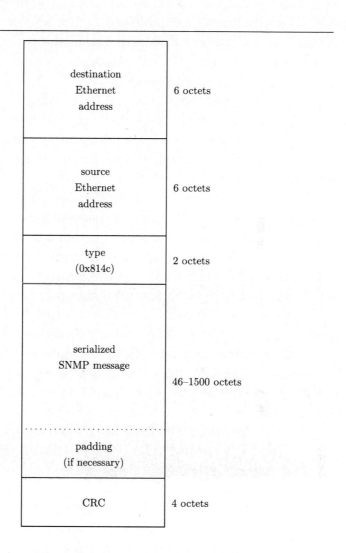

Figure 5.2: SNMP over Ethernet

5.6.4   Mapping onto the OSI COTS

This mapping is defined in [52]. Mapping onto a connection-oriented transport is more detailed as a transport connection to the receiving SNMP entity must be established before SNMP messages can be sent. Thus, the mapping consists of establishing a transport connection, sending one or more SNMP messages on that connection, and then releasing the transport connection.

Consistent with the fundamental axiom, the initiator of a connection should not require that responses to a request be returned on that connection. However, if a responder to a connection sends messages on that connection, these MUST be in response to requests received on that connection.

Ideally, the transport connection *should* be released only by the initiator, however, note that the responder may release the connection due to resource limitations. Further note that the amount of time a connection remains established is implementation-specific. Implementors should take care to choose an appropriate dynamic algorithm.

Also consistent with the fundamental axiom, the initiator should not associate any reliability characteristics with the use of a connection. Issues such as message retransmission, etc., always remain with the SNMP entity, not with the transport service.

Choice of the transport address varies, depending on the underlying *transport-stack* (transport and network protocols) used to offer the COTS.

If an X.25–based COTS is used, demultiplexing is performed on the basis of X.25 protocol-ID. By convention, the value 0x03018200 is used for agents, and SNMP entities listening for traps use a protocol-ID of 0x0301900.

Otherwise, demultiplexing is performed on the basis of transport selector. By convention, the SNMP agent resides at selector "`snmp`", and SNMP entities listening for traps reside at selector "`snmp-trap`."

5.7 SNMP MIB

In MIB-II, a set of managed objects were defined for SNMP application entities:

```
snmp OBJECT IDENTIFIER ::= { mib 11 }
```

In addition to the objects shown in Figure 5.3 on page 164, the other objects in the SNMP group are:

snmpInTooBigs: PDUs received with `error-status` of `tooBig`

snmpInNoSuchNames: PDUs received with `error-status` of `noSuchName`

snmpInBadValues: PDUs received with `error-status` of `badValue`

snmpInReadOnlys: PDUs received with `error-status` of `readOnly`

snmpInGenErrs: PDUs received with `error-status` of `genErr`

snmpInTotalReqVars: number of MIB objects retrieved

snmpInTotalSetVars: number of MIB objects changed

snmpOutTooBigs: PDUs sent with `error-status` of `tooBig`

snmpOutNoSuchNames: PDUs sent with `error-status` of `noSuchName`

snmpOutBadValues: PDUs sent with `error-status` of `badValue`

snmpOutReadOnlys: PDUs sent with `error-status` of `readOnly`

snmpOutGenErrs: PDUs sent with `error-status` of `genErr`

snmpEnableAuthTraps: enable/disable the generation of `authenticationFailure` traps

Figure 5.3: Case Diagram for the SNMP Group

5.8 Historical Perspective

The *Simple Gateway Monitoring Protocol* (SGMP) [49] is of historical interest only. The primary differences between SGMP and SNMP are:

- SGMP contained the definition of objects useful for monitoring gateways, whilst SNMP contains no object definitions, as these are defined in the MIB (and pertain to both hosts and gateways);

- SNMP contains a "set" mechanism, SGMP also had such a mechanism but it was embryonic.

- SNMP contains a formal framework for authentication and authorization; and,

- SNMP uses a separate UDP port for trap traffic.

The first two changes explain the difference between the names of the two protocols, SGMP was used for gateway monitoring; SNMP is used for network management.

5.9   An Interesting Change

A weakness of the OBJECT-TYPE macro is that it does not describe how
SNMP forms instance identifiers. The reason for this is historical, at
the time the macro was defined, there were two management protocols
which were supposed to use the Internet-standard SMI.

This leads us to wonder if a new macro could be defined that had
a clause indicating how the instance-identifier were to be formed, e.g.,

```
ifEntry SNMP-OBJECT-TYPE
        SYNTAX   IfEntry
        ACCESS   read-only
        STATUS   mandatory
        INSTANCE { ifIndex }
        ::= { ifTable 1 }
```

which is identical to the way the OBJECT-TYPE macro is used except the INSTANCE clause provides the additional information. Such
a macro has not yet been defined, but the concept does bear some
consideration.

5.10   Data Encoding

It is now time to describe how instances of data types defined using
ASN.1 are *serialized* into strings of octets. Just as ASN.1 defines
an abstract syntax notation, there is a corresponding *transfer syntax
notation* termed the *Basic Encoding Rules* (BER) [53].[6] It is clearly
beyond the scope of *The Simple Book* to present a thorough treatment
of the BER; the reader should consult Chapter 8 of *The Open Book*
for a detailed exposition. Thus, the remainder of this chapter, which
is condensed from *The Open Book*, will introduce the BER only to
the extent that it is used by the mangement framework.

Although an encoding may be quite complex overall, the actual
rules used to produce the encodings are small in number and quite
simple to describe. The Basic Encoding Rules is simply a recursive
algorithm that can produce a compact octet encoding for any ASN.1
value.

It must be emphasized that the BER is largely a rote topic, as it is
a heavily used and well understood technology. Whilst it is important
to gain an understanding of the issues that the BER must tackle, the
myriad details are usually taken care of by (hopefully well-debugged)
programs.

5.10.1   Top-Level

At the top-level, the BER describes how to encode a single ASN.1
type. This may be a simple type such as an **INTEGER**, or an arbitrarily complex type. Conceptually, the key to applying the BER is to
understand that the most complex ASN.1 type is nothing more than
a number of smaller, less complex ASN.1 types. If this decomposition
continues, then ultimately an ASN.1 simple type such as **INTEGER** is
encoded.

Using the BER, each ASN.1 type is encoded as three fields:

- a *tag* field, which indicates the ASN.1 type;

- a *length* field, which indicates the size of the ASN.1 value encoding which follows;

---

[6]Not to be confused with *bit error rate*.

- a *value* field, which is the ASN.1 value encoding.

Thus, any ASN.1 type is encoded in three fields:

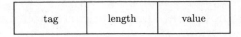

It turns out that each of these fields is of variable length. Because ASN.1 may be used to define arbitrarily complex types, the BER must be able to support arbitrarily complex encodings.

Bit Ordering

Before looking at the details, it is important to appreciate how the BER views octets. Each octet consists of 8–bits — obviously! But, how are the bits numbered? With the BER, the high-order (most significant) bit is called bit 8, whilst the low-order (least significant) bit is called bit 1. This is important to apply consistently because different machine architectures use different ordering rules (some view the high-order bit as being on the left edge of the octet, others view the high-order bit as being on the octet's right edge). Briefly put:

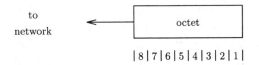

Numeric Representations

Furthermore, a large number of fields encoded by the BER are integer values expressed as binary numbers. There are two ways of representing these numbers, depending on whether negative numbers need to be represented.

To encode an integer that may take on any value (positive, negative, or zero), a *two's-complement* representation is used. In this scheme, a string of bits comprises the number. Bit 8 of the first octet contains the most significant bit, whilst bit 1 of the last octet contains the least significant bit. Although conceptually it is often easier to think of the representation as being octet-aligned, this needn't be the case. For example, the BER may specify that some fields are only

7 bits long. As long as the most significant previously unused bit in the first octet is used as the most significant bit of the string, and the least significant bit unused in the last octet is used as the least significant bit of the string, no ambiguity arises.

Note that a single contents octet can encode an integer value from $-128 \leq x \leq 127$, whilst two contents octets can encode an integer value from $-65536 \leq x \leq 65535$. (In general, with b bits in the string, numbers from $-2^{b-1} \leq x \leq 2^{b-1} - 1$ may be encoded.) In order to ensure that encodings are as compact as possible, the BER does not permit the first 9 bits to be zero- or one-filled. (The first octet is redundant in these cases.)

The second representation is used to encode non-negative integer values. This is a simple variation, termed an *unsigned* representation, in which the high-order bit contributes to the counter rather than decrementing from it:

$$x = \left(\sum_{i=0}^{n-1} bit(i) * 2^i \right)$$

for a string of n bits. Because an extra bit is available for representing the magnitude of the integer value, larger numbers may be represented, in the same number of bits, than with a two's-complement encoding. Numbers from $0 \leq x \leq 2^b - 1$ may be encoded. With most applications of the unsigned representation, the BER permits the leading octets to be zero-filled. This is done for compatibility with the 1984 CCITT X.409 Recommendation.

5.10.2 Tag Field

The *tag* field is encoded as one or more *identifier octets*. This encoding must somehow capture the definition of the corresponding ASN.1 type. The BER does this by encoding the ASN.1 tag of the type. Recall that a tag is associated with each type defined using ASN.1.

As noted earlier, there are four classes of tags in ASN.1:

- *universal* tags, for the well-known data types (Table 3.1 on page 85 shows these);

- *application-wide* tags, which are defined within a single ASN.1 module;

- *context-specific* tags, which are used to provide distinguishing information in constructor types; and,

- *private-use* tags, which are used by consenting parties.

In addition to belonging to one of these groups, a tag has associated with it a non-negative integer. Thus, the tag field, officially termed the *identifier octets*, generated by the BER must encode not only the tag's class but also the tag's number.

In addition, the tag field must encode one other bit of information. As noted earlier, an ASN.1 type might be primitive or it might be constructed. Although we think of it as natural that the value of a primitive type should be encoded as a single collection of octets, it may be more efficient for the sending process to break the value up into smaller, more manageable parts. For example, suppose a facsimile image is being encoded. This is represented in ASN.1 using a `BIT STRING`. If the image was large, it would probably be convenient to apply the BER to only a part of the image at a time. This may be done using a constructed encoding: after the BER was applied, the resulting octet-aligned encodings would be sent, the next part of the image fetched and then encoded. This would continue until the image had been entirely consumed. If the sender wishes to use this scheme, then it must indicate to the receiving process that it is doing so. Thus, if an ASN.1 type is primitive, it may usually be sent either in a primitive form, or in a constructed form. However, if the ASN.1 type is constructed, then it is always sent in constructed form.

So, encoding the tag field as a sequence of octets is rather simple. The tag field consists of one or more octets. The first octet encodes the tag's class along with an indication as to whether the encoding is constructed. Since there are four classes of tags, this can be represented in two of the eight bits in the octet.

Finally, the primitive/constructed indication will require a third bit, which for brevity is termed f:

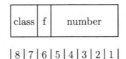

$$|8|7|6|5|4|3|2|1|$$

The encoding of the two high-order bits (bits 8 and 7) are:

Class	Bit 8	Bit 7
Universal	0	0
Application-wide	0	1
Context-specific	1	0
Private	1	1

Thus, five bits are left over for encoding the non-negative tag number. These could be used to encode a non-negative integer from 0 to 63. But, this would be rather short-sighted: many more than 64 types are possible! Thus, the BER uses the following rule:

- if the tag's number is less than 31, then it is encoded in the five bits that remain, using the unsigned representation discussed earlier;

- otherwise, bits 5 through 1 are set to all ones, which indicates that the octets that follow contain the tag's number.

So, in many cases (and clearly for all the Universal tags defined thus far), a single octet is sufficient to encode the tag field. In the other cases, one or more octets follow the first octet. The high-order bit (bit 8), if set to zero, indicates whether this particular octet is the last octet of the tag field:

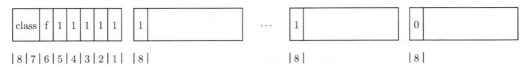

$$|8|7|6|5|4|3|2|1| \quad |8| \qquad\qquad |8| \qquad\qquad |8|$$

Thus, in the case where the tag's number is greater than or equal to 31, the value is encoded using the unsigned integer representation found by concatenating the 7–bit values that follow the initial identifier octet.

5.10.3   Length Field

The *length* field is encoded as one or more *length octets*. This encoding indicates how many of the octets that follow make up the value of the ASN.1 type being encoded.

Observant readers have probably noticed a contradiction in the BER. Earlier, it was noted that it may be useful to encode a primitive type using a constructed encoding if it was difficult to have the entire primitive type available during encoding. If this is the case, then how can the length field be calculated and sent *before* the value? There are two possible solutions to this dilemma, and the BER permits both of them!

The first solution is to provide for a special value for the length field, termed the *indefinite* form. This means that the length of the encoding is not known ahead of time and that the receiving process should look for a special sequence of octets to indicate the end of the value, termed the *end-of-contents*. Obviously, the BER must ensure that no encoding of an ASN.1 type will be able to generate this sequence as its value.

The second solution is to note that it is possible, although potentially inefficient, to make two passes through the data: the first to calculate the length, and the second to do the actual encoding.

If the length of the encoding is known, this is termed the *definite* form. In this case, the length field consists of one or more octets encoding the integer-valued length. If the number of octets of the encoding is less than 128, a single octet can be used to encode the length:

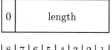

$$|8|7|6|5|4|3|2|1|$$

If the length is longer, then more than one octet is used. The first octet has the high-order bit (bit 8) set to one. The remaining seven bits comprise a number saying how many octets follow in the length field (anywhere from 1 to 126 octets).[7] The length is encoded using the unsigned integer representation found by concatenating the octets

---

[7]The value 127 for bits 7–1 is reserved for possible future extension.

that follow the initial length octet. Since all eight bits are used, up to $126 * 8$ or 1008 bits may be used. Since $2^{1008} - 1$ is larger than the address space on any computer likely to be built for quite some time, this is probably enough bits (a polite understatement). Even so, the BER still provides for future extensibility.

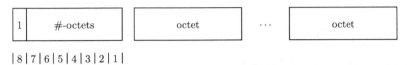

If an indefinite form encoding is used, the length field consists of a single octet that has the high-order bit set to one and the remaining bits set to zero. After this octet, the value field is encoded, consisting of zero or more ASN.1 encodings. To mark the end of the encoding, the end-of-contents octets are sent.

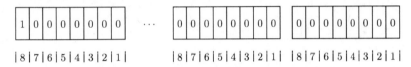

As can be seen, the end-of-contents markers are simply two zero-valued octets. This is equivalent to encoding an ASN.1 type with universal tag value 0 and no length. Since there is no ASN.1 type with this tag, the BER will never produce an ambiguous encoding. Of course, in order to interpret these octets correctly, the BER must know "where to start looking." For this reason, the indefinite length can only be used with constructed encodings. (This will become more clear as the discussion progresses.)

SNMP specifically *disallows* the use of indefinite length form for all messages along with the management information carried by those messages. The indefinite length form places a large burden on the receiving SNMP entity. Since the definite length form is always needed for primitive encodings, use of the indefinite length form is prohibited.

5.10.4   Value Field

We now consider how the ASN.1 types used in the management framework have their values encoded. The value field is encoded as zero or more *contents octets*.

Simple Types

The simple types provide the fundamental encodings that are used by the BER.

Simple Types – INTEGER

An INTEGER value is encoded as one or more contents octets, always in primitive form. The value is encoded using the two's-complement encoding which you will recall prohibits having the first 9 bits as zero- or one-filled, to eliminate redundancy.

For example, the value 100 (decimal) is encoded as:

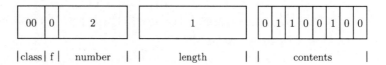

which, ignoring the bits with value zero, is:

$$2^6 + 2^5 + 2^2 = 64 + 32 + 4 = 100$$

Simple Types – OCTET STRING

An OCTET STRING value is encoded as zero or more contents octets, in either primitive or constructed form.

Here is a primitive form encoding for the value "anon":

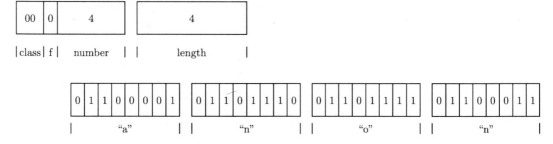

A constructed form of an OCTET STRING value is simply a collection of smaller OCTET STRINGs. Each substring will have its tag field take the value for OCTET STRING.

Note that the SMI prohibits using the constructed form when encoding instances of the IpAddress data type.

Simple Types – NULL

A NULL value is encoded as zero contents octets. It is syntactically similar to the end-of-contents octets, but it has a different tag:

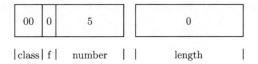

Simple Types – OBJECT IDENTIFIER

An OBJECT IDENTIFIER value is encoded as one or more contents octets, always in primitive form.

Recall that an OBJECT IDENTIFIER is a sequence of non-negative integer values. The BER mandates certain characteristics of any OBJECT IDENTIFIER it encodes: the first element must take the value 0, 1, or 2; and, the second element must take a value less than 40 if the first element is 0 or 1. The reason for these limitations is administrative. Recall that exactly three subordinates to the root node have been defined, coincidentally having values 0, 1, or 2. Since naming authority for these subordinates reside with ISO and CCITT, they are responsible for ensuring that any immediate subordinates are not assigned a number greater than 39.

For the purposes of encoding using the BER:

- the first two elements in the sequence form a *sub-identifier* with the value $X * 40 + Y$, where X is the value of the first element, and Y is the value of the second element; and,

- each element following in the sequence also forms a *sub-identifier* with a value equal to that element's value.

For example,

    1.0.8571.5.1

consists of four sub-identifiers: 40 $(40 * 1 + 0)$, 8571, 5, and 1.

Each sub-identifier is encoded using the unsigned representation in one or more octets. However, the most significant bit of each octet is set to one if another octet follows. Thus, the sub-identifier is represented by concatenating one or more 7–bit values together and treating the resulting string of bits as an unsigned number. In order to ensure a compact encoding, the leading octet may not have bit 8 set to one and all the remaining bits set to zero (i.e., the first seven bits of the encoding must have a non-zero value).

Hence, in order to encode

        1.0.8571.5.1

four numbers, 40, 8571, 5, and 1 must be encoded. Three of these can be represented in seven or fewer bits, and therefore each can be encoded in a single octet. The other, 8571, requires 14 bits, and hence is encoded using two octets. (If 15 bits had been required to encode the sub-identifier using the unsigned representation, then three octets would be needed for the encoding, as a bit in each octet indicates if another octet is used.)

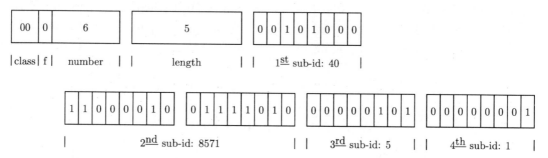

Constructor Types

As the ASN.1 language defined complex types in terms of combining simple types with constructors, so the BER encodes complex types by encoding a constructor whose value portion consists of encodings of simpler types.

The complexity in generating an encoding of the constructor types lies in knowing what value to use for the length field. This was one of the key reasons that the notation of an indefinite length was developed — when encoding a constructor type, the sending process generates the tag and length fields (using the indefinite length), generates the encoding for each element of the constructor type, and then generates the end-of-contents octets to "wrap things up." This mechanism allows the sending process to be vastly simplified at the expense of the receiving process, which must now "know how to deal with such things."

Consistent with the fundamental axiom, SNMP requires that the definite form be used at all times.

Constructor Types – SEQUENCE

A SEQUENCE value is encoded as zero or more contents octets, always in constructed form. Basically, the tag and length fields are generated. Then, for each element present in the SEQUENCE, the BER is recursively applied.

The order of the encodings must match the order that the elements were defined in the ASN.1 module for this type.

Consider an encoding of:

```
VarBind ::=
    SEQUENCE {
        name
            ObjectName,

        value
            ObjectSyntax
    }
```

Without knowing what types ObjectName and ObjectSyntax are, the encoding for VarBind must look something like this:

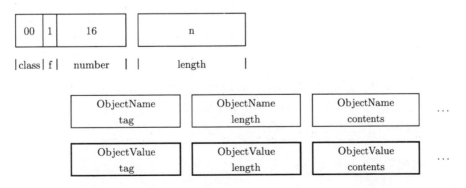

if the definite length is used, or

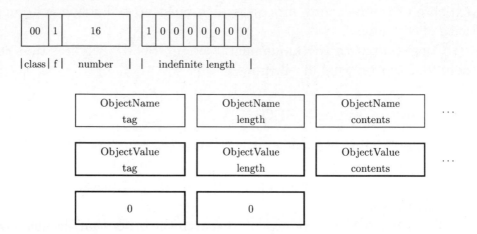

if the indefinite length is used.

Constructor Types – SEQUENCE OF

A `SEQUENCE OF` value is encoded identically to a `SEQUENCE` value; even the tags are the same. Note that the tags of the elements are truly redundant here. However, they must be encoded to maintain the TLV format.

Tagged Types

A tagged type of the form:

```
SomeType ::=
    [tag]
        IMPLICIT OtherType
```

is encoded using the rules for `OtherType`, the difference being that a new value was used in the tag field.

This is straight-forward, but leads us to consider how a definition of the form

```
SomeType ::=
    [tag]
        OtherType
```

might be encoded (there is no IMPLICIT keyword). The answer is that a tagged definition of this form is treated as a constructor analogous to:

```
SomeType ::=
    [tag]
        IMPLICIT SEQUENCE {
            OtherType
        }
```

The idea is that the tagging information of OtherType is retained intact, being contained within another type that has the new tag. Although the BER does not state the encoding rules for tagged types in this fashion, using this conceptualization tends to make the encoding rules appear much more intuitive.

Thus, an encoding of:

```
SomeType ::=
    [APPLICATION 0]
        OtherType
```

always looks something like this:

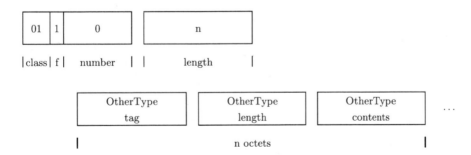

Although the example here does not show use of the indefinite length, this is permitted by the BER, as it would be with any type that could be encoded using the constructed form. In the interest of simplicity, indefinite length encodings are not allowed by the Internet-standard Network Management Framework, so an example is not given here.

5.10.5   The Controversy about TLV encodings

Although the BER generates compact encodings, it is not particularly
efficient in terms of processing. In fact, other encoding mechanisms
are often 20 times (or more) faster than using the BER. Whilst these
mechanisms are not used to encode ASN.1 data types, they nonetheless exist in highly useful, well deployed systems.

Thus, there has always been some argument as to whether use of
the BER (and ASN.1) invokes too high a price on a managed agent.
As of this writing, this issue remains debated but largely irrelevant.

5.10.6   An Example

The discussion now turns to an example that shows how the BER
may be applied to the ASN.1 data types used in the management
framework. Referring back to Figure 5.1 which started on page 149,
consider the ASN.1 value:

```
example Message ::=
    {
        version version-1,
        community "public",
        data {
            get-response {
                request-id 17,
                error-status noError,
                error-index 0,
                variable-bindings {
                    {
                        name 1.3.6.1.2.1.1.1.1.0,
                        value {
                            simple {
                                string "unix"
                            }
                        }
                    }
                }
            }
        }
    }
```

In generating an encoding using the BER for this value, the first step
(conceptually) is to view the value as being composed of ASN.1 simple

and constructor types:

```
{
    0,
    "public",
    [2] {
        17,
        0,
        0,
        {
            {
                1.3.6.1.2.1.1.1.1.0,
                "unix"
            }
        }
    }
}
```

This gives a more concrete view of the data values to be encoded.

The next step is to actually construct the encoding.

A `Message` consists of three parts. The tag field is easy to generate. By scanning the components of the message, and calculating their lengths, it is determined that 43 octets will be needed for the value portion.[8] Thus, the first two octets of the encoding are as follows:

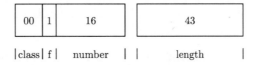

Next, the version number, an **INTEGER**, is encoded:

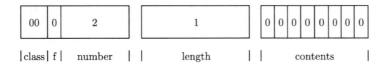

---

[8]A simple recursive algorithm may be used to determine this. Actually, there are many possible implementation strategies that might be used, e.g., generating the value field first and then generating the tag and length fields.

Following this, the community name, an **OCTET STRING**, is encoded:

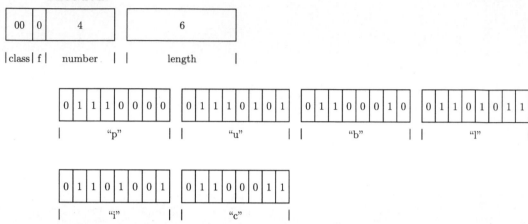

Following this, an instance of the `PDUs` data type is encoded. Since this is a **CHOICE**, whichever data is specified by the value is encoded instead: in this case, an instance of the `GetResponse-PDU`. This is an **IMPLICITly** tagged type, so in turn, a `PDU` value is encoded, but with a different tag. A `PDU` data type is a **SEQUENCE**, so it must use the constructed form. We begin by generating the tag and length fields:

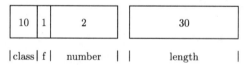

Next, the request identifier, error status, and error index fields are encoded. All three of these are integers:

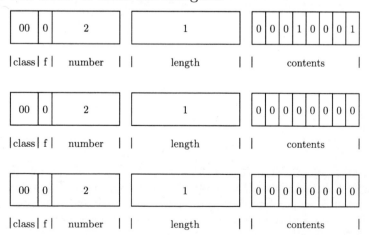

Finally, the variable bindings, a **SEQUENCE OF** value, is encoded. Once again, the tag and length fields are generated:

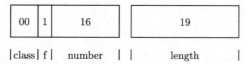

Each element of the **SEQUENCE OF** value is a `VarBind` value, which is a **SEQUENCE**. Since there is only one element in the **SEQUENCE OF**, only one such value need be encoded. As usual, the tag and length fields are generated:

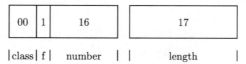

Finally, the components of the `VarBind` value are generated, starting with an `ObjectName` value. This is an **OBJECT IDENTIFIER** with value `1.3.6.1.2.1.1.1.1.0`, having 9 sub-identifiers:

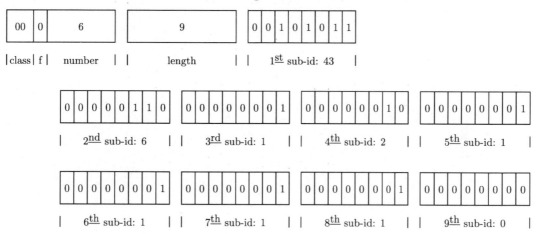

This is followed with an `ObjectValue` value, which is an **OCTET STRING**:

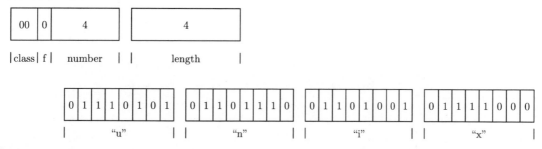

Putting this all together, here are the 45 octets that are generated (in hexadecimal):

```
30 2b
    02 01 00
    04 06 70 75 62 6c 69 63
    a2 1e
        02 01 11
        02 01 00
        02 01 00
        30 13
            30 11
                06 09 2b 06 01 02 01 01 01 01 00
                04 04 75 6e 69 78
```

5.11 In Perspective

It is now time to contrast the Internet-standard Network Management Framework to the OSI view of network management. Three areas will now be considered in turn.

5.11.1 Transport Mappings

SNMP assumes only a basic CL-mode access to underlying layers whilst, the OSI Common Management Information Protocol (CMIP), uses a connection-oriented model as a part of an application layer entity.

The OSI approach is general, in that network management uses the same framework as all the other OSI applications. However, critics of this approach argue that network management is unlike "normal" applications and that it requires special mechanisms. For example, at either the transport and network layers, sophisticated algorithms are used to ensure reliability of the transmission. Unfortunately, these mechanisms, which are designed to hide problems in the network, are intended for applications like file transfer and electronic mail. When the network is collapsing, this behavior is most likely inappropriate when trying to manage the network!

Thus the SNMP approach is more appropriate: CL-mode access means that there are no hand-shaking packets required before management can occur, and that each management application controls the level of retransmission. Considering that the basic unit of commerce in an internet is the datagram, it should be easy to grasp that the management protocol must have a direct mapping onto an underlying datagram service.

5.11.2 Operations

Although both SNMP and CMIP use request-reply interactions, there are fewer operations with SNMP. This is because functionality of the `action`, `create`, and `delete` operations of the OSI Common Management Information Service (CMIS), can be performed by the single

SNMP `set` operation.   Any imperative action can be modeled by a set, as can any addition or deletion.

The trade-off here is one of defining complexity in the operators or operands. The SNMP approach focuses on a few simple operators, whilst the CMIS approach focuses on more numerous, more complicated operators. This distinction is often characterized by Chuck Davin, one of the authors of SNMP, as a "RISC vs. CISC" argument.

5.11.3   Identifying Management Information

Whilst both SNMP and CMIP use the `OBJECT IDENTIFIER` to name individual object types, CMIP introduces complex scoping and filtering mechanisms to identify object instances. As a consequence, in a single management operation, it is impractical to reference two objects in different parts of the information tree. For example, additional management traffic is required when referencing something from both the system group and the IP routing table.

In contrast, SNMP uses a very focused approach to identify object instances, and provides the powerful `get-next` operator to efficiently traverse the tree. Experience has shown that this capability provides substantive advantages in comparison to the theoretical benefits of the scoping and filtering approach.

Of course, in each area, SNMP has been guided by the fundamental axiom used in the Internet-standard Network Management Framework. In constrast, CMIP has been formed by the generalist approach of OSI.

soap...   Given this perspective, perhaps a more apt name for the SNMP would have been the *Moderate Network Management Protocol* or simply the MNMP. This has often been suggested by the the eminent Professor Case.   Continuing in this vein, the author suspects that CMIP is really an abbreviation for the *(overly) Complex Management*
...soap *Information Protocol.*

Chapter 6

Policy: Applications

Thus far, discussion has focused on the core services of the Internet-standard Management Framework. They provide a set of services by which the devices in an internet can be managed.

It is now time to consider the hardest part of the problem: building tools based on these services in order to perform management. Unfortunately, this is the least understood aspect of *any* management system. How does one develop an integrated set of management policies in which operators, programs, and agents cooperate to keep an internet running smoothly? The author is honest in admitting that he doesn't have the answers.

In this chapter an approach to building these policies is described. As the approach is developed, actual NOC applications are presented.

6.1   The Big Picture

In order to take a proactive role, it is necessary to monitor and corre-late. Thus, the first step is to identify the key elements to be managed.

In the case of a network provider, the key elements are the core routers of the backbone along with any co-located distribution routers. In contrast, in the case of a single site, the key elements are probably the routers connecting the site to the rest of the internet.

Regardless, the NOC runs a management application which con-tinuously monitors these key elements and graphically displays the state of the network. The number of objects which are monitored, along with the frequency, depend on the sophistication of the man-agement application. On page 189, an example of the display of such an application is shown.

Note that in the discussion that follows, the term "management application" is purposefully vague. It may be a single program or a collection of programs. Implementation matters of this level are unimportant for the discussion at hand.

6.1.1   Trouble-Shooting

Once the management application has reached steady-state, using only the Internet-standard MIB, it is in a good position to detect and analyze problems.

Link-Level Problems

For each element, the monitor keeps track of the state of each attach-ment (called a link) on the element by scanning the interfaces table and examining `ifOperStatus` for each row. As the agents are usually configured to send traps to the NOC, the management application also monitors the trap log for messages from the agents.

When the management application observes that a link has transi-tioned to the `down` state, it might perform several tasks immediately:

- log this information for archival purposes;

- inform the network operator by changing the network display;

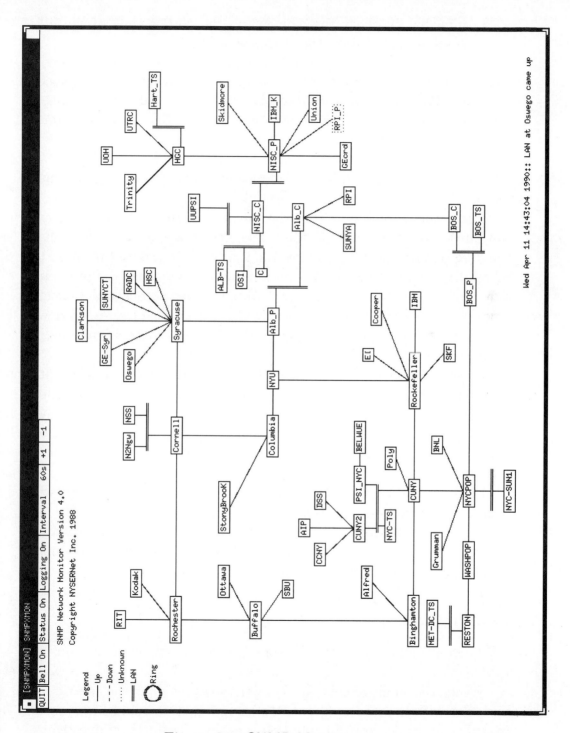

Figure 6.1: SNMP Monitor

189

- immediately query the element on the "other end" of the link to see what it thinks the status is; and,

- if an *interface-specific* MIB has been defined for the link (either in `ifSpecific` or a private MIB variable), and if the management application has knowledge of that MIB, then additional procedures can be invoked.

The procedures followed by the operations staff vary widely, depending on the technology used for the link.

The reader should note that the use of trap-directed polling places the burden of "thinking" on the management application. As it has the "big picture" of the key elements, it alone is in the best position to correlate seemingly unrelated events in order to localize the problem. Of course, if the link is along a critical path, then second-order effects (such as changes in routing tables) will manifest themselves, as news of the outage is propagated through the routing protocols running in the internet.

Depending on how much redundancy there is in the connectivity between the management station and the device "beyond" a failed link, one link failure may cause nodes to become unreachable, causing their status to change in the display. Of course, the application may notice the latter change first, and the true problem may become evident only after further information is available.

Finally, it is worth noting that the management application will probably take action when a link transitions back to the up state. In particular, a link which rapidly changes state back and forth probably indicates something bad is happening (and this usually causes more problems than the link remaining down).

Routing Problems

For each element, the monitor keeps track of portions of the routing table.

When the management application observes that the metric associated with a route is frequently changing, this could be a warning of a network problem, possibly nearby. To further investigate, the management application must observe both `ipRouteNextHop` and `ipRouteMetric1` as shown in Figure 6.2 on page 192.

If fluctuations occur rapidly, the management application could start following the next-hop thread in order to determine what is going on. In fact, this is precisely the action taken when the NOC receives a report that two hosts are unable to communicate. A management application, similar to the *traceroute* program mentioned way back in Section 2.7.2 on page 66, is run. However, this application needn't reside on the source host. Rather the NOC can use SNMP to query each element, starting with the source host. For each, the routing table is examined in order to determine the next-hop thread. A routing loop is easily detected by keeping track of the agents visited during the traversal. Skipping ahead a bit, Figure 7.7 on page 243 shows an algorithm which might be used.

Of course, since IP traffic between two hosts is not fixed along one path, it is possible that the management application will traverse only one of several possible paths. Knowing this, the NOC might run the route tracing application along the reverse path, starting with the destination host, and look for routing inconsistencies.

Congestion Problems

Finally, for each element, the monitor might also keep track of both the throughput and errors encountered on each link on the element.

When either reaches a threshold, the monitor might inform the operator who may wish to examine the situation more closely. At this point, the management application might begin polling for these variables more frequently to gain a better estimate of the instantaneous level of activity on the link. This information might be shown in a bar graph plotting activity against time, as shown in Figure 6.3.

As might be expected, querying the element on the "other end" of the link might produce information useful for contrast.

```
┌─────────────────────────────────────────────────────────────────────┐
│ ■  [SNMPXRTMETRIC] SNMPXRTMETRIC                                    ▊│
├─┐                                                                    │
│Q│                                                                    │
│ SNMP Route Metric Monitor Version 3.0                               │
│ Agent: 128.145.100.2                                                │
│             0   1   2   3   4   5   6   7   8   9  10  11  12  13  14  15  16 │
│        SUNYA───────────────────────                                 │
│          AIP───────────────────────────                             │
│       Alfred───────────────────────────────────────────────────────│
│   Binghamton───────────────────────────────────────────────────────│
│   Brookhaven───────────────────────────────────────────────────────│
│      Buffalo───────────────────────────────────────────────────────│
│         CCNY───────────────────────────────────────────────────────│
│     Clarkson─────                                                   │
│     Columbia───────────────────                                     │
│ Cooper_Union─────────────────────────                               │
│         CUNY─────────────────────────                               │
│          DSS───────────────────────────                             │
│           EI─────────────────────────                               │
│       GE_CRD─────────────────────────                               │
│  GE_Syracuse─────                                                   │
│      Grumman───────────────────────────────                         │
│ Hart.Grad.Ctr.─────────────────────────────────                     │
│          HSC─────────────                                           │
│    U.Hartford─────────────────────────                              │
│  IBM_Kingston─────────────────────────                              │
│  IBM_Yorktown─────────────────────────                              │
│     Karlsruhe─────────────────────────                              │
│        Kodak───────────────────────                                 │
│          NYU─────────────────────────                               │
│       Oswego─────                                                   │
│       Ottowa───────                                                 │
│   Polytechnic─────────────────────────────────                      │
│         RADC────────────                                            │
│       Reston───────────────────────────────────────                 │
│          RIT───────────────────────                                 │
│    Rochester─────────                                               │
│   Rockefeller─────────────────────────                              │
│          RPI─────────────────────────                               │
│          SBU─────────────────────────                               │
│     Skidmore───────────────────────────                             │
│    SmithKline─────────────────────────                              │
│   StonyBrook─────────────────────────                               │
│     Syracuse─────                                                   │
│       SUNYCT───────                                                 │
│      Trinity───────────────────────────                             │
│        Union───────────────────────────                             │
│  United-Tech───────────────────────────                             │
│                                                                     │
└─────────────────────────────────────────────────────────────────────┘
```

Figure 6.2: SNMP Route Metric Monitor

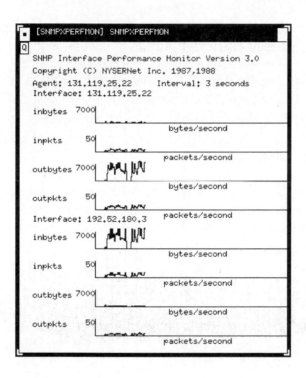

Figure 6.3: SNMP Performance Monitor

In perspective

It is important to appreciate that these techniques all introduce traffic onto the internet. Care must be taken to avoid (or at least identify) three pitfalls:

- problematic connectivity between the NOC and the elements (e.g., having management traffic traverse a flakey link to ask the another element what it thinks is going on);

- the so-called *Hawthorne Effect*, in which monitoring traffic skews the data being retrieved; and,

- the lesser-known *Davin Corollary*, which observes that the granularity of management information is always relative to the network transit time of the management requests (management of the network always occurs relative to the transit time of the management traffic).

Of course, the Hawthorne Effect is really just an example of a Heisenberg measurement property (you can't observe something without interfering with it), and the Davin Corollary is just another name for one of the axioms of control theory.

6.1.2   Statistics Gathering

It is straight-forward to build an application which gathers management information from network elements. The problem is always one of deciding

what to ask for: this is determined by the importance of planning for future growth, along with the need to analyze chronic problems;

what to do with it: the sheer bulk of the data will require the NOC staff to process it prior to analysis, the type of processing done depends on what's being looked for; and,

how long to keep it: this is determined by the availability of secondary storage resources.

In order to determine information about `Counter` objects, the NOC will have to keep track both of the previous values of those objects along with the previous value of the `sysUpTime` object. This is necessary to determine the actual change during a sampling interval. Of course, if the new value of `sysUpTime` is smaller or the delta between the old and new values is too small, then the agent has restarted. In this case, then management information has been lost.

In general, statistics gathering is a database retrieval problem: there's a lot of archival data available, being able to find it and use it effectively is the hard part.

6.2   Multiple Administrative Domains

The discussion thus far has acted as though a NOC has full access to
the agents in an internet. In the case where the internet is under a
single administration, this is a valid assumption. In the more general
case, a problem will cross two or three administrative domains.

In cases such as these, bilateral agreements between the NOCs responsible for each domain must be in place. These agreements must
define the communities which are used for cross-domain management.
With multi-domain internet management, and particularly when the
basic mechanism has only weak authentication, trust must be in abun-
dance.

6.2.1   The Proxy Solution

In many cases, a solution is to build a "management firewall" between management domains. Consider a situation in which domains
A and B wish to cooperate in managing problems which cross their
management domains.

The NOC for A will run a proxy agent which has read-only access
to the key network elements in A. The agent will support multiple
communities, each corresponding to one of the key network elements
in A. Finally, the NOC for A will configure the proxy agent so that
the NOC for B is a member of these communities.

When a user in B reports a problem that crosses the boundaries
between A and B, the NOC for B might consult the proxy agent as
a member of the appropriate community. The most notable benefit
of this approach is that it allows A to determine the limitations to
which the NOC for B is allowed to manage A: a sophisticated proxy
agent can implement sophisticated policies.

There are also two interesting side-effects: first, the administrative
configurations (community knowledge) for each network element in A
is kept simple: each element need only know about the NOC for A
and the proxy agent; and, second, the proxy agent may cache answers
from the network elements so as to reduce unnecessary network traffic.

For example, the proxy agent might provide access to precisely
the core routers of the backbone in A. If A has connections to many

domains, then it is likely that there will be many requests from many sources to examine the routing tables of the core routers. The proxy agent, if so implemented and configured, can cache this information.

In fact, the proxy solution generalizes quite nicely to third-party management. It is possible that traffic between the source and destination might traverse several management domains. In this case, effective management requires that agreements be in place between the source domain and each intervening domain.

Chapter 7

An Implementation

The Internet-standard Network Management Framework has been implemented on many platforms. Because of this, it is difficult to characterize the nature of these implementations in all but the most general terms.

At a first cut, one can distinguish between agent and manager implementations. At the risk of being too simplistic, agent implementations fall into one of two categories:

- *tightly-integrated*, in which performance is optimized by placing the management instrumentation and protocol into the logical process containing the entities implementing the useful protocols; and,

- *loosely-integrated*, in which flexibility is optimized by separating the implementations of the management protocol and administrative framework from the rest of the protocol entities.

The first approach is appropriate for devices such as routers and other special-purpose network entities. The second approach is used for general-purpose computing engines.

Each tightly-integrated implementation is highly tuned and optimized to run on a particular platform.

These implementations are not portable across the product lines of different vendors, and may not even be portable within a single vendor's product line! It should be noted that the benefits of the fundamental axiom are most appreciated in these implementations.

A loosely-integrated implementation is usually meant to be of general use. Portability is enhanced by structuring the implementation so that it is applicable to a large number of platforms, at the expense of using a generalized, and usually slow, means for interacting with the other protocol entities.

Because of the wide range of needs, all manager implementations tend to be implemented in the same style as loosely-integrated agent systems.

The discussion now turns to consider an implementation of an agent and manager built using this latter style of implementation. The *4BSD/ISODE SNMP* package is an implementation of the management framework for Berkeley **UNIX** systems. It is a part of the *ISO Development Environment* (ISODE), which was developed primarily as a tool for studying the upper-layers of OSI.[1] The reader might consider it strange that ISODE includes an implementation of SNMP. Inasmuch as the continued survival of the Internet hinges on all nodes becoming network manageable, the SNMP software was developed using ISODE and will be freely distributed with future releases of Berkeley **UNIX**. Although the package contains a full agent implementation, it does not contain a full NOC implementation. Rather, the manager side of the implementation consists of tools for *rapid-prototyping* network management applications.

The discussion begins by considering common data structures and mechanisms. Following this, the agent and manager software are discussed in turn. ISODE is coded in the *C* programming language and runs on several variants of the **UNIX** operating system. Hence, when reading the sections on implementation, it will be helpful to be familiar with the basics of the **UNIX** operating system.

For the remainder of this chapter, the reader should keep in mind that an *implementation* of SNMP is being discussed. The data structures and access mechanisms are part of the implementation, they are most certainly not part of the SNMP definition.

---

[1]Ordering information for ISODE can be found in Appendix D.

7.1 Core

The core of the package consists of a MIB-compiler and a supporting run-time library.

7.1.1 MOSY

The *mosy* compiler reads the ASN.1 definitions of a MIB module, and produces a simple file used by the run-time library. The name *mosy* stands for the Managed Object Syntax-compiler (YACC-based).

The user runs *mosy* on each MIB module of interest and then concatenates the resulting output files to the file produced by running *mosy* on the SMI module. For example:

```
% mosy smi.my
mosy 6.0 #2 (cheetah) of Sat Mar 24 10:51:51 PST 1990
RFC1155-SMI identifiers: internet directory mgmt
            experimental private enterprises

RFC1155-SMI types: ObjectName ObjectSyntax SimpleSyntax
            ApplicationSyntax NetworkAddress IpAddress
            Counter Gauge TimeTicks Opaque

% mosy mib.my
mosy 6.0 #2 (cheetah) of Sat Mar 24 10:51:51 PST 1990
RFC1156-MIB identifiers: mib system interfaces at ip
            icmp tcp udp egp

RFC1156-MIB objects: sysDescr sysObjectID sysUpTime
            ifNumber ifTable ifEntry

    ...

% cat smi.defs mib.defs > objects.defs
```

might be used to create a file containing definitions for MIB-I. This file is then installed in a system area and is read by the run-time library when a management application (or agent) initializes itself.

The syntax of the file is largely unimportant as it is read only by the run-time library. It is essentially a "flat" representation of the information defined in the OBJECT-TYPE macro.

7.1.2   Run-time Library

The run-time library consists of routines to keep track of the managed objects in the configuration file. This is divided into three areas: syntax, objects, and instances.

The library is initialized by calling the routine readobjects, e.g.,

```
#include <isode/snmp/objects.h>


    ...


if (readobjects ("objects.defs") == NOTOK)
    error ("readobjects: %s", PY_pepy);
```

Object Syntax

The C structure used to model an object's syntax is:

```
typedef struct object_syntax {
    char    *os_name;        /* syntax name */

    IFP     os_encode;       /* data -> PE */
    IFP     os_decode;       /* PE -> data */
    IFP     os_free;         /* free data */

    IFP     os_parse;        /* str -> data */
    IFP     os_print;        /* data -> tty */


    ...
}               object_syntax, *OS;
#define NULLOS  ((OS) 0)
```

where IFP is a pointer to a function returning an integer value, and PE is an internal form used to represent data values already encoded for network transmission.

The run-time library contains definitions for all of the syntaxes defined in the SMI:

syntax	C structure
INTEGER	integer
OCTET STRING	struct qbuf *
OBJECT IDENTIFIER	struct OIDentifier *
NULL	char *
IpAddress	struct sockaddr_in *
NetworkAddress	struct sockaddr_in *
Counter	integer
Gauge	integer
TimeTicks	integer
DisplayString	struct qbuf *

These are all simple data structures defined in the run-time library.

Object Syntax – integer

This is used for these syntaxes:

```
INTEGER
Counter
Gauge
TimeTicks
```

The definition on most systems is:

```
typedef int integer;
```

which is hardly surprising.

Object Syntax – struct qbuf

This is used for these syntaxes:

```
OCTET STRING
DisplayString
```

The definition is:

```
struct qbuf {
    struct qbuf *qb_forw; /* doubly-linked list */
    struct qbuf *qb_back; /*    .. */

    int     qb_len;        /* length of data */
    char    *qb_data;      /* current pointer into data */
    char    qb_base[1];    /* extensible... */
};
```

(If the string was encoded using the constructed form, there are multiple qbufs in the ring.)

The macro QBFREE is used to traverse the qb_forw field to free all qbufs in the ring:

```
QBFREE (qb)
struct qbuf *qb;
```

To allocate a new string from a ring of qbufs, use

```
char *qb2str (q)
struct qbuf *q
```

The resulting string is terminated with a null character. Note, however, that the repertoire for the string needn't be ASCII.

To allocate a new qbuf which contains a given string, use

```
struct qbuf str2qb (s, len, 1)
char    *s;
int     len;
```

and to free an allocated qbuf, use qb_free which calls QBFREE and then free on its argument.

Object Syntax – struct OIDentifier

This is used for these syntaxes:

    OBJECT IDENTIFIER

The definition is:

```
typedef struct OIDentifier {
    int     oid_nelem;  /* number of sub-identifiers */

    unsigned int *oid_elements;
                /* the (ordered) list of sub-identifiers */
}                       OIDentifier, *OID;
#define NULLOID ((OID) 0)
```

To compare two OIDs, use

```
int     oid_cmp (p, q)
OID     p,
        q;
```

which returns -1 if $p < q$, 1 if $p > q$, and 0 otherwise.

To allocate a new OID and copy it from another, use

```
OID     oid_cpy (p)
OID     p;
```

and to free an allocated OID, use `oid_free`.

To take an OID and produce a string in numeric form use

```
char    *sprintoid (oid)
OID     oid;
```

The result is returned in a static area, so subsequent calls will over-write this value. The inverse routine is:

```
OID     str2oid (s)
char    *s;
```

which returns an OID from a static area.

Object Syntax – struct sockaddr_in

This is used for these syntaxes:

```
IpAddress
NetworkAddress
```

The definition of this structure is well-known to any familiar with Berkeley UNIX [54].

Defining a new Syntax

New syntaxes are added by defining a new C structure and then five routines which manipulate the structure. Consider Figure 7.1 which shows how the INTEGER syntax is realized.

The only structure not defined thus far is a PE or *presentation element*. This is a C data structure which is an intermediary form between the structures used by the programmer and the encoding used on the network.

From a high-level perspective, a PE is nothing more than a modestly complex C structure that represents an ASN.1 value as either a string of octets or bits (primitive types) or as a linked list of other presentation elements (constructor types). Layered on top of this are numerous routines that convert between PEs and the data structures used by a target architecture. These routines are usually accessed by code generated by the mechanisms described in Section 7.2.4 on page 224.

Obviously, use of presentation elements introduces an inherent inefficiency: at some point two (or perhaps three) copies of data reside in the system. Further, the current implementation of presentation elements is memory-resident. This means that large ASN.1 structures, when converted to and from PEs, must remain entirely in memory. However, the generality is substantial; by using a common internal form, many tools can be built that manipulate them. This encourages reuse and rapid prototyping. By having one set of well-debugged routines that manipulate PEs, developers focus their time on other, higher-level, issues.

```
integer_encode (x, pe)
integer *x;
PE      *pe;
{
    return ((*pe = int2prim (*x)) == NULLPE ? NOTOK : OK);
}

integer_decode (x, pe)
integer **x;
PE      pe;                                                               10
{
    integer    i = prim2num (pe);

    if ((i == NOTOK && pe -> pe_errno != PE_ERR_NONE)
            || (*x = (integer *) malloc (sizeof **x)) == NULL)
        return NOTOK;
    **x = i;

    return OK;
}                                                                        20

integer_free (x) integer *x; { free ((char *) x); }

integer_parse (x, s)
integer **x;
char    *s;
{
    long    l;

    if (scanf (s, "%ld", &l) != 1                                        30
            || (*x = (integer *) malloc (sizeof **x)) == NULL)
        return NOTOK;
    **x = (integer) l;

    return OK;
}

integer_print (x, os) integer *x; OS os; { printf ("%d", *x); }

...                                                                      40

add_syntax ("INTEGER", integer_encode, integer_decode, integer_free, integer_parse, integer_print);
```

Figure 7.1: Realizing the INTEGER syntax

Object Types

The C structure used to model an object type is:

```
typedef struct object_type {
    char    *ot_text;        /* descriptor */
    OID     ot_name;         /* identifier */

    OS      ot_syntax;       /* SYNTAX */

    int     ot_access;       /* ACCESS */
#define OT_NONE          0x00
#define OT_RDONLY        0x01
#define OT_WRONLY        0x02
#define OT_RDWRITE       0x03

    int     ot_status;       /* STATUS */
#define OT_OBSOLETE      0x00
#define OT_MANDATORY     0x01
#define OT_OPTIONAL      0x02
#define OT_DEPRECATED    0x03

    IFP     ot_getfnx;       /* agent pointer */
    caddr_t ot_info;         /*   .. for object */

    ...
}                   object_type, *OT;
#define NULLOT  ((OT) 0)
```

The library provides several routines to find the MIB objects which
have been read in from configuration files.

The routine **name2obj** takes an **OBJECT IDENTIFIER** and returns
the corresponding *prototype*. What this means is that if an object
is exactly named, or an instance of that object is named, then the
structure corresponding to that object is returned. Thus (taking a
few liberties with the C language), a call to

```
name2obj ( OID { ipNextHop.0.0.0.0 } )
```

returns the object type for **ipNextHop**.

The routine `text2obj` takes a string and returns the exact object type, e.g.,

```
text2obj ("ipNextHop")
```

will succeed, but

```
text2obj ("ipNextHop.0.0.0.0")
```

will fail.

The routine `text2oid` takes a string and returns the name (i.e., `OBJECT IDENTIFIER`) associated with the corresponding object. The string can be numeric, symbolic, or combined, so all three of these calls

```
text2oid ("1.3.6.1");

text2oid ("internet");

text2oid ("iso.3.6.1");
```

return the same `OID`.

Finally, the routine **oid2ode** takes an `OID` and returns a string suitable for pretty-printing, in symbolic form (whenever possible).

Object Instances

The *C* structure used to model an object instance is:

```
typedef struct object_instance {
    OID      oi_name;      /* instance OID */
    OT       oi_type;      /* prototype */
}                object_instance, *OI;
#define NULLOI  ((OI) 0)
```

There are three routines to manipulate MIB instances.

The routine **name2inst** takes a variable name and returns the corresponding instance, e.g.,

```
name2inst ( OID { ipNextHop.0.0.0.0 } )
```

will return an **OI** with the **oi_name** field set to its argument and **oi_type** set to the object type for **ipNextHop**.

The routine **next2inst** finds the closest object type before the variable name and returns an OI corresponding to that object type. This is used by an agent with a two-level algorithm (discussed later on) implementing the powerful **get-next** operator.

Finally, the routine

```
OI      text2inst (text)
char    *text;
```

calls **text2oid** to get the **OID** corresponding to the argument, then calls **name2obj** to get the object type associated with that **OID**, and copies the information into a static area.

7.2 Agent Implementation

Since the protocol entities in Berkeley UNIX reside in the kernel, user-processes, such as the SNMP agent, *snmpd*, must go to special lengths in order to carry out the directives of the management protocol. However, as a user-process, *snmpd* is permitted more freedom than a kernel-resident entity when additional configuration information is required. Further, a failure in *snmpd* should not result in either UNIX or the protocol entities failing. On balance, the performance loss and extra machinations required are acceptable.

7.2.1 Initialization

In its initialization phase, the agent:

1. Examines its command line arguments for directives from the user. This allows for debugging and special configurations to be accomplished. For example, it may be useful to run a test version of the agent on a non-standard UDP port so as not to interfere with the normal SNMP service.

2. If invoked during system start-up, the program then detaches and performs the usual daemon-initialization functions.

3. The run-time library for managed objects is initialized.

4. Next, the MIB subsystem in the agent is initialized. For each object supported by the agent, the corresponding object type is fetched from the library and the `ot_getfnx` field is set to the address of a procedure which will access instances of the object.

5. Next, the agent configuration file is read.

6. The agent then starts listening on each transport address it is responsible for. Normally this is simply UDP port 161 on the local host. For the remainder of this discussion, only this normal case will be considered, although the agent implementation also supports mappings onto the OSI COTS and OSI CLTS.

7. Finally, a `coldStart` trap is sent to the NOC announcing that the agent is up and running.

Not all of the information defined in the MIB can be found in the UNIX kernel. Thus, *snmpd* needs some help from the system administrator. A configuration file is used for this purpose.

As shown in Figure 7.2, each line of the file contains a directive and one or more arguments:

community: defines a community for the agent. The arguments are:

- the community name (which is an ASCII string);
- the IP address of the manager which uses this community (if absent, or if the value `0.0.0.0` is used, then any manager may use this community);
- the access mode, one of `readOnly`, `writeOnly`, `readWrite`, or `none`; and,
- the view name associated with the community.

view: defines a collection of manageable objects. The arguments are:

- the view name (which is an `OBJECT IDENTIFIER`); and,
- zero or more "subtree" names, the union of which compose the view.

If no subtrees are specified, then the view contains all objects known to the agent.

trap: defines a community which traps are sent to. The arguments are:

- the community name;
- the destination IP address; and,
- the associated view.

logging: tailors the logging package used by the agent.

```
community        public

community        system          0.0.0.0              readOnly
1.17.2
view             1.17.2          system unix

trap             traps           192.33.4.20

logging          file=snmpd.log  size=50
logging          slevel=fatal    slevel=exceptions    slevel=notice
logging          sflags=close    sflags=create        sflags=zero

variable         sysContact      "Marshall Rose <mrose@psi.com>"
variable         sysLocation     "Troy machine room"
variable         sysServices     72

variable         interface lo0   ifType=24            ifSpeed=0
variable         interface le0   ifType=6
```

Figure 7.2: Example Agent Configuration File

variable *name***:** which sets the value of a leaf object.

variable interface: which sets the value of those columns in the interfaces table which are not instrumented by the Berkeley UNIX kernel. The arguments are:

- a kernel-level name; and,
- one or more attribute-value pairs.

For example, the kernel does not store information indicating what kind of hardware is associated with a particular interface. The system administrator, who presumably is cognizant about such things, can supply this information to the agent.

7.2.2   Main Loop

The main-loop of *snmpd* is straight-forward: the agent waits for an incoming datagram. Upon receiving one:

1. It reads the datagram from UDP and notes the transport address of the sending entity.

2. A special integer-value variable, `quantum`, is incremented. This keeps track of the logical request-id being processed by the agent.

3. It de-serializes the datagram into an ASN.1 structure. If an error occurs, this is logged and the packet is discarded.

4. The ASN.1 structure is then translated into an SNMP `Message`. If an error occurs, this is logged and the packet is discarded.

5. A check is made on the `version-number` field. If a version mismatch has occurred, this is logged and the packet is discarded.

6. The community name is looked up. If the community is unknown to the agent, and the agent is enabled to send authentication traps, then such a trap is sent. Regardless, this is logged and the packet is discarded.

7. Otherwise, the agent loops through the list of variables in the request: first it finds the prototype by calling `name2inst`. For `get` and `set` operations, if there is no prototype then a `get-response` with error `noSuchName` is returned, and the packet is discarded. For the powerful `get-next` operation, the routine `next2inst` is called to find the next prototype.

   Once a prototype is found, the operation is checked against the community profile. If a mismatch occurs, then a `get-response` with error `noSuchName` or `readOnly` is returned, and the packet is discarded.

   Otherwise, the agent invokes an access routine to perform the desired operation:

- If an error occurs, no further processing is done; instead, a `get-response` with the appropriate error is returned and the packet is discarded.

- If the powerful `get-next` operation is being invoked, it is possible that there are no instances which are lexicographically greater than the variable given (e.g., the end of a table has been reached). In this case, a special value is returned by the access routine. The agent then calls `next2inst` to find the next object type supported by the agent, and the access routine associated with that object is invoked.

  If `next2inst` knows of no later objects, then `noSuchName` is returned in a `get-response`, and the packet is discarded.

8. After exhausting the list of variables in the request, the agent returns a `get-response` and discards the packet.

Throughout the actions above, the appropriate variables in the SNMP MIB (described in Section 5.7 on page 163) are updated.

Earlier it was noted that the *C* structure used to model an object type has a field, `ot_getfnx`, which points to an access routine that can be used to perform an SNMP operation on a variable. It was also noted that, during agent startup, this field is initialized for each variable supported by the agent. The routine is free to use the `ot_info` field in order to handle several MIB objects. For example, the routine `o_ip` handles all the non-tabular objects in the IP group. Linkage between the agent and the access routine might be accomplished like this:

```
#define ipForwarding    0
...
extern  int    o_ip ();


...


OT     ot;

if (ot = text2obj ("ipForwarding")) {
    ot -> ot_getfnx = o_ip;
```

```
        ot -> ot_info = (caddr_t) ipForwarding;
    }
    ...
```

It is now time to see how these access routines are implemented. Since the agent, at present, supports only read-only access, only two operations need be examined. Both operations are invoked in the same way:

```
int     result = (*ot -> ot_getfnx) (oi, v, offset)
OI      oi;
struct type_SNMP_VarBind *v;
int     offset;
```

where:

- the `oi` parameter contains the name of the variable along with a pointer to the prototype object structure;

- the `v` parameter also contains the name of the variable, and a field to store the value:

```
struct type_SNMP_VarBind {
    OID     name;

    PE      value;
};
```

and,

- the `offset` parameter identifies which operation is to be performed, either `get` or the powerful `get-next`.

It turns out that these access routines are written in one of two ways, depending on whether the routine is used to access a tabular variable. Both cases are now considered in turn.

Non-tabular variables

Figure 7.3 starting on page 218 sketches how the `o_ip` routine is implemented. The first action is to determine which leaf object is being referenced. The corresponding symbolic constant is placed in the variable `ifvar`. Then a switch is made based on the operation:

- For the `get` operation, all instances are identified by the object type followed by `.0` (e.g., `ipForwarding.0`).

  The code checks to see if the `OID` associated with the object instance is exactly one longer than the `OID` associated with the object type, and that the extra sub-identifier has the value 0.

- For the powerful `get-next` operation, there are really two cases, depending on whether some instance identifier is present.

  If an instance is present, then for a non-tabular leaf object, the next variable *must* belong to some other object type, so the access routine simply returns the value `NOTOK`, and the calling routine in the agent will find the next object, as described earlier.

  Otherwise, if no instance is identified, a new `OID` is constructed and initialized. The old `OID` is `free`'d and the new one inserted in its place.

Now that the correct instance has been identified, a check is made to see if the **UNIX** kernel should be consulted. (The agent will read a kernel data structure *at most* once for each SNMP message it processes.) Finally, the instance value is encoded and the access routine returns.

The agent contains several routines to encode instance values for the standard syntaxes. For example,

```
int     o_number (oi, v, number)
OI      oi;
struct type_SNMP_VarBind *v;
integer number;
```

is used to stuff a numeric value into a variable. First the prototype and object syntax corresponding to the instance are extracted. Then the `os_encode` routine is called to create a presentation element corresponding to the number. If a value is already present in the variable, it is `free`'d. Regardless, the variable's value is then set to the newly created presentation element. If an error occurs in processing, then the appropriate SNMP error is returned.

```
static  int     lastq = −1;

static  int     ipforwarding;
#define FORW_GATEWAY 1
#define FORW_HOST     2

static  struct ipstat ipstat;


static int  o_ip (oi, v, offset)                                              10
OI      oi;
register struct type_SNMP_VarBind *v;
int     offset;
{
    int     ifvar;
    register struct ipstat *ips = &ipstat;
    register OID    oid = oi −> oi_name;
    register OT     ot = oi −> oi_type;

    ifvar = (int) ot −> ot_info;                                              20
    switch (offset) {
        case type_SNMP_SMUX_PDUs_get_request:
            if (oid −> oid_nelem != ot −> ot_name −> oid_nelem + 1
                    || oid −> oid_elements[oid −> oid_nelem − 1] != 0)
                return int_SNMP_error_status_noSuchName;
            break;

        case type_SNMP_SMUX_PDUs_get_next_request:
            if (oid −> oid_nelem == ot −> ot_name −> oid_nelem) {
                OID     new;                                                  30

                if ((new = oid_extend (oid, 1)) == NULLOID)
                    return int_SNMP_error_status_genErr;
                new −> oid_elements[new −> oid_nelem − 1] = 0;

                if (v −> name)
                    free_SNMP_ObjectName (v −> name);
                v −> name = new;
            }
            else                                                             40
                return NOTOK;
            break;

        default:
            return int_SNMP_error_status_genErr;
    }
```

Figure 7.3: Get and Get-Next of Non-Tabular Objects

```
        if (quantum != lastq) {
            lastq = quantum;

            if (getkmem (nl + N_IPFORWARDING, (caddr_t) &ipforwarding,
                        sizeof ipforwarding) == NOTOK
                    || getkmem (nl + N_IPSTAT, (caddr_t) ips, sizeof *ips)
                            == NOTOK)
                return int_SNMP_error_status_genErr;
        }
                                                                            10
        switch (ifvar) {
            case ipForwarding:
                return o_integer (oi, v, ipforwarding ? FORW_GATEWAY : FORW_HOST);

    ...


            default:
                return int_SNMP_error_status_noSuchName;
        }
    }
                                                                            20
```

Figure 7.3: **Get and Get-Next of Non-Tabular Objects (cont.)**

Tabular variables

Figure .25 starting on page 221 sketches how the `o_ip_route` routine
is implemented. This routine is used to realize the IP routing table.

The first action is to call a routine called **get_routes**. This checks
to see if the routing tables should be copied from the kernel. If so, a
data structure is created containing this information.

The next action is to determine which leaf object is being referenced. The corresponding symbolic constant is placed in the variable
`ifvar`. Then a switch is made based on the operation. Because these
are tabular objects, the instance refers to a row in the table (and the
leaf object refers to a column in the table, of course).

- For the **get** operation, all instances are identified by the object
  type followed by the destination IP address for the route (e.g.,
  `ipRouteNextHop.192.33.4.21`).

  The code checks to see if the `OID` associated with the object
  instance is of the right length (exactly 4 sub-identifiers longer
  than the `OID` associated with the object type).

  If so, the **get_rtent** routine is called to retrieve this entry from the data structure built by a previous call to `get_routes`. Otherwise, a `noSuchName` error is returned.

- For the powerful `get-next` operation, the first action is to "normalize" the instance identifier. Exactly four octets are expected, so if an instance identifier is present, but is less than four octets, a normalized name is constructed.

  Next, there are really two cases, depending on whether some instance identifier is present.

  If no instance is identified, a new `OID` is constructed and initialized for the first row of the table. The prior previous call to `get_routes` put the routing entry corresponding to the lexicographically smallest instance identifier in the variable `rts_inet`. The old `OID` is `free`'d and the new one inserted in its place.

  Otherwise, if some instance identifier is present, the `get_rtent` routine is called to find the routing entry corresponding to the row whose instance identifier is larger than, but closest to, the indicated instance identifier.

  If no such row is found, the next variable belongs to some other object type, so the access routine simply returns the value `NOTOK`, and the calling routine in the agent will find the next object, as described earlier.

Now that the correct routing entry has been identified, the instance value is encoded and the access routine returns.

The problem with this approach is the overhead in reading the routing table from the **UNIX** kernel. In particular, `get_routes` will retrieve the entire routing table *at most* once for each SNMP message. This means that if a request is for many routing variables, accurate answers can be returned from this one *kernel dive*, and the only overhead incurred is when the *first* routing variable in a request is referenced. A reference to any other routing variable can be satisfied by the cache built by `get_routes`.

Unfortunately, the amount of interaction between a user-process and the kernel in order to retrieve the *entire* routing table is substantive, typically three system calls must be made for *each* route.

```
static int  o_ip_route (oi, v, offset)
OI         oi;
register struct type_SNMP_VarBind *v;
int        offset;
{
    int        ifvar;
    register int    i;
    register unsigned int *ip,
                          *jp;
    register struct rtetab *rt;                                    10
    register OID    oid = oi −> oi_name;
    OID        new;
    register OT      ot = oi −> oi_type;

    if (get_routes (offset) == NOTOK)
          return int_SNMP_error_status_genErr;
```

Figure 7.4: Get and Get-Next of Tabular Objects

On systems with a large routing table, the overhead is notable. In a future version of Berkeley UNIX, a new interface to the kernel may be introduced to reduce this problem. In the meantime, the agent current uses a simplistic caching algorithm optimized for traversing the entire routing table using the powerful **get-next** operator.

```
ifvar = (int) ot -> ot_info;
switch (offset) {
    case type_SNMP_PDUs_get_request:
        if (oid -> oid_nelem != ot -> ot_name -> oid_nelem + IFN_SIZE)
            return int_SNMP_error_status_noSuchName;
        if ((rt = get_rtent (oid -> oid_elements + oid -> oid_nelem
                                        - IFN_SIZE, IFN_SIZE, rts_inet, 0))
                == NULL)
            return int_SNMP_error_status_noSuchName;
        break;                                                                     10

    case type_SNMP_PDUs_get_next_request:
        if ((i = oid -> oid_nelem - ot -> ot_name -> oid_nelem) != 0 && i < IFN_SIZE) {
            for (jp = (ip = oid -> oid_elements + ot -> ot_name -> oid_nelem - 1) + i;
                    jp > ip; jp--)
                if (*jp != 0)
                    break;
            if (jp == ip)
                oid -> oid_nelem = ot -> ot_name -> oid_nelem;
            else {                                                                 20
                if ((new = oid_normalize (oid, IFN_SIZE - i, 255)) == NULLOID)
                    return int_SNMP_error_status_genErr;
                if (v -> name)
                    free_SNMP_ObjectName (v -> name);
                v -> name = oid = new;
            }
        }

        if (oid -> oid_nelem == ot -> ot_name -> oid_nelem) {
            if ((rt = rts_inet) == NULL)                                           30
                return NOTOK;
            if ((new = oid_extend (oid, IFN_SIZE)) == NULLOID)
                return int_SNMP_error_status_genErr;
            ip = new -> oid_elements + new -> oid_nelem - IFN_SIZE;
            if (v -> name)
                free_SNMP_ObjectName (v -> name);
            v -> name = new;
        }
        else
            if ((rt = get_rtent (ip = oid -> oid_elements                          40
                                        + oid -> oid_nelem - IFN_SIZE,
                                IFN_SIZE, rts_inet, 1)) == NULL)
                return NOTOK;
        jp = rt -> rt_instance;
        for (i = IFN_SIZE; i > 0; i--)
            *ip++ = *jp++;
        break;

    default:
        return int_SNMP_error_status_genErr;                                       50
}
```

Figure 7.4: Get and Get-Next of Tabular Objects (cont.)

```
switch (ifvar) {
    case ipNextHop:
        return o_ipaddr (oi, v, (struct sockaddr_in *) &rt -> rt_gateway);

    ...

    default:
        return int_SNMP_error_status_noSuchName;
    }
}
```
                                                                        10

Figure 7.4: Get and Get-Next of Tabular Objects (cont.)

7.2.3   Implementing Sets in an Agent

Even though the agent implementation supports only read-only views at present, there are some implementation issues to note with respect to implementing the `set` operation:

- Since either all or none of the individual objects must be set, in an implementation where individual functions are used for the different objects, the `set` function must be done in two passes: on the first pass, all error checking is done including resource-reservation as necessary such that the second pass can be either a *commit* phase which is "guaranteed not to fail," or a *release* phase in which the reserved resources can be released.

  One possibility is for the first pass to actually do the set, but also to save the previous values, and the second pass can then restore those values if necessary. Of course, for deleting table entries, as described in Section 5.4.2 on page 144, this may not be the best approach.

- To further complicate matters, some MIB objects, when being set, may require that they can only be set in combination with other MIB objects in the same request (e.g., for adding table entries, as described in Section 5.4.1 on page 144). In this case, there is a requirement for interaction between the functions implementing sets for different MIB objects.

7.2.4   Encoding and Decoding SNMP Messages

The last topic to be discussed is how SNMP messages are encoded into strings of octets for transmission and decoded into C structures upon reception. These routines were automatically generated!

ISODE contains a series of compilers which read ASN.1 modules and produce equivalent C structures. In addition, these compilers generate C routines to translate between presentation elements and the C structures. Finally, the run-time library in ISODE contains routines to encode and decode presentation elements for network transmission and reception.

Thus, the applications programmer deals exclusively in *C* structures. All of the infrastructure required to send and receive these structures on the network is automatically processed. (Section 8.4 of *The Open Book* discusses these concepts more fully.)

For now, it is important to realize that sending is a two-step process:

- a routine is called to convert the *C* structure to a presentation element; then,

- a routine is called to serialize the presentation element onto a transport service, such as TCP or UDP.

The receiving process is inverted.

The advantage of this approach is that it is flexible, predictable, and doesn't require any thought from the applications programmer. The disadvantage is that it makes a second copy of the data (the presentation element) during the transmission or reception process.

There are of course, many other approaches. The usage of ASN.1 in the management framework is specifically focused on allowing efficient hand-coded routines to be written. These can achieve significant performance approaches over the ISODE approach, at the risk of substantively reduced functionality.

7.3   Exporting MIB modules

On kernel/user systems such as Berkeley UNIX, an agent is often implemented as a user-process which reads kernel variables in order to realize the MIB. Indeed, the previous section discussed the expense involved with such an approach.

This approach is workable as long as all of the information needed by the agent resides in either the kernel or in stable storage (i.e., UNIX files). However, when other user-processes are employed to implement other network services, such as the mail queue, communication between the agent and other processes is problematic.

To provide a solution, the 4BSD/ISODE SNMP package introduces a *local* mechanism, based on a new protocol, the *SNMP Multiplexing* (SMUX) protocol. When a user-process, termed a *SMUX peer*, wishes to export a MIB module, it initiates a SMUX association to the local agent, registers itself, and (later) fields management operations for objects in the MIB module.

Carrying this approach to its fullest, it is possible to generalize the agent so that it knows about only the SNMP group of the Internet-standard MIB. All other portions of the agent's view can be implemented by another process. This is quite useful, for example, when a computer manufacturer wishes to provide SNMP access for its operating system in binary form.

Of course, it would also be useful to define a MIB for the SMUX. This is given in an example in Section B.2.3 on page 277 in Appendix B.

7.3.1   Architecture

There are two approaches that can be taken when trying to integrate arbitrary MIB modules with the agent:

- The *request-response* model simply propagates the SNMP requests received by the agent to the user process which exported the MIB module. The SMUX peer then performs the operation and returns a response. In turn, the agent propagates this response back to the manager.

The request-response model is said to be *agent-driven* since, after registration, the SNMP agent initiates all transactions.

- The *cache-ahead* model requires that the SMUX peer, after registration, periodically updates the agent with the subtree for the MIB module which has been registered. The agent, upon receiving an SNMP request, locally performs the operation, and returns a response to the manager. (Of course, the effect of the set operation must never be cached.)

  The cache-ahead model is said to be *peer-driven* since, after registration, the SMUX peer initiates all transactions.

There are advantages and disadvantages to both approaches. The architecture envisioned supports both models in the following fashion: the protocol between the SNMP agent and the SMUX peer is based on the request-response model. However, the SMUX peer, may itself be a user-process which employs the cache-ahead model with other user-processes, and each SMUX peer is free to define a cache-ahead protocol specific for the application at hand.

Obviously, the SMUX peer which employs the cache-ahead model acts as a "management firewall" for those user-processes which actually implement the managed objects in the given MIB module.

7.3.2 SMUX Protocol

The ASN.1 definition of the SMUX protocol is found in Figure 7.5 starting on page 228.

The SMUX protocol is simple: the SNMP agent listens for incoming connections. Upon establishing a connection, the SMUX peer issues an `OpenPDU` to initialize the SMUX association. If the agent declines the association, it issues a `closePDU` and closes the connection. If the agent accepts the association, no response is issued.

For each subtree defined in a MIB module that the SMUX peer wishes to register (or unregister), the SMUX peer issues a `RReqPDU`. In turn, the agent issues a corresponding `RRspPDU`. The agent returns `RRspPDUs` in the same order as the `RReqPDUs` were received.

SMUX **DEFINITIONS** ::= **BEGIN**

IMPORTS
    ObjectName
            FROM RFC1155–SMI

    PDUs
            FROM RFC1157–SNMP;

                                                                                    10
–– tags for SMUX–specific PDUs are application–wide to
–– avoid conflict with tags for current (and future)
–– SNMP–generic PDUs

SMUX–PDUs ::=
    CHOICE {
            open   *–– SMUX peer uses*
                OpenPDU,   *–– immediately after TCP open*

            close   *–– either uses immediately before TCP close*   20
                ClosePDU,

            registerRequest *–– SMUX peer uses*
                RReqPDU,

            registerResponse *–– SNMP agent uses*
                RRspPDU,

            PDUs   *–– note that roles are reversed:*
                            ––   SNMP agent does get/get–next/set   30
                            ––   SMUX peer does get–response/trap
    }

Figure 7.5: SNMP Multiplexing Protocol

```
-- open PDU
-- currently only simple authentication

OpenPDU ::=
  CHOICE {
        simple
            SimpleOpen
  }

SimpleOpen ::=                                                    10
  [APPLICATION 0] IMPLICIT
        SEQUENCE {
          version     -- of SMUX protocol
                INTEGER {
                    version-1(0)
                },

          identity    -- of SMUX initiator, authoritative
            OBJECT IDENTIFIER,
                                                                 20
          description -- of SMUX initiator, implementation-specific
                DisplayString,

          password    -- zero length indicates no authentication
                OCTET STRING
        }

-- close PDU

ClosePDU ::=                                                      30
  [APPLICATION 1] IMPLICIT
        INTEGER {
            goingDown(0),
            unsupportedVersion(1),
            packetFormat(2),
            protocolError(3),
            internalError(4),
            authenticationFailure(5)
        }
```

Figure 7.5: SNMP Multiplexing Protocol (cont.)

-- insert PDU

RReqPDU ::=
   [**APPLICATION** 2] **IMPLICIT**
      SEQUENCE {
        subtree
           ObjectName,

        priority   *-- the lower the better, "-1" means default*
           INTEGER ($-1..2147483647$),   10

        operation
           INTEGER {
             delete(0),
             readOnly(1),
             readWrite(2)
           }
      }

RRspPDU ::=   20
   [**APPLICATION** 3] **IMPLICIT**
      INTEGER {
        failure(-1)
               -- on success the non-negative priority is returned
      }

END

Figure 7.5: SNMP Multiplexing Protocol (cont.)

When the SMUX peer wishes to issue a trap, it issues an SNMP `Trap-PDU`. When the agent receives such a PDU, it propagates this to the management stations that it is configured to send traps to.

When the agent receives an SNMP `get`, the powerful `get-next`, or `set` request from a manager, and that request includes one or more variables within a subtree registered by a SMUX peer, the agent sends an equivalent SNMP PDU containing only those variables within the subtree registered by that SMUX peer. When the SMUX peer receives such a PDU, it applies the indicated operation and issues a corresponding `get-response`. The agent then correlates this result and propagates the resulting `get-response` to the network management station.

When either the agent or the SMUX peer wishes to release the SMUX association, the `ClosePDU` is issued and the connection is closed.

Tricky Things

Although the protocol, as evidenced above, is straight-forward, there are a few nuances.

Tricky Things – Registration

Associated with each registration is an integer priority, which takes a value in the range from 0 to $2^{31} - 1$. The lower the value, the higher the priority.

Multiple SMUX peers may register the same subtree. However, they must do so at different priorities (i.e., a subtree and a priority uniquely identifies a SMUX peer). So, if a SMUX peer wishes to register a subtree at a priority which is already taken, the agent repeatedly increments the integer value until an unused priority is found.

When registering a subtree, the special value -1 may be used, which selects the highest available priority. Of course, the agent may select an arbitrarily worse priority for a SMUX peer, based on local (configuration) information.

Note that when a subtree is registered, the SMUX peer with the highest registration priority is exclusively consulted for all operations on that subtree. Further note that agents must enforce the *subtree mounting effect*, which hides the registrations by other SMUX peers of objects within the subtree. For example, if a SMUX peer registered `sysDescr`, and later another SMUX peer registered `system` (which scopes `sysDescr`), then all requests for `sysDescr` would be given to the latter SMUX peer.

An agent should disallow any attempt to register at or within the SNMP and SMUX subtrees of the MIB. Other subtrees may be disallowed as an implementation-specific option.

Tricky Things – Removing Registration

A SMUX peer may remove registrations for only those subtrees which it has registered. If the priority given in the `RReqPDU` is −1, then the registration of highest priority is selected for deletion. Otherwise, only that registration with the precise registration is selected.

Tricky Things – Variables in Requests

When constructing an SNMP PDU for a SMUX peer, the agent may send one, or more than one variable in a single request. In all cases, the agent should process each variable sequentially, and block accordingly when a SMUX peer is contacted.

Tricky Things – Request-ID

When the agent constructs an SNMP PDU for a SMUX peer, the `request-id` field of the PDU takes a special meaning. Basically, this field should take a different value for each SNMP PDU received by the agent. If an agent generates multiple PDUs for a SMUX peer, upon receipt of a single PDU from the network management station, then the `request-id` field of the PDUs sent to the SMUX peer takes the same value (which need bear no relationship to the value of the `request-id` field of the PDU originally received by the agent.)

Tricky Things – The Powerful Get-Next

Each SMUX peer acts as though it contains the entire MIB when processing the powerful `get-next` operator. This means that the agent must check each variable named in the response generated by the SMUX peer and see if it is in the subtree of the managed object corresponding to the original SNMP request. If not, the agent will apply the powerful `get-next` operator to the next managed object in the community profile. This may result in contacting a different SMUX peer, depending on the registration topology.

Tricky Things – Sets

Given the discussion in Section 7.2.3 on page 224, it should be noted that implementing the `set` operation appears to be difficult using the SMUX. In theory this is true: the SMUX does not directly allow a two-pass implementation of the `set` operation. In practice however, it is likely that all of the objects in the `set` request will be handled by the same process (either the SNMP agent or a single SMUX peer), so this may not be an actual deficiency.

Mappings on Transport Service

The SMUX protocol may be mapped onto any CO-mode transport service. At present, only one such mapping is defined:

When using TCP to provide the transport-backing for the SMUX protocol, the agent listens on TCP port 199. Each SMUX PDU is serialized using the Basic Encoding Rules and sent over TCP. As ASN.1 objects are self-delimiting when encoded using the BER, no packetization protocol is required.

7.3.3   Implementation

The SMUX protocol is fully implemented in the 4BSD/ISODE SNMP package, and is supported by the agent. In addition, a SMUX library is available to aid programmers in instrumenting their programs with the SMUX protocol.

7.4   Manager Implementation

The 4BSD/ISODE SNMP package does not contain a full NOC implementation. Rather, it consists of tools for the rapid-prototyping of network management applications.

At the simplest level, an SNMP initiator program *snmpi*, is available which makes each SNMP operation (except **trap**) available to the user. For example,

```
% snmpi -a 192.33.4.21 -c secret
snmpi> get sysUptime.0
sysUpTime.0=45366736 (5 days, 6 hours, 1 minutes, 7.36 seconds)
snmpi>
```

tells *snmpi* to direct management traffic to the agent at the specified IP address using the given community name.

In addition, there is a **dump** command which is used to examine a subtree in the community profile. For example, to see the SNMP group:

```
snmpi> dump snmp
snmpInPkts.0=732
snmpOutPkts.0=732
snmpInBadVersions.0=0
snmpInBadCommunityNames.0=0
snmpInBadCommunityUses.0=0
snmpInASNParseErrs.0=0
snmpInBadTypes.0=0
snmpInTotalReqVars.0=736
snmpInTotalSetVars.0=0
snmpInGetRequests.0=1
snmpInGetNexts.0=741
snmpInSetRequests.0=0
snmpOutTooBigs.0=0
snmpOutNoSuchNames.0=2
snmpOutBadValues.0=0
snmpOutReadOnlys.0=0
snmpOutGenErrs.0=0
snmpOutGetResponses.0=748
snmpOutTraps.0=0
snmpEnableAuthTraps.0=enabled(1)
snmpi>
```

does the trick. Note that for those integer-valued objects which have enumerated labels, *snmpi* prints both the label and the value (because it is hard-wired to do so).

Although the `dump` command is useful for walking a portion (or the entire) community profile, *snmpi* is of only minimal use.

Rather than supplying NOC applications, a language for building new applications is defined. This is done by modifying one of the common UNIX commands used for rapid-prototyping, the *awk* program. In particular, the GNU version of *awk*, *gawk*, was selected. The result is called "SNMP-capable gawk."

The *gawk* program is a pattern scanning and processing language used to interpret "scripts" that contain

```
pattern     { action }
```

pairs. For each line of input, *gawk* checks to see if it matches the pattern, if so, the action, which is written in a language very much like C, is executed. In addition, there are two special patterns,

```
BEGIN     { actions }
```

and

```
END     { actions }
```

which are executed at the beginning and end, respectively, of the input.

This structure allows a programmer to test out ideas with very fast turn-around. Once an idea is proven, it can then be recoded entirely in C to achieve a performance boost. Of course, many programmers never bother with the second step: many *awk* scripts perform quite adequately in a production environment.

7.4.1   SNMP-capable gawk

Basically, SNMP-capable *gawk* reads a compiled MIB file, and recognizes the leaf objects (both tabular and non-tabular) as special variables.

The current implementation assumes all MIB variables are read-only. This means that MIB objects must occur only as *rvalues* in expressions.

Non-tabular variables

To retrieve an object which does not occur inside a table, the name of the object is used, and the instance identifier is automatically calculated, e.g.,

```
% gawk 'BEGIN { print sysDescr; }'
```

results in the SNMP operation

```
get (sysDescr.0)
```

being invoked and the value returned by the agent being printed.

Since an SNMP operation might fail, there are two special variables that may be examined:

- **DIAGNOSTIC**, which returns a textual description of any problem which occurred with the last SNMP operation; and,

- **ERROR**, which contains the **error-status** returned by the last SNMP operation.

Hence:

```
% gawk 'BEGIN { print "sysDescr: ", sysDescr, DIAGNOSTIC; }'
```

prints either the system description of the agent, or a diagnostic, depending on what happened with the SNMP interaction.

Tabular variables

A value of an object occurring in a table can be retrieved in one of two ways.

First, the instance identifier can be written as an array reference, e.g.,

```
ifDescr[1]
```

which is equivalent to an **get** operation on the variable

```
ifDescr.1
```

or

```
ipRouteNextHop["10.0.0.0"]
```

which is equivalent to a **get** operation on the variable

```
ipRouteNextHop.10.0.0.0
```

This is called the "subscript notation."

Second, the table can be traversed. This is done with the *gawk* **for-in** construct, e.g.,

```
for (i in ipRouteDest) {
    printf "route to %s via %s\n",
        ipRouteDest, ipRouteNextHop;
}
```

which says to traverse the table containing the object `ipRouteDest`. The for-loop body will be executed once for each row of the table; for each iteration, the control variable will be assigned the value of the instance-identifier for that row (**not** the value of the column in that row). This allows other parts of the MIB to be referenced using the same instance-identifier, e.g.,

```
for (i in ipRouteDest) {
    printf "ipRoutingTable[%s]: to %s via %s\n",
        i, ipRouteDest, ipRouteNextHop;
}
```

The **for-in** construct retrieves a row of a table using a single powerful **get-next** operation. If a particular column is unsupported by the agent, then referencing the corresponding variable will return the empty string. Note that within the for-loop body, repeated references to a column of a table will not result in additional SNMP operations. If, for some reason, it is desirable to refresh a variable's value, the subscript notation is used, e.g.,

```
for (i in ipRouteDest) {
    printf "route to %s via %s\n",
        ipRouteDest, ipRouteNextHop[i];
}
```

which causes each iteration to use the powerful **get-next** operation to bind values to each column in the `ipRoutingTable`, and the corresponding instance-identifier is assigned to i. Then, when the **printf** statement is executed, a separate **get** operation will be used to supply a (possibly) new value for `ipRouteNextHop`. Usually, the subscript notation is used when it is necessary to look at a variable in another table, e.g.,

```
for (i in ipRouteDest) {
    printf "route to %s via %s on %s (interface #%d)\n",
        ipRouteDest, ipRouteNextHop,;
        ifDescr[ipRouteIfIndex], ipRouteIfIndex;
}
```

which causes each iteration to use the powerful **get-next** operation to bind values to each column in the `ipRoutingTable`, and the corresponding instance-identifier is assigned to i. Then, when the **printf** statement is executed, a separate **get** operation will be used to supply the corresponding value of `ifDescr`.

Of course, there's always the question of dealing with agents which may not support the table or when an error occurs. Usually, the following code fragment is sufficient:

```
didone = 0;
for (i in tabularVariable) {
    didone = 1;
#   handle each row of the table here...
}
if (didone == 0) {
    if (DIAGNOSTIC) {
#       handle table error here...
    }
    else {
#       handle empty table here...
    }
}
else
    if (DIAGNOSTIC) {
#       handle partial table here...
    }
```

Finding an empty or partial table is often unimportant, so the boiler-plate usually is:

```
didone = 0;
for (i in tabularVariable) {
    didone = 1;

#    handle each row of the table here...
}
if (!didone && DIAGNOSTIC)
    printf "table: %s\n", DIAGNOSTIC;
```

If the subscript notation is not used, it is illegal to reference a tabular variable outside of a `for-in` loop.

Non-tabular variables (revisited)

If a script is accessing a lot of non-tabular variables sharing a common parent (e.g., within the **system** group), the `for-in` construct can be used to traverse this degenerate tree, e.g.,

```
for (i in sysDescr) {
#    this for-loop is executed at most once...
}
```

will cause all the non-tabular variables having the same immediate parent as `sysDescr` to be retrieved in a single powerful `get-next` operation, and the corresponding instance-identifier (i.e., 0) is assigned to `i`.

This syntax is used only for optimization of network traffic.

Data typing

The *gawk* program has two kinds of data types: numbers and strings. When mapping MIB objects to these data types, the following conventions are used:

Syntax	Type	Format
INTEGER	number	
OCTET STRING	string	`"%02x: ... : %02x"`
DisplayString	string	
OBJECT IDENTIFIER	string	`"%u. ... .%u"`
NULL	string	`"NULL"`
IpAddress	string	`"a.b.c.d"`
NetworkAddress	string	`"a.b.c.d"`
Counter	number	
Gauge	number	
TimeTicks	number	

New Variables

There are a few built-in, read-write variables available in SNMP-capable *gawk*:

Variable	Type	Value of	Default
AGENT	string	SNMP agent name or address	localhost
COMMUNITY	string	SNMP community name	public
DIAGNOSTIC	string	last thing to go wrong	
ERROR	number	last SNMP error status	
RETRIES	number	times to retry SNMP operation	3
TIMEOUT	number	seconds between retries	10

The `DIAGNOSTIC` and `ERROR` variables are set after each SNMP operation. If no error occurs, the `DIAGNOSTIC` variable is set to the empty string, and the `ERROR` varaible is set to zero.

New Functions

There are a few built-in functions added available in SNMP-capable *gawk*:

- The `bitwise_and(i,j)` function returns the bit-wise AND of the two unsigned long quantities, i and j.

- The `bitwise_or(i,j)` function returns the bit-wise OR of the two unsigned long quantities, i and j.

7.4.2 Two Examples

In order to put everything in perspective, consider Figure 7.6. This prints out information about each interface on a managed node, e.g.,

```
% gawk -f mib.interfaces
Name Mtu   Net/Dest    Address     Ipkts   Ierrs Opkts   Oerrs
le0  1500  192.33.4.0  192.33.4.21 1460533 122   1309675 0
lo0  1536  127.0.0.0   127.0.0.1   48599   0     48599   0
%
```

The interesting part in this script is how the IP address for each interface is determined. A nested `for-in` construct is used to traverse the IP address table. Once the desired address is found, the `break` statement is used to terminate the loop early.

Of course, a script can be much more interesting. Earlier, in Section 6.1.1 on page 190, it was noted how SNMP could be used to trace the route taken by IP datagrams in an internet. Figure 7.7 shows how this is realized. Note that this script does not take into account the `ipRouteNetMask` object.

7.4.3 Query Language

It should be noted that SNMP-capable *gawk* is only one of many possible programming paradigms for the management framework. For example, an SNMP *query language* has been defined and implemented, as described in [55]. In this work, a model for network management is developed based on relational database theory, which uses elementary query simplification in order to reduce the number of SNMP operations required to resolve queries.

7.4.4 Implementing Sets in a Manager

Even though the manager implementation supports only read-only activities at present, there are some implementation issues to note with respect to invoking the `set` operation:

- As noted in Section 7.2.3 on page 224, care should be taken when grouping objects in a single `set` request. For example, if one of the objects to be set has the effect of resetting the agent,

```
BEGIN {
    printf "%-4s %-4s %-14s %-15s %-7s %-5s %-7s %-5s\n",
            "Name", "Mtu", "Net/Dest", "Address", "Ipkts", "Ierrs",
            "Opkts", "Oerrs";

    didone = 0;
    for (i in ifIndex) {
        didone = 1;

        dest = "";
        addr = "";
        for (j in ipAdEntAddr) {
            if (ipAdEntIfIndex == ifIndex) {
                split(addr = ipAdEntAddr, a, ".");
                split(ipAdEntNetMask, b, ".");
                dest = bit_and(a[1],b[1]) "." \
                        bit_and(a[2],b[2]) "." \
                        bit_and(a[3],b[3]) "." \
                        bit_and(a[4],b[4]);
                break;
            }
        }

        printf (length(ifDescr) <= 4 ? "%-4s " : "%s\n        "),
            ifDescr;
        printf "%-4d %-14s %-15s %-7d %-5d %-7d %-5d %-4d %-5d\n",
                ifMtu, dest, addr, ifInUcastPkts+ifInNUcastPkts,
                ifInErrors, ifOutUcastPkts+ifOutNUcastPkts,
                ifOutErrors;
    }
    if (!didone && DIAGNOSTIC)
        printf "ifTable: %s\n", DIAGNOSTIC;
}
```

Figure 7.6: Example Script for SNMP-capable gawk

```
BEGIN   {
    printf "from %s to %s:\n", AGENT, DEST;
    tried[AGENT] = 1;
    INVALID = 2; DIRECT = 3;

    while (DEST != AGENT) {
        dr = 0;
        if ((hop = ipRouteNextHop[addr = DEST]) \
                && (type = ipRouteType[addr]) == INVALID)
            hop = 0;
        if (!hop \
                && (hop = ipRouteNextHop[addr = "0.0.0.0"]) \
                && (type = ipRouteType[addr]) != INVALID)
            dr = 1;
        if (hop) {
            printf "    via %-15s metric %2d%s\n",
                    hop, ipRouteMetric1[addr],
                    dr ? " (default route)" : "";
        }
        else {
            printf "\nno path to %s from %s\n%s\n",
                    DEST, AGENT, DIAGNOSTIC;
            exit(1);
        }

        if (type == DIRECT)
            exit(0);

        if (hop in tried)
            printf "\nrouting loop!\n";
        else
            tried[hop] = 1;
        AGENT = hop;
    }
}
```

Figure 7.7: Using SNMP-capable gawk to trace routes

then including other objects in that `set-request` is probably ineffective.

- For some objects, a `set-request` should not be re-transmitted, just because a `get-response` was not received, without issuing an intervening `get-request` to test whether the original `set` operation took effect.

- Recall that the underlying transport service need not guarantee non-duplication nor in-order delivery. Consequently, when the operation of one `set-request` depends upon the success of a previous `set-request`, the second request must be delayed until it is certain that the packets carrying the first request no longer exist in the network. In the case of a UDP-based mapping, the manager must wait until the **time-to-live** field of the IP datagrams used to carry the first request have expired.

- As noted in Section 5.4.1 on page 144, when adding a table entry all columns in the table must be set in the same request. However, some agents support only a subset of the columns, whilst other agents support all columns. In this case, all agent implementations should be somewhat flexible.

Chapter 8

The Future

It's often been noted that

soap...

> *The future is easy to predict, the hard part is being right.*

Nonetheless, it seems appropriate to try and forecast up to the mid-90s.

Authentication

The single most pressing need in the Internet-standard Network Management Framework is secure authentication techniques. A working group of the IETF has been chartered to specify this technology, and there is some hope that it may be implemented in prototypes by the end of 1990. If so, then within five years it is possible that large portions of the Internet will employ authenticated SNMP entities as a normal part of their operations.

   If secure authentication becomes commonplace, the control aspects of network management in the Internet can become much stronger. This will allow the creation of many powerful new applications that can automatically take a proactive role in the network.

MIB

With the lessons learned from MIB-II, it seems clear that heavy use of the experimental-space for MIBs will occur.[1] As these are proven and consensus is reached, future versions of the Internet-standard MIB will incorporate these versions.

Even so, the Internet-standard MIB will probably change slowly. Vendors will balk if this core definition changes too quickly. (Perhaps a "mature" industry can be gauged by the increase in the length of its product cycle?)

However, there is a movement to require *all* of the protocols in the Internet suite to have a corresponding MIB module. If this reaches fruition, then all aspects of the protocol suite will have well-defined hooks for monitoring and control.

This is exciting: if a MIB for electronic mail were defined, then one could write a program that would report whenever someone was exploiting a security hole in the Berkeley UNIX *sendmail* program. However, considering the insecurity of *sendmail* and UNIX in general, such a system would generate so many traps that even a network with a T-3 backbone would be congested in short-order!

SNMP

Full deployment of SNMP in TCP/IP-based internets seems imminent given the high-level of success it is enjoying.

SNMP has traditionally avoided issues involved in the archival and retrieval of historical information, preferring to emphasize operational issues (keeping the network running). Hopefully some attention will be focused in this area.

There are now definitions both for mapping SNMP onto the OSI transport services, along with a MIB module for the OSI CL-mode network layer. The MIB module is quite similar to the IP group in the Internet-standard MIB, in the hope of leveraging the existing tools that are capable of managing IP-based networks.

---

[1] There is even talk of using the SNMP for controlling kitchen toasters, compact-disc players, and other home appliances!

Implementations of "SNMP over OSI" and the "CLNS MIB" now exist. Thus, whilst SNMP might not be an OSI standard, it might become the *de facto* protocol of choice for managing OSI networks. This statement might be somewhat controversial.

Administrative Domains

There is a need to provide a framework for management across administrative boundaries. According to many network operators, this is perhaps the key barrier to effective end-to-end management. Hopefully more mature implementations combined with a secure authentication framework will alleviate this problem.

8.1   In Conclusion

Regardless of the "spin" one places on the future, it is clear that internets *require* network management. It is also clear that the Internet-
standard Network Management Framework and its fundamental axiom have produced a useful, and more importantly, a workable, system
for internet management.

8.1.1   The Cost of Working Systems

A quotation I use from time to time comes from the eminent Professor
Case:

> *I want my dog hunting raccoon, not skinning them!*

What this means is that routers should route, terminal servers should
provide terminal service, and printers should print. They should not
spend all (or even much) of their time doing activities related to network management. The management framework used in the Internet
suite of protocols reflects these requirements quite faithfully.

Such focus does not come without a price. For example, the role of
chair of the SNMP Working Group is little more than political arbiter.
Technical work is performed by a few key members of the group, and
the chair tries to provide an environment to allow this. As current
chair, there are a couple of simple-minded tricks I use. For example,
meetings are scheduled in locations off the beaten track, simply to
reduce attendence by hangers-on and standards go'ers — who attend
to make seminal contributions and enjoy many fine lunches and din-
ners. One meeting was scheduled in Tennessee at 9:00am Monday
morning, with only ten business days notice given (but we still had
over 30 attendees).

Why discourage mass attendance? The reason is both to achieve
focus and to try to get a small variance in the skill sets of the attendees. There seems to be a propensity among new members not
to read past minutes or previous contributions, or to gain a rudimen-
tary understanding of the technology by attending industry tutorials,
workshops, reading RFCs, articles, and so on. Little is accomplished

at meetings when a new member would rather be spoon-fed the technology "for free," at the expense of all other participants who have taken the steps to become familiar with it. At one meeting, it was suggested that "flashcards" be produced containing the answers to many commonly raised issues. Meetings could then be expedited by raising these cards at the appropriate time.

Of course, it's not just new players that cause problems. For example, during the work on MIB-I, there was a lengthy discussion on what should go into the address translation group. During this discussion, one of the "OSI management gurus" contributed frequently. Finally, after thirty minutes of argument, the same so-called guru asked:

> *What's in those ARP tables anyway?*

So here we have someone who's been arguing with everyone else for half an hour as to what goes into this table, and he doesn't even know what is supposed to be modeled! Considering that this was supposedly an experienced professional, the reader should appreciate how difficult judging the levels of competence of the attendees can be.

The Internet *network management wars* were particularly unpleasant, largely due to the politics and shenanigans involved, coupled with the indecisiveness of the (then) standardization process. As noted in the first issue of the eleemosynary publication, *The INTERNET Crucible*:

> *"... after spending a year trying to achieve consensus on the successor to the current Internet-standard SMI/MIB, the MIB working group was disbanded without ever producing anything: the political climate prevented them from resolving the matter. (Many congratulatory notes were sent to the chair of the group thanking him for his time. This is an interesting new trend for the Internet — congratulating ourselves on our failures.)"*

Of course, it was not the chair that failed, but the process: the situation was simply politically intractible.[2]

---

[2]The CRUCIBLE is an anonymously-authored Internet tabloid, with the distinction of having been called both "the one true light of the Internet" and "jealous garbage," albeit by different sources.

To resolve contentious issues, the experimental subtree is now heavily used (as described in Section 4.2.1 on page 112). This allows the working group to settle arguments by forcing the matter of implementation. Since one can learn as much (if not more) from a failed experiment than from a success, this approach has much promise.

Finally, each meeting requires that the chair toss out "doggie biscuits" to most of the participants, so that at the end of the meeting he can ask each person around the table if they are happy with the outcome. Thus, the job of the chair is to make the process appear to be "open and friendly," whilst making sure that none of the "doggie biscuits" tossed about have any bad effects on the working aspects of the technology.[3]

While this view might seem somewhat jaundiced, it is entirely *honest*; but, more importantly it is *necessary*: as evidenced by the last decade, technology by committee must be firmly guided if workable technology is to be produced. The mechanisms developed and now used for management of TCP/IP-based internets are entirely workable and useful. I believe that it was the combination of savvy technology and political doggedness from several parties, that made this happen.

8.1.2   The Folly of Management by Committee

In contrast, other management frameworks, most notably the OSI framework, seem bent on management through:

administrative fiat: They belive that because it's a standard, it will be implemented.

unnecessary generality: Even though experience has shown that the critical nature of network management is unlike any other class of application, OSI treats network management as just another application in the general framework.

isolated environments: Proponents of OSI network management argue that demonstration at trade shows is enough of a proof of concept to validate their approach.

---

[3]Once a "standards person" attended a meeting of the SNMP Working Group. He commented on how well things went, and how everyone got to participate!

> **theoretical concerns:** The committees keep refining the management model instead of worrying about how to effectively manage networks.

A favorite quote of the author is a statement which appeared in the minutes of a group that was trying to produce a CMOT demo for the INTEROP® trade-show in October of 1988:

> *Excellent progress is being made: we are proceeding through the documents one by one.*

This underscores, quite eloquently, the difference between the groups. While the CMOT people were busy analyzing documents and producing implementation agreements, the SNMP people were just implementing. Is it any wonder that proponents of OSI in the Internet are viewed with such contempt?

This is particularly worrisome to the author, who has long been a proponent of OSI, and has fielded many *successful* OSI services. The honest OSI'er (to use a title bestowed by Paul Mockapetris), isn't happy being categorized with the crowd that tried (and failed) to introduce OSI network management into the Internet. The author believes in using the appropriate philosophy when trying to solve a problem. As such, it makes sense to use OSI for things like message handling and directory services: these are services which can benefit from the generality offered by OSI. In contrast, the OSI view of network management seems tragically detached from the realities of managing networks.

Whilst this may seem unfair, it is, however sadly accurate. By striving for generality and theoretical completeness in all things, proponents of OSI network management are producing a system which will likely be unable to respond to critical failures in OSI-based internets. Fortunately, SNMP can now be used to manage OSI networks, so, when OSI-based internets do arise, a management solution will be at hand.

So, with this solid basis of the Internet-standard Network Management Framework, the 90s should be a productive and exciting time for the management of internets of all kinds!

⎡ . . .soap ⎤

Appendix A

Relevant Internet Documents

The *Request for Comments* document series provides for the dissemination of information about the Internet suite of protocols. Not all RFCs arc standards, quite the reverse: relatively few RFCs have any standardization status at all. Rather, the majority of RFCs are research notes intended for discussion.

RFCs are available in both printed and electronic form. The printed copies are available, for a modest fee, from the DDN Network Information Center:

> Postal: DDN Network Information Center
> SRI International
> 333 Ravenswood Avenue
> Menlo Park, CA 94025
> US

> Phone: +1 800–235–3155
> +1 415–859–3695

> Mail: NIC@NIC.DDN.MIL

In electronic form, users may use "anonymous" FTP to the host
NIC.DDN.MIL (residing at [192.67.67.20]) and retrieve files from the
directory "RFC:", e.g.,

```
% ftp nic.ddn.mil
Connected to nic.ddn.mil
220 NIC.DDN.MIL FTP Service Process
Name (nic.ddn.mil:mrose): anonymous
331 ANONYMOUS user ok, send real ident as password.
Password (nic.ddn.mil:anonymous): guest
230 User ANONYMOUS logged in at Sat 7-Apr-90 11:18-PDT, job 23.
ftp> cd rfc:
331 Default name accepted. Send password to connect to it.
ftp> ascii
220 Type A ok.
ftp>
```

Certainly the first RFC to retrieve is the Index of RFCs:

```
ftp> get rfc-index.txt
200 Port 16.23 at host 192.33.44.21 accepted.
150 ASCII retrieve of TS:<RFC>RFC-INDEX.TXT started.
226 Transfer completed. 140290 (8) bytes transferred.
140290 bytes received in 23.58 seconds (5.8 Kbytes/s)
ftp> quit
%
```

If your site does not have IP-connectivity to the Internet, but does
have electronic mail access, then you can send a message to the mailbox

```
Service@NIC.DDN.MIL
```

and in the subject field indicate the RFC number, e.g.,

```
Subject: RFC 1130
```

A reply to your message will contain the desired RFC.

If your site has electronic mail access to the Internet, and you
desire notification when new RFCs are published, send a note to the
mailbox

```
RFC-request@NIC.DDN.MIL
```

and ask to be added to the RFC notification list.

Internet Drafts

Internet Drafts are available only in electronic form. Use "anonymous" FTP to the host nnsc.nsf.net (residing at [192.31.103.6]) and retrieve files from the directory internet-drafts/, e.g.,

```
% ftp nnsc.nsf.net
Connected to nnsc.nsf.net
220 nnsc.nsf.net FTP server
Name (nnsc.nsf.net:mrose): anonymous
331 guest login ok, send ident as password.
Password (nnsc.nsf.net:anonymous): guest
230 Guest login ok, access restrictions apply.
ftp> cd internet-drafts
250 CWD command successful.
ftp> ascii
220 Type set to A.
ftp>
```

If your site has electronic mail access to the Internet, and you desire notification when new Internet Drafts are published, send a note to the mailbox

```
ietf-request@venera.isi.edu
```

and ask to be added to the ietf list.

A.1   Administrative RFCs

The key administrative RFCs are:

RFC	Name	Status
1140	IAB Official Protocol Standards	Required
1060	Assigned Numbers	Required
1011	Official Protocols	Required
1009	Gateway Requirements	Required
1122	Host Requirements — Communications	Required
1123	Host Requirements — Applications	Required

Note that these RFCs are periodically updated. As with the rest of the RFC series, the most recent document always takes precedence. In particular, note that the Official Protocols RFC is updated quarterly.

The information which follows is taken from the IAB Official Standards RFC [23], published in May, 1990. By the time of this reading, a new version of this RFC will no doubt have been published.

A.2 Core Protocol RFCs

The RFCs pertaining to the core of the Internet suite of protocols are:

RFC	Name	Status
791	Internet Protocol	Required
950	Subnet Extension	Required
919	Broadcast Datagrams	Required
922	Broadcast Datagrams with Subnets	Required
792	Internet Control Message Protocol	Required
768	User Datagram Protocol	Recommended
793	Transmission Control Protocol	Recommended
1034	Domain Name System Concepts and Facilities	Recommended
1035	Domain Name System Implementation and Specification	Recommended
854	TELNET Protocol	Recommended
959	File Transfer Protocol	Recommended
821	Simple Mail Transfer Protocol	Recommended
974	Mail Routing and the Domain Name System	Recommended
822	Format of Electronic Mail Messages	Recommended

A.3   Interface-Specific RFCs

The RFCs pertaining to transmission of the IP over various media are:

RFC	Name	Status
826	Address Resolution Protocol	Elective
903	Reverse Address Resolution Protocol	Elective
907	Wideband Network	Elective
877	Public Data Networks	Elective
894	Ethernet networks	Elective
895	Experimental Ethernet networks	Elective
1042	IEEE802 networks	Elective
1044	Hyperchannel	Elective
1051	ARCNET	Elective
1055	Serial Links	Elective
1088	NetBIOS (Novell)	Elective
1103	FDDI	Elective
1149	Avian networks	Elective

Although the status of these standards is *elective*, if a device elects to transmit IP datagrams over one of the media above, then it is *required* to use the procedures defined in the relevant RFC(s).

A.4 Network Management RFCs

These RFCs form the basis of the *Internet-standard Network Management Framework*:

RFC	Name	Status
1155	Structure of Management Information	Recommended
1156	Management Information Base	Recommended
1157	Simple Network Management Protocol	Recommended

All of these documents are full "Standard Protocols" with "Recommended" status. In addition, MIB-II, the intended successor to the Internet-standard MIB, is currently a *proposed* Internet-standard, and is defined in RFC1158[47].

Further, new network management RFCs are emerging which are specific to particular tasks:

RFC	Name	Status
1147	Network Management Tools Catalog	Informational
1161	SNMP over OSI	Experimental
1162	CLNS MIB	Experimental

Note that none of these are currently "Standards Protocols."

A.4.1   List of Assigned Experiments

The list of registered names under the

```
experimental OBJECT IDENTIFIER ::= { internet 3 }
```

subtree, as of June, 1990, are:

Number	Descriptor	Description	Contact
0	(none)	(reserved)	[JKR1]
1	CLNS	ISO CLNS Objects	[GS2]
2	T1-Carrier	T1 Carrier Objects	[FB77]
3	IEEE802.3	Ethernet-like Objects	[JXC]
4	IEEE802.5	Token Ring-like Objects	[EXD]
5	DECNet-PHIV	DECnet Phase IV Objects	[JXS2]
6	Interface	Generic Interface Objects	[KZM]
7	IEEE802.4	Token Bus-like Objects	[KZM]
8	FDDI	FDDI Objects	[JDC20]
9	LANMGR-1	LAN Manager V1	[JXG1]
10	LANMGR-TRAPS	LAN Manager Traps	[JXG1]

Detailed contact information can be found in the Assigned Numbers
RFC.

To register a new experiment, one must first coordinate with the
Area Director for Network Management in the Internet Engineering
Steering Group. (The Internet Assigned Numbers Authority can provide this contact information.) The Area Director will coordinate
with the IANA to request an experimental number.

Once contact is made with the Area Director, a working group of
the IETF will be formed (if appropriate) to oversee the experiment. In
particular, the working group must author an Internet Draft, defining
the experimental MIB. This draft will be made available for public
review, as discussed in Section A on page 255.

To aid authors of enterprise-specific MIB modules, a template is
available on host `nisc.nyser.net`. Use "anonymous" FTP and retrieve files from the directory "`pilot/snmp-wg/`".

A.4.2 List of Assigned Enterprises

Table A.1 starting on page 262 shows the list of registered names under the

```
enterprises OBJECT IDENTIFIER ::= { private 1 }
```

subtree, as of May, 1990. Detailed contact information can be found in the Assigned Numbers RFC.

Some enterprise-specific MIB modules are available for FTP on the host `venera.isi.edu`. Use "anonymous" FTP and retrieve files from the directory "`mib/`".

To have an enterprise-specific MIB module placed in this area, mail a copy to the Internet Assigned Numbers Authority. At a minimum the module must contain an SMI-compliant description of the MIB. In addition, a textual description of the MIB module may be included. The MIB module will be checked for compliance with the Internet-standard SMI, and then placed in the `mib/` area by the IANA. Note that MIB modules in this area are not "registered" in any sense, they are simply available for public inspection (unlike experimental MIB modules which are registered as Internet Drafts).

Number	Descriptor	Contact
0	(reserved)	[JKR1]
1	Proteon	[GSM11]
2	IBM	[JXR]
3	CMU	[SXW]
4	Unix	[KXS]
5	ACC	[AB20]
6	TWG	[KZM]
7	CAYMAN	[BP52]
8	PSI	[MS9]
9	cisco	[GXS]
10	NSC	[GS123]
11	HP	[RDXS]
12	Epilogue	[KA4]
13	U of Tennessee	[JDC20]
14	BBN	[RH6]
15	Xylogics, Inc.	[JRL3]
16	Unisys	[UXW]
17	Canstar	[SXP]
18	Wellfleet	[JCB1]
19	TRW	[GGB2]
20	MIT	[JR35]
21	EON	[MXW]
22	Spartacus	[YXK]
23	Excelan	[RXB]
24	Spider Systems	[VXW]
25	NSFNET	[HWB]
26	Hughes LAN Systems	[KZM]
27	Intergraph	[SXC]
28	Interlan	[FJK2]
29	Vitalink Communications	[FXB]
30	ULANA	[BXA]
31	NSWC	[SRN1]
32	Santa Cruz Operation	[KR35]
33	Xyplex	[BXS]
34	Cray	[HXE]

Table A.1: List of Assigned Enterprises

Number	Descriptor	Contact
35	Bell Northern Research	[GXW]
36	DEC	[RXB1]
37	Touch	[BXB]
38	Network Research Corp.	[BXV]
39	Baylor College of Medicine	[SB98]
40	NMFECC-LLNL	[SXH]
41	SRI	[DW181]
42	Sun Microsystems	[DXY]
43	3Com	[TB6]
44	CMC	[DXP]
45	SynOptics	[BXB1]
46	Cheyenne Software	[RXH]
47	Prime Computer	[MXS]
48	MCNC/North Carolina Data Network	[KXW]
49	Chipcom	[JXC]
50	Optical Data Systems	[JXF]
51	gated	[JXH]
52	Cabletron Systems	[RXD]
53	Apollo Computers	[JXB]
54	DeskTalk Systems, Inc.	[DXK]
55	SSDS	[RXS]
56	Castle Rock Computing	[JXS1]
57	MIPS Computer Systems	[CXM]
58	TGV, Inc.	[KAA]
59	Silicon Graphics, Inc.	[RXJ]
60	University of British Columbia	[DXM]
61	Merit	[BXN]
62	FiberCom	[EXR]
63	Apple Computer Inc	[JXH1]
64	Gandalf	[HXK]
65	Dartmouth	[PXK]
66	David Systems	[DXM]
67	Reuters	[BXZ]
68	Cornell	[DC126]
69	TMAC	[MLS34]

Table A.1: List of Assigned Enterprises (cont.)

Number	Descriptor	Contact
70	Locus Computing Corp.	[AXS]
71	NASA	[SS92]
72	Retix	[AXM]
73	Boeing	[JXG]
74	AT&T	[AXC2]
75	Ungermann-Bass	[DXM]
76	Digital Analysis Corp.	[SXK]
77	LAN Manager	[JXG1]
78	Netlabs	[JB478]
79	ICL	[JXI]
80	Auspex Systems	[BXE]
81	Lannet Company	[EXR]
82	Network Computing Devices	[DM280]
83	Raycom Systems	[BXW1]
84	Pirelli Focom Ltd.	[SXL]
85	Datability Software Systems	[LXF]
86	Network Application Technology	[YXW]
87	LINK (Lokales Informatik-Netz Karlsruhe)	[GXS]
88	NYU	[BJR2]
89	RND	[RXN]
90	InterCon Systems Corporation	[AW90]
91	LearningTree Systems	[JXG2]
92	Webster Computer Corporation	[RXE]
93	Frontier Technologies Corp.	[PXA]
94	Nokia Data Communications	[DXE]
95	Allen-Bradley Company, Inc.	[BXK]
96	CERN	[JXR]
97	Sigma Network Systems, Inc.	[KXV]
98	Emerging Technologies, Inc.	[DXB2]
99	SNMP Research	[JDC20]
100	Ohio State University	[SXA1]

Table A.1: List of Assigned Enterprises (cont.)

A.5 Contact Information

The RFC Editor can be reached at:

> Postal: Jonathan B. Postel
> RFC Editor
> USC/Information Sciences Institute
> 4676 Admiralty Way
> Marina del Rey, CA 90292-6695
> US
>
> Phone: +1 213–822–1511
>
> Mail: postel@isi.edu

The Internet Assigned Numbers Authority can be reached at:

> Postal: Joyce K. Reynolds
> Internet Assigned Numbers Authority
> USC/Information Sciences Institute
> 4676 Admiralty Way
> Marina del Rey, CA 90292-6695
> US
>
> Phone: +1 213–822–1511
>
> Mail: iana@isi.edu

Appendix B

The Lore of Internet Management

Standardized network management of TCP/IP-based internets is only a few years old and has seen explosive growth in the participation process. A lot of time is spent via electronic mail "bringing people up to speed."

Thus the motivation for this Appendix, which answers the questions most commonly asked about Internet management. Following this, guidelines for MIB authors are presented.

B.1   Commonly Asked Questions

The Internet mailbox

    snmp@nisc.nyser.net

is the discussion group for management of TCP/IP internets in general, and for SNMP in particular. All the mail sent to this mailbox is forwarded to a large number of people interested in SNMP. If you have mail access to the Internet and you wish to be added to this list, send your request to:

    snmp-request@nisc.nyser.net

History repeats itself every three months on the snmp list. The same questions keep popping up. Here are the most commonly asked questions, with the answers.

about MIBs

- *How do I get an enterprise number?*

  Request one from the Internet Assigned Numbers Authority. Contact information is given on page 265.

- *Why doesn't my management station know about the private MIB variables of my router, which is from another vendor? How can it find out?*

  You must ask your router vendor to provide a description of the MIB for the router to the vendor of your management station. You must then ask the vendor of your management station to support this MIB. Alternately, you can buy a management station from your router vendor, as this presumably knows about the router's MIB. Alternately, you can "vote with your feet."

  Private MIBs are just that, *private*. The Internet-standard MIB was defined so that all conformant management products would interoperate when managing the core aspects of the Internet suite of protocols. A vendor-specific MIB contains only objects which are specific to that particular implementation. It is not surprising that other vendors might have little interest in supporting that particular MIB in their own management stations. (If portions of the private MIB are of general use, the vendor can submit them for possible inclusion in a future revision of the Internet-standard MIB.)

about the Internet-Standard MIB

- *What do the counters in the interfaces group really count?*

  They measure the activity of the protocols used to transmit IP datagrams. In the case of a physical medium, this is usually frames. If other protocol technologies are used, then packets might be counted.

- *What values do Counters have on a system restart?*

  Most agents set them to zero, but they don't have to; counters can be set to any value on an agent restart.

- *Using SNMP, is there any way to obtain an IP address for a specific interface number of a gateway?*

  Say that i is the value of `ifIndex` for the interface in question. Traverse the IP address table, looking for a value of `ipAdEntIfIndex` which is equal to i. The answer is the value of `ipAdEntAddr` for that row of the table. An example of this is shown in Section 7.4.2 on page 241.

about SNMP

- *How do I add or delete a row in a table?*

  See Section 5.4 on page 144.

- *Can I retrieve an object with has type SEQUENCE using SNMP, thus allowing retrieval of an entire row of a table at once?*

  No. Only leaf objects are available for retrieval.

- *How is the powerful get-next operator used?*

  See Section 5.3.1 on page 140.

- *and why is it called "powerful"?*

See the soapbox on page 142.

- *What is the response to a powerful get-next operator when I come to the end of a table?*

An instance from another object is returned. The only exception is if the table was the last object in the view. In this case, you get a `noSuchName` error.

- *What does error status of `noSuchName` mean?*

For the `get` and `set` operator, it means that the instance you specified does not exist in the community profile.

For the powerful `get-next` operator, it means that there is no instances in the community profile which is lexicographically greater than the one you specified.

about Communities

- *What is the relationship between an agent and a manager?*

It's called a community.

- *What value goes into the community field of an SNMP message and what does it mean?*

The community field names an administrative relationship between an agent and one or more management stations. See Section 5.2 on page 135 for the details.

- *What do I do if the community name in the received SNMP message is invalid?*

What do you mean by invalid? If you mean that the community is unknown to the agent, or the authentication entity says that the sender of the message isn't a member of that community, you might generate an `authenticationFailure` trap. Regardless, you simply ignore the message.

If the community is known, but the desired operation can't be performed (e.g., trying to do a `set` when the community allows only reading), then you generate a `get-response` containing the appropriate error.

- *Can a community have different access rights depending on the MIB view it supports?*

  This is a non-sensical question. See Section 5.2.2 on page 135 for how authorization works in SNMP.

about Traps

- *How do I ask that Trap messages be sent to me?*

  You don't. The agent should have some local configuration information which defines which management stations it will send traps to.

- *Why isn't there a Trap in SNMP for random-event "whatever"?*

  As a vendor you can get your own enterprise number, write your own enterprise-specific MIB, and define your own traps, placing the trap number in the `specific-trap` field of the `Trap-PDU`.

- *How can I, as a vendor, define 1000's of my own traps so I don't have to waste bandwidth polling?*

  When your agent wants to generate one of your own traps, it generates an `enterpriseSpecific` trap, and sets the value of the `specific-trap` variable to the appropriate trap number.

- *How do `warmStart` and `coldStart` traps differ?*

  If the managed objects corresponding to the "useful protocols" may have changed as a result of the initialization, it's called a `coldStart`.

- *When do I send an authentication trap?*

  When your agent receives an SNMP message containing either a community it does not know about, or if your agent determines that the sender of the message is not a member of the community.

Also, note that your agent must be locally configurable so that there is a way to turn off the generation of these traps.

- *What variables go into a* **trap** *message? Does there have to be any?*

  It depends on what kind of trap it is. Section 5.5.3 on page 156 indicates this. Once you have included any mandatory variables, it's up to you whether others are included. So, if the trap doesn't require any variables, you don't have to send any.

about ASN.1 and the BER

- *Does somebody have an example of an encoded SNMP message?*

  See Section 5.10.6 on page 180.

- *Why does the encoding of object identifiers contain the added calculation for compressing the first two components?*

  Because that's the way the standards committee defined it. Actually, the number of values that can occur in the first two components (termed sub-identifiers) is limited. Consequently, it's possible to encode the object identifiers in one less octet (big deal).

about Implementations

- *How many agents can exist on a single network element?*

  As many as you want. In particular, if the agents are proxying for other devices, then each agent will support different views.

- *My router has one SNMP agent. Which of its IP addresses do I send my SNMP queries to?*

  It doesn't matter which one (unless your network has routing problems such that only a subset of the router's addresses is reachable).

- *What public-domain sofware is available?*

  There are three packages available:

    - the CMU SNMP distribution;
    - the MIT SNMP development kit; and,
    - the 4BSD/ISODE SNMP package.

  Appendix D tells how to order the last package. To find out about the other two, read the next question and answer.

- *Is there a list of SNMP products?*

  Yes. Get a copy of RFC 1147, *Tools for Monitoring and Debugging TCP/IP Internets and Interconnected Devices.*

and finally

- *How can I manage my OSI systems?*

  You have OSI systems that work? How novel!

  See Section 5.6 on page 159.

B.2 How to Write a MIB Module

The first step is to determine the OBJECT IDENTIFIER prefix that will be used for the MIB module.

If the MIB module is being defined on a multilateral, experimental basis (e.g., for an Internet protocol), then Section A.4.1 on page 260 says how to ask for an experiment number.

Otherwise, if the MIB module is specific to an enterprise, then contact the Internet Assigned Numbers Authority and ask for an *enterprise* number (assuming one already hasn't been assigned).

B.2.1 MIB Skeleton

The next step is to define the skeleton for the MIB module. For an experimental MIB, it will look something like this:

```
FIZBIN-MIB DEFINITIONS ::= BEGIN

IMPORTS
    experimental, OBJECT-TYPE
        FROM RFC1155-SMI;

fizBin OBJECT IDENTIFIER ::= { experimental 99 }

END
```

Otherwise, for an enterprise-specific MIB, it might look something like this:

```
FIZZBIN-MIB DEFINITIONS ::= BEGIN

IMPORTS
    enterprises, OBJECT-TYPE
        FROM RFC1155-SMI;

cheetah OBJECT IDENTIFIER ::= { enterprises 9999 }
fizBin  OBJECT IDENTIFIER ::= { cheetah 1 }

END
```

Regardless of the kind of MIB module, the last `OBJECT IDENTIFIER` in the skeletons above points to the root of the subtree which will be used to define objects.

B.2.2 MIB Objects

Next, define the MIB objects that comprise the module. Here are the guidelines:

- Group the objects to add more hierarchy to the definitions.

- For each tabular object, decide how the instance-identifiers are formed for the leaves of that table.

  The rules are pretty simple: determine which column(s) in the table will unambiguously distinguish a row. The syntax of those columnar objects indicate how to form the instance-identifier:

  - integer-valued: a single sub-identifier taking the integer value (this works only for non-negative integers);

  - string-valued, fixed-length strings: n sub-identifiers, where n is the length of the string (each octet of the string is encoded in a separate sub-identifier);

  - string-valued, variable-length strings: $n + 1$ sub-identifiers, where n is the length of the string (the first octet is n itself, following this, each octet of the string is encoded in a separate sub-identifier); or,

  - `OBJECT IDENTIFIER`-valued: $n + 1$ sub-identifiers, where n is the number of sub-identifiers in the value (the first octet is n itself, following this, sub-identifier in the value is copied).

  Of course, if multiple columns are needed to distinguish between rows, then the ordering of the columns should reflect the way the table is most usefully traversed.

- For each tabular object that will allow row deletion, be sure to define a column called **xxType** which is integer-valued. One of the labels associated with the object type should be `invalid`, e.g.,

```
ipRouteType OBJECT-TYPE
    SYNTAX INTEGER {
            other(1),
            invalid(2),
            direct(3),
            remote(4)
        }
    ...
```

By convention, the label with value 1 is called `other`, and the label with value 2 is called `invalid`.

- Be sure to mark each tablular and row (entry) object as being `not-accessible` — only leaf objects are accessed with the SNMP.

- For each leaf object, include a textual definition of the variable. For example, the definition of a counter would indicate when it is incremented, what it counts, and so on. Consider using a Case Diagram to indicate the relationship between counters and the useful protocol being managed.

- If there is a possibility that the module might someday be a part of the Internet-standard MIB, there are few conventions to recall from earlier discussion:

    - Objects may not have a status of *optional*. If a group of related variables may, or may not, be implemented, define a group and make that optional.

    - Objects must conform to the syntax defined by the Internet-standard SMI, as outlined in Section 4.1.3. In particular, pay attention to the conventions regarding enumerated integers.

      For consistency purposes, it's a good idea to run the MIB module through an ASN.1 compiler that knows about the SMI. For example, the *mosy* program described in Section 7.1.1 on page 201 can be used for this purpose.

- It is good practice for objects to follow the conventions of the Internet-standard MIB. In particular, recall that the symbolic descriptions of objects (the textual names) are all unique within a MIB module, and that the textual names of counters end with the letter "s."

- Be sure to distinguish between the syntaxes for strings. Binary information (such as media addresses) should be defined using the `OCTET STRING`; textual information should be defined using the `DisplayString`.

B.2.3   An Example

The MIB module for the SMUX protocol introduced in Section 7.3 on page 226 is shown in Figure B.1, starting on page 279.

In addition, the following text, which defines the identification of object instances for use with SNMP, accompanies the MIB module definition:

Instance Identification with SNMP

The names for all object types in this MIB module are defined explicitly either in the Internet-standard MIB or in other documents which conform to the naming conventions of the Internet-standard SMI. The SMI requires that conformant management protocols define mechanisms for identifying individual instances of those object types for a particular network element.

Each instance of any object type defined in this MIB module is identified in SNMP operations by a unique name called its *variable name*. In general, the name of an SNMP variable is an `OBJECT IDENTIFIER` of the form $x.y$, where x is the name of a non-aggregate object type and y is an `OBJECT IDENTIFIER` fragment that, in a way specific to the named object type, identifies the desired instance.

This naming strategy admits the fullest exploitation of the semantics of the *powerful* SNMP get-next operator, because it assigns names for related variables so as to be contiguous in the lexicographical ordering of all variable names known in the MIB module.

The type-specific naming of object instances is defined below for a number of classes of object types. Instances of an object type to which none of the following naming conventions are applicable are named by OBJECT IDENTIFIERs of the form $x.0$, where x is the name of said object type in the MIB module.

For example, suppose one wanted to identify an instance of the variable sysDescr. The object class for sysDescr is:

```
iso org dod internet mgmt mib system sysDescr
 1   3   6     1       2    1     1        1
```

Hence, the object type, x, would be

```
1.3.6.1.2.1.1.1
```

to which is appended an instance sub-identifier of 0. That is,

```
1.3.6.1.2.1.1.1.0
```

identifies the one and only instance of sysDescr.

smuxPeerTable Object Type Names

The name of a SMUX peer relationship, s, is the OBJECT IDENTIFIER value of the form i, where i has the value of that instance of the smuxPindex object type associated with s.

For each object type, t, for which the defined name, n, has a prefix of smuxPeerEntry, an instance, i, of t is named by an OBJECT IDENTIFIER of the form $n.s$, where s is the name of the SMUX peer relationship about which i represents information.

For example, suppose one wanted to identify the instance of the variable smuxPidentity associated with peer relationship number 2. Accordingly,

```
smuxPidentity.2
```

would identify the desired instance.

SMUX–MIB **DEFINITIONS** ::= **BEGIN**

IMPORTS
      enterprises, **OBJECT–TYPE**, ObjectName
         FROM RFC1155–SMI;

unix   **OBJECT IDENTIFIER** ::= { enterprises 4 }

                                                                 10

smux   **OBJECT IDENTIFIER** ::= { unix 4 }

Figure B.1: MIB module for the SMUX Protocol

smuxTreeTable Object Type Names

The name of a SMUX subtree relationship, s, is the OBJECT IDENT-IFIER value of the form $i.j$, where i has the value of that instance of the smuxTsubtree object type, and j has the value of that instance of the smuxTpriority object type, associated with s.

For each object type, t, for which the defined name, n, has a prefix of smuxTreeEntry, an instance, i, of t is named by an OBJECT IDENT-IFIER of the form $n.s.t.u$, where s is the number of sub-identifiers in the corresponding instance of smuxTsubtree, t is the value of the instance of smuxTsubtree corresponding to this entry, and u is the value of the instance of smuxTpriority corresponding to this entry.

For example, suppose one wanted to identify the instance of the variable smuxTindex associated with the subtree 1.3.6.1.5 for priority 3. Accordingly,

    smuxTindex.5.1.3.6.1.5.3

would identify the desired instance.

```
smuxPeerTable    OBJECT-TYPE
        SYNTAX  SEQUENCE OF SmuxPeerEntry
        ACCESS  not-accessible
        STATUS  mandatory
        ::= { smux 1 }


smuxPeerEntry    OBJECT-TYPE
        SYNTAX  SmuxPeerEntry
        ACCESS  not-accessible
        STATUS  mandatory                                            10
        ::= { smuxPeerTable 1}


SmuxPeerEntry ::=
    SEQUENCE {
        smuxPindex
            INTEGER,
        smuxPidentity
            OBJECT IDENTIFIER,
        smuxPdescription
            DisplayString,                                           20
        smuxPstatus
            INTEGER
    }


smuxPindex       OBJECT-TYPE
        SYNTAX  INTEGER
        ACCESS  read-write
        STATUS  mandatory
        ::= { smuxPeerEntry 1 }

                                                                     30
smuxPidentity    OBJECT-TYPE
        SYNTAX  OBJECT IDENTIFIER
        ACCESS  read-write
        STATUS  mandatory
        ::= { smuxPeerEntry 2 }


smuxPdescription OBJECT-TYPE
        SYNTAX  DisplayString
        ACCESS  read-write
        STATUS  mandatory                                           40
        ::= { smuxPeerEntry 3 }


smuxPstatus      OBJECT-TYPE
        SYNTAX  INTEGER { valid(1), invalid(2), connecting(3) }
        ACCESS  read-write
        STATUS  mandatory
        ::= { smuxPeerEntry 4 }
```

Figure B.1: MIB module for the SMUX Protocol (cont.)

```
smuxTreeTable    OBJECT-TYPE
        SYNTAX SEQUENCE OF SmuxTreeEntry
        ACCESS not-accessible
        STATUS mandatory
        ::= { smux 2 }


smuxTreeEntry    OBJECT-TYPE
        SYNTAX SmuxTreeEntry
        ACCESS not-accessible
        STATUS mandatory                                      10
        ::= { smuxTreeTable 1}

SmuxTreeEntry ::=
    SEQUENCE {
        smuxTsubtree
            ObjectName
        smuxTpriority
            INTEGER,
        smuxTindex
            INTEGER,                                           20
        smuxTstatus
            INTEGER
    }


smuxTsubtree    OBJECT-TYPE
        SYNTAX ObjectName
        ACCESS read-write
        STATUS mandatory
        ::= { smuxTreeEntry 1 }
                                                              30
smuxTpriority OBJECT-TYPE
        SYNTAX INTEGER (0..2147483647)
        ACCESS read-write
        STATUS mandatory
        ::= { smuxTreeEntry 2 }


smuxTindex OBJECT-TYPE
        SYNTAX INTEGER (0..2147483647)
        ACCESS read-write
        STATUS mandatory                                      40
        ::= { smuxTreeEntry 3 }


smuxTstatus    OBJECT-TYPE
        SYNTAX INTEGER { valid(1), invalid(2) }
        ACCESS read-write
        STATUS mandatory
        ::= { smuxTreeEntry 4 }

END
```

Figure B.1: MIB module for the SMUX Protocol (cont.)

Appendix C

MIB-II

Below is a listing of the MIB-II definition, taken from RFC 1158[47]. Note that at present, MIB-II is only a *proposed* Internet-standard. It is possible, though unlikely, that the MIB-II definition might change. Always consult the Official Protocols RFCs to determine the actual RFC to use for the Internet-standard MIB.

RFC1158−MIB **DEFINITIONS** ::= **BEGIN**

IMPORTS
      mgmt, **OBJECT−TYPE**, NetworkAddress, IpAddress, Counter, Gauge,
        TimeTicks
          FROM RFC1155−SMI;

mib−2   **OBJECT IDENTIFIER** ::= { mgmt 1 }   *−− MIB−II (same prefix as MIB−I)*

system   **OBJECT IDENTIFIER** ::= { mib−2 1 }   10
interfaces **OBJECT IDENTIFIER** ::= { mib−2 2 }
at   **OBJECT IDENTIFIER** ::= { mib−2 3 }
ip   **OBJECT IDENTIFIER** ::= { mib−2 4 }
icmp   **OBJECT IDENTIFIER** ::= { mib−2 5 }
tcp   **OBJECT IDENTIFIER** ::= { mib−2 6 }
udp   **OBJECT IDENTIFIER** ::= { mib−2 7 }
egp   **OBJECT IDENTIFIER** ::= { mib−2 8 }
−− cmot   OBJECT IDENTIFIER ::= { mib−2 9 }
transmission **OBJECT IDENTIFIER** ::= { mib−2 10 }
snmp   **OBJECT IDENTIFIER** ::= { mib−2 11 }   20

−− object types

−− the System group

sysDescr **OBJECT−TYPE**
      SYNTAX DisplayString (**SIZE** (0..255))

283

       ACCESS read−only
       STATUS mandatory
       ::= { system 1 }

sysObjectID **OBJECT−TYPE**
       SYNTAX OBJECT IDENTIFIER
       ACCESS read−only
       STATUS mandatory
       ::= { system 2 }

sysUpTime **OBJECT−TYPE**
       SYNTAX TimeTicks
       ACCESS read−only
       STATUS mandatory
       ::= { system 3 }

sysContact **OBJECT−TYPE**
       SYNTAX DisplayString (**SIZE** (0..255))
       ACCESS read−write
       STATUS mandatory
       ::= { system 4 }

sysName **OBJECT−TYPE**
       SYNTAX DisplayString (**SIZE** (0..255))
       ACCESS read−write
       STATUS mandatory
       ::= { system 5 }

sysLocation **OBJECT−TYPE**
       SYNTAX DisplayString (**SIZE** (0..255))
       ACCESS read−only
       STATUS mandatory
       ::= { system 6 }

sysServices **OBJECT−TYPE**
       SYNTAX INTEGER (0..127)
       ACCESS read−only
       STATUS mandatory
       ::= { system 7 }

−− *the Interfaces group*

ifNumber **OBJECT−TYPE**
       SYNTAX INTEGER
       ACCESS read−only
       STATUS mandatory
       ::= { interfaces 1 }

−− *the Interfaces table*

ifTable **OBJECT−TYPE**
       SYNTAX SEQUENCE OF IfEntry
       ACCESS read−only
       STATUS mandatory
       ::= { interfaces 2 }

```
ifEntry OBJECT-TYPE
        SYNTAX  IfEntry
        ACCESS  read-only
        STATUS  mandatory
        ::= { ifTable 1 }                                    90

IfEntry ::=
    SEQUENCE {
        ifIndex
            INTEGER,
        ifDescr
            DisplayString,
        ifType
            INTEGER,
        ifMtu                                                100
            INTEGER,
        ifSpeed
            Gauge,
        ifPhysAddress
            OCTET STRING,
        ifAdminStatus
            INTEGER,
        ifOperStatus
            INTEGER,
        ifLastChange                                         110
            TimeTicks,
        ifInOctets
            Counter,
        ifInUcastPkts
            Counter,
        ifInNUcastPkts
            Counter,
        ifInDiscards
            Counter,
        ifInErrors                                           120
            Counter,
        ifInUnknownProtos
            Counter,
        ifOutOctets
            Counter,
        ifOutUcastPkts
            Counter,
        ifOutNUcastPkts
            Counter,
        ifOutDiscards                                        130
            Counter,
        ifOutErrors
            Counter,
        ifOutQLen
            Gauge,
        ifSpecific
            OBJECT IDENTIFIER
    }

ifIndex OBJECT-TYPE                                          140
```

```
        SYNTAX INTEGER
        ACCESS read−only
        STATUS mandatory
        ::= { ifEntry 1 }

ifDescr OBJECT−TYPE
        SYNTAX DisplayString (SIZE (0..255))
        ACCESS read−only
        STATUS mandatory
        ::= { ifEntry 2 }                                                      150

ifType OBJECT−TYPE
        SYNTAX INTEGER {
                other(1),                    −− none of the following
                regular1822(2),
                hdh1822(3),
                ddn−x25(4),
                rfc877−x25(5),
                ethernet−csmacd(6),
                iso88023−csmacd(7),                                            160
                iso88024−tokenBus(8),
                iso88025−tokenRing(9),
                iso88026−man(10),
                starLan(11),
                proteon−10Mbit(12),
                proteon−80Mbit(13),
                hyperchannel(14),
                fddi(15),
                lapb(16),
                sdlc(17),                                                      170
                t1−carrier(18),
                cept(19),                    −− european equivalent of T−1
                basicISDN(20),
                primaryISDN(21),
                propPointToPointSerial(22),    −− proprietary serial
                ppp(23),
                softwareLoopback(24),
                eon(25),                     −− CLNP over IP
                ethernet−3Mbit(26),
                nsip(27),                    −− XNS over IP                    180
                slip(28)                     −− generic SLIP
              }
        ACCESS read−only
        STATUS mandatory
        ::= { ifEntry 3 }

ifMtu OBJECT−TYPE
        SYNTAX INTEGER
        ACCESS read−only
        STATUS mandatory                                                      190
        ::= { ifEntry 4 }

ifSpeed OBJECT−TYPE
        SYNTAX Gauge
        ACCESS read−only
        STATUS mandatory
```

```
        ::= { ifEntry 5 }

ifPhysAddress OBJECT-TYPE
        SYNTAX OCTET STRING                                              200
        ACCESS read-only
        STATUS mandatory
        ::= { ifEntry 6 }

ifAdminStatus OBJECT-TYPE
        SYNTAX INTEGER {
                up(1),        -- ready to pass packets
                down(2),
                testing(3)    -- in some test mode
                }                                                        210
        ACCESS read-write
        STATUS mandatory
        ::= { ifEntry 7 }

ifOperStatus OBJECT-TYPE
        SYNTAX INTEGER {
                up(1),        -- ready to pass packets
                down(2),
                testing(3)    -- in some test mode
                }                                                        220
        ACCESS read-only
        STATUS mandatory
        ::= { ifEntry 8 }

ifLastChange OBJECT-TYPE
        SYNTAX TimeTicks
        ACCESS read-only
        STATUS mandatory
        ::= { ifEntry 9 }
                                                                        230
ifInOctets OBJECT-TYPE
        SYNTAX Counter
        ACCESS read-only
        STATUS mandatory
        ::= { ifEntry 10 }

ifInUcastPkts OBJECT-TYPE
        SYNTAX Counter
        ACCESS read-only
        STATUS mandatory                                                240
        ::=  { ifEntry 11 }

ifInNUcastPkts OBJECT-TYPE
        SYNTAX Counter
        ACCESS read-only
        STATUS mandatory
        ::= { ifEntry 12 }

ifInDiscards OBJECT-TYPE
        SYNTAX Counter                                                  250
        ACCESS read-only
        STATUS mandatory
```

```
            ::= { ifEntry 13 }

ifInErrors OBJECT-TYPE
        SYNTAX Counter
        ACCESS read-only
        STATUS mandatory
        ::= { ifEntry 14 }
```

260

```
ifInUnknownProtos OBJECT-TYPE
        SYNTAX Counter
        ACCESS read-only
        STATUS mandatory
        ::= { ifEntry 15 }

ifOutOctets OBJECT-TYPE
        SYNTAX Counter
        ACCESS read-only
        STATUS mandatory
        ::= { ifEntry 16 }
```

270

```
ifOutUcastPkts OBJECT-TYPE
        SYNTAX Counter
        ACCESS read-only
        STATUS mandatory
        ::= { ifEntry 17 }

ifOutNUcastPkts OBJECT-TYPE
        SYNTAX Counter
        ACCESS read-only
        STATUS mandatory
        ::= { ifEntry 18 }
```

280

```
ifOutDiscards OBJECT-TYPE
        SYNTAX Counter
        ACCESS read-only
        STATUS mandatory
        ::= { ifEntry 19 }
```

290

```
ifOutErrors OBJECT-TYPE
        SYNTAX Counter
        ACCESS read-only
        STATUS mandatory
        ::= { ifEntry 20 }

ifOutQLen OBJECT-TYPE
        SYNTAX Gauge
        ACCESS read-only
        STATUS mandatory
        ::= { ifEntry 21 }
```

300

```
ifSpecific OBJECT-TYPE
        SYNTAX OBJECT IDENTIFIER
        ACCESS read-only
        STATUS mandatory
        ::= { ifEntry 22 }
```

nullSpecific **OBJECT IDENTIFIER** ::= { 0 0 }

310

-- the Address Translation group (deprecated)

atTable **OBJECT-TYPE**
    SYNTAX SEQUENCE OF AtEntry
    ACCESS read-write
    STATUS deprecated
    ::= { at 1 }

atEntry **OBJECT-TYPE**
    SYNTAX AtEntry
    ACCESS read-write
    STATUS deprecated
    ::= { atTable 1 }

320

AtEntry ::=
  SEQUENCE {
    atIfIndex
      INTEGER,
    atPhysAddress
      OCTET STRING,
    atNetAddress
      NetworkAddress
  }

330

atIfIndex **OBJECT-TYPE**
    SYNTAX INTEGER
    ACCESS read-write
    STATUS deprecated
    ::= { atEntry 1 }

340

atPhysAddress **OBJECT-TYPE**
    SYNTAX OCTET STRING
    ACCESS read-write
    STATUS deprecated
    ::= { atEntry 2 }

atNetAddress **OBJECT-TYPE**
    SYNTAX NetworkAddress
    ACCESS read-write
    STATUS deprecated
    ::= { atEntry 3 }

350

-- the IP group

ipForwarding **OBJECT-TYPE**
    SYNTAX INTEGER {
        gateway(1), *-- entity forwards datagrams*
        host(2)   *-- entity does NOT forward datagrams*
      }
    ACCESS read-write
    STATUS mandatory
    ::= { ip 1 }

360

ipDefaultTTL **OBJECT−TYPE**
        SYNTAX INTEGER
        ACCESS read−write
        STATUS mandatory
        ::= { ip 2 }   370

ipInReceives **OBJECT−TYPE**
        SYNTAX Counter
        ACCESS read−only
        STATUS mandatory
        ::= { ip 3 }

ipInHdrErrors **OBJECT−TYPE**
        SYNTAX Counter
        ACCESS read−only   380
        STATUS mandatory
        ::= { ip 4 }

ipInAddrErrors **OBJECT−TYPE**
        SYNTAX Counter
        ACCESS read−only
        STATUS mandatory
        ::= { ip 5 }

ipForwDatagrams **OBJECT−TYPE**   390
        SYNTAX Counter
        ACCESS read−only
        STATUS mandatory
        ::= { ip 6 }

ipInUnknownProtos **OBJECT−TYPE**
        SYNTAX Counter
        ACCESS read−only
        STATUS mandatory
        ::= { ip 7 }   400

ipInDiscards **OBJECT−TYPE**
        SYNTAX Counter
        ACCESS read−only
        STATUS mandatory
        ::= { ip 8 }

ipInDelivers **OBJECT−TYPE**
        SYNTAX Counter
        ACCESS read−only   410
        STATUS mandatory
        ::= { ip 9 }

ipOutRequests **OBJECT−TYPE**
        SYNTAX Counter
        ACCESS read−only
        STATUS mandatory
        ::= { ip 10 }

ipOutDiscards **OBJECT−TYPE**   420

SYNTAX Counter
ACCESS read−only
STATUS mandatory
::= { ip 11 }

ipOutNoRoutes **OBJECT−TYPE**
    SYNTAX Counter
    ACCESS read−only
    STATUS mandatory
    ::= { ip 12 }

430

ipReasmTimeout **OBJECT−TYPE**
    SYNTAX INTEGER
    ACCESS read−only
    STATUS mandatory
    ::= { ip 13 }

ipReasmReqds **OBJECT−TYPE**
    SYNTAX Counter
    ACCESS read−only
    STATUS mandatory
    ::= { ip 14 }

440

ipReasmOKs **OBJECT−TYPE**
    SYNTAX Counter
    ACCESS read−only
    STATUS mandatory
    ::= { ip 15 }

ipReasmFails **OBJECT−TYPE**
    SYNTAX Counter
    ACCESS read−only
    STATUS mandatory
    ::= { ip 16 }

450

ipFragOKs **OBJECT−TYPE**
    SYNTAX Counter
    ACCESS read−only
    STATUS mandatory
    ::= { ip 17 }

460

ipFragFails **OBJECT−TYPE**
    SYNTAX Counter
    ACCESS read−only
    STATUS mandatory
    ::= { ip 18 }

ipFragCreates **OBJECT−TYPE**
    SYNTAX Counter
    ACCESS read−only
    STATUS mandatory
    ::= { ip 19 }

470

−− *the IP Interface table*

ipAddrTable **OBJECT−TYPE**

```
        SYNTAX  SEQUENCE OF IpAddrEntry
        ACCESS  read−only
        STATUS  mandatory
        ::= { ip 20 }                                                480

ipAddrEntry OBJECT−TYPE
        SYNTAX  IpAddrEntry
        ACCESS  read−only
        STATUS  mandatory
        ::= { ipAddrTable 1 }

IpAddrEntry ::=
    SEQUENCE {
        ipAdEntAddr                                                  490
            IpAddress,
        ipAdEntIfIndex
            INTEGER,
        ipAdEntNetMask
            IpAddress,
        ipAdEntBcastAddr
            INTEGER,
        ipAdEntReasmMaxSize
            INTEGER (0..65535)
    }                                                                500

ipAdEntAddr OBJECT−TYPE
        SYNTAX  IpAddress
        ACCESS  read−only
        STATUS  mandatory
        ::=  { ipAddrEntry 1 }

ipAdEntIfIndex OBJECT−TYPE
        SYNTAX  INTEGER
        ACCESS  read−only                                           510
        STATUS  mandatory
        ::=  { ipAddrEntry 2 }

ipAdEntNetMask OBJECT−TYPE
        SYNTAX  IpAddress
        ACCESS  read−only
        STATUS  mandatory
        ::=  { ipAddrEntry 3 }

ipAdEntBcastAddr OBJECT−TYPE                                         520
        SYNTAX  INTEGER
        ACCESS  read−only
        STATUS  mandatory
        ::= { ipAddrEntry 4 }

ipAdEntReasmMaxSiz OBJECT−TYPE
        SYNTAX  INTEGER (0..65535)
        ACCESS  read−only
        STATUS  mandatory
        ::= { ipAddrEntry 5 }                                       530

−− the IP Routing table
```

ipRoutingTable **OBJECT−TYPE**
    SYNTAX SEQUENCE OF IpRouteEntry
    ACCESS read−write
    STATUS mandatory
    ::= { ip 21 }

ipRouteEntry **OBJECT−TYPE**   540
    SYNTAX IpRouteEntry
    ACCESS read−write
    STATUS mandatory
    ::= { ipRoutingTable 1 }

IpRouteEntry ::=
SEQUENCE {
    ipRouteDest
      IpAddress,
    ipRouteIfIndex   550
      INTEGER,
    ipRouteMetric1
      INTEGER,
    ipRouteMetric2
      INTEGER,
    ipRouteMetric3
      INTEGER,
    ipRouteMetric4
      INTEGER,
    ipRouteNextHop   560
      IpAddress,
    ipRouteType
      INTEGER,
    ipRouteProto
      INTEGER,
    ipRouteAge
      INTEGER,
    ipRouteMask
      IpAddress
}   570

ipRouteDest **OBJECT−TYPE**
    SYNTAX IpAddress
    ACCESS read−write
    STATUS mandatory
    ::= { ipRouteEntry 1 }

ipRouteIfIndex **OBJECT−TYPE**
    SYNTAX INTEGER
    ACCESS read−write   580
    STATUS mandatory
    ::= { ipRouteEntry 2 }

ipRouteMetric1 **OBJECT−TYPE**
    SYNTAX INTEGER
    ACCESS read−write
    STATUS mandatory
    ::= { ipRouteEntry 3 }

ipRouteMetric2 **OBJECT−TYPE**   590
    SYNTAX INTEGER
    ACCESS read−write
    STATUS mandatory
    ::= { ipRouteEntry 4 }

ipRouteMetric3 **OBJECT−TYPE**
    SYNTAX INTEGER
    ACCESS read−write
    STATUS mandatory
    ::= { ipRouteEntry 5 }   600

ipRouteMetric4 **OBJECT−TYPE**
    SYNTAX INTEGER
    ACCESS read−write
    STATUS mandatory
    ::= { ipRouteEntry 6 }

ipRouteNextHop **OBJECT−TYPE**
    SYNTAX IpAddress
    ACCESS read−write   610
    STATUS mandatory
    ::= { ipRouteEntry 7 }

ipRouteType **OBJECT−TYPE**
    SYNTAX INTEGER {
        other(1),   −− *none of the following*
        invalid(2),   −− *an invalidated route*
        direct(3),   −− *route to directly connected (sub−)network*
        remote(4)   −− *route to a non−local host/network/sub−network*
    }   620
    ACCESS read−write
    STATUS mandatory
    ::= { ipRouteEntry 8 }

ipRouteProto **OBJECT−TYPE**
    SYNTAX INTEGER {
        other(1),   −− *none of the following*
        local(2),   −− *non−protocol information, e.g., manually configured entries*
        netmgmt(3),   −− *set via a network management protocol*
        icmp(4),   −− *obtained via ICMP, e.g., Redirect*   630
                 −− *the following are gateway routing protocols*
        egp(5),
        ggp(6),
        hello(7),
        rip(8),
        is−is(9),
        es−is(10),
        ciscoIgrp(11),
        bbnSpfIgp(12),
        ospf(13),   640
        bgp(14)
    }
    ACCESS read−only
    STATUS mandatory

```
           ::= { ipRouteEntry 9 }

ipRouteAge OBJECT−TYPE
       SYNTAX INTEGER
       ACCESS read−write
       STATUS mandatory                                    650
       ::= { ipRouteEntry 10 }

ipRouteMask OBJECT−TYPE
       SYNTAX IpAddress
       ACCESS read−write
       STATUS mandatory
       ::= { ipRouteEntry 11 }

−− the IP Address Translation tables
                                                           660
ipNetToMediaTable OBJECT−TYPE
       SYNTAX SEQUENCE OF IpNetToMediaEntry
       ACCESS read−write
       STATUS mandatory
       ::= { ip 22 }

ipNetToMediaEntry OBJECT−TYPE
       SYNTAX IpNetToMediaEntry
       ACCESS read−write
       STATUS mandatory                                    670
       ::= { ipNetToMediaTable 1 }

IpNetToMediaEntry ::=
   SEQUENCE {
       ipNetToMediaIfIndex
           INTEGER,
       ipNetToMediaPhysAddress
           OCTET STRING,
       ipNetToMediaNetAddress
           IpAddress,                                      680
       ipNetToMediaType
           INTEGER
   }

ipNetToMediaIfIndex OBJECT−TYPE
       SYNTAX INTEGER
       ACCESS read−write
       STATUS mandatory
       ::= { ipNetToMediaEntry 1 }
                                                           690
ipNetToMediaPhysAddress OBJECT−TYPE
       SYNTAX OCTET STRING
       ACCESS read−write
       STATUS mandatory
       ::= { ipNetToMediaEntry 2 }

ipNetToMediaNetAddress OBJECT−TYPE
       SYNTAX IpAddress
       ACCESS read−write
       STATUS mandatory                                    700
```

```
              ::= { ipNetToMediaEntry 3 }

ipNetToMediaType OBJECT-TYPE
        SYNTAX INTEGER {
                other(1),      -- none of the following
                invalid(2),    -- an invalidated mapping
                dynamic(3),
                static(4)
            }
        ACCESS read-write                                      710
        STATUS mandatory
        ::= { ipNetToMediaEntry 4 }


-- the ICMP group

icmpInMsgs OBJECT-TYPE
        SYNTAX Counter
        ACCESS read-only
        STATUS mandatory                                       720
        ::= { icmp 1 }

icmpInErrors OBJECT-TYPE
        SYNTAX Counter
        ACCESS read-only
        STATUS mandatory
        ::= { icmp 2 }

icmpInDestUnreachs OBJECT-TYPE
        SYNTAX Counter                                         730
        ACCESS read-only
        STATUS mandatory
        ::= { icmp 3 }

icmpInTimeExcds OBJECT-TYPE
        SYNTAX Counter
        ACCESS read-only
        STATUS mandatory
        ::= { icmp 4 }
                                                               740
icmpInParmProbs OBJECT-TYPE
        SYNTAX Counter
        ACCESS read-only
        STATUS mandatory
        ::= { icmp 5 }

icmpInSrcQuenchs OBJECT-TYPE
        SYNTAX Counter
        ACCESS read-only
        STATUS mandatory                                       750
        ::= { icmp 6 }

icmpInRedirects OBJECT-TYPE
        SYNTAX Counter
        ACCESS read-only
        STATUS mandatory
```

::= { icmp 7 }

icmpInEchos **OBJECT−TYPE**
    SYNTAX Counter
    ACCESS read−only
    STATUS mandatory
    ::= { icmp 8 }

icmpInEchoReps **OBJECT−TYPE**
    SYNTAX Counter
    ACCESS read−only
    STATUS mandatory
    ::= { icmp 9 }

icmpInTimestamps **OBJECT−TYPE**
    SYNTAX Counter
    ACCESS read−only
    STATUS mandatory
    ::= { icmp 10 }

icmpInTimestampReps **OBJECT−TYPE**
    SYNTAX Counter
    ACCESS read−only
    STATUS mandatory
    ::= { icmp 11 }

icmpInAddrMasks **OBJECT−TYPE**
    SYNTAX Counter
    ACCESS read−only
    STATUS mandatory
    ::= { icmp 12 }

icmpInAddrMaskReps **OBJECT−TYPE**
    SYNTAX Counter
    ACCESS read−only
    STATUS mandatory
    ::= { icmp 13 }

icmpOutMsgs **OBJECT−TYPE**
    SYNTAX Counter
    ACCESS read−only
    STATUS mandatory
    ::= { icmp 14 }

icmpOutErrors **OBJECT−TYPE**
    SYNTAX Counter
    ACCESS read−only
    STATUS mandatory
    ::= { icmp 15 }

icmpOutDestUnreachs **OBJECT−TYPE**
    SYNTAX Counter
    ACCESS read−only
    STATUS mandatory
    ::= { icmp 16 }

icmpOutTimeExcds **OBJECT−TYPE**
    SYNTAX Counter
    ACCESS read−only
    STATUS mandatory
    ::= { icmp 17 }

icmpOutParmProbs **OBJECT−TYPE**
    SYNTAX Counter
    ACCESS read−only
    STATUS mandatory
    ::= { icmp 18 }

820

icmpOutSrcQuenchs **OBJECT−TYPE**
    SYNTAX Counter
    ACCESS read−only
    STATUS mandatory
    ::= { icmp 19 }

830

icmpOutRedirects **OBJECT−TYPE**
    SYNTAX Counter
    ACCESS read−only
    STATUS mandatory
    ::= { icmp 20 }

icmpOutEchos **OBJECT−TYPE**
    SYNTAX Counter
    ACCESS read−only
    STATUS mandatory
    ::= { icmp 21 }

840

icmpOutEchoReps **OBJECT−TYPE**
    SYNTAX Counter
    ACCESS read−only
    STATUS mandatory
    ::= { icmp 22 }

icmpOutTimestamps **OBJECT−TYPE**
    SYNTAX Counter
    ACCESS read−only
    STATUS mandatory
    ::= { icmp 23 }

850

icmpOutTimestampReps **OBJECT−TYPE**
    SYNTAX Counter
    ACCESS read−only
    STATUS mandatory
    ::= { icmp 24 }

860

icmpOutAddrMasks **OBJECT−TYPE**
    SYNTAX Counter
    ACCESS read−only
    STATUS mandatory
    ::= { icmp 25 }

icmpOutAddrMaskReps **OBJECT−TYPE**
    SYNTAX Counter

```
        ACCESS read−only
        STATUS mandatory                                         870
        ::= { icmp 26 }


−− the TCP group

tcpRtoAlgorithm OBJECT−TYPE
        SYNTAX INTEGER {
                other(1),    −− none of the following
                constant(2), −− a constant rto
                rsre(3),     −− MIL−STD−1778, Appendix B      880
                vanj(4)      −− Van Jacobson's algorithm
        }
        ACCESS read−only
        STATUS mandatory
        ::= { tcp 1 }

tcpRtoMin OBJECT−TYPE
        SYNTAX INTEGER
        ACCESS read−only
        STATUS mandatory                                         890
        ::= { tcp 2 }

tcpRtoMax OBJECT−TYPE
        SYNTAX INTEGER
        ACCESS rcad  only
        STATUS mandatory
        ::= { tcp 3 }

tcpMaxConn OBJECT−TYPE
        SYNTAX INTEGER                                           900
        ACCESS read−only
        STATUS mandatory
        ::= { tcp 4 }

tcpActiveOpens OBJECT−TYPE
        SYNTAX Counter
        ACCESS read−only
        STATUS mandatory
        ::= { tcp 5 }
                                                                 910
tcpPassiveOpens OBJECT−TYPE
        SYNTAX Counter
        ACCESS read−only
        STATUS mandatory
        ::= { tcp 6 }

tcpAttemptFails OBJECT−TYPE
        SYNTAX Counter
        ACCESS read−only
        STATUS mandatory                                         920
        ::= { tcp 7 }

tcpEstabResets OBJECT−TYPE
        SYNTAX Counter
```

      ACCESS read−only
      STATUS mandatory
      ::= { tcp 8 }

tcpCurrEstab **OBJECT−TYPE**
      SYNTAX Gauge
      ACCESS read−only
      STATUS mandatory
      ::= { tcp 9 }

930

tcpInSegs **OBJECT−TYPE**
      SYNTAX Counter
      ACCESS read−only
      STATUS mandatory
      ::= { tcp 10 }

940

tcpOutSegs **OBJECT−TYPE**
      SYNTAX Counter
      ACCESS read−only
      STATUS mandatory
      ::= { tcp 11 }

tcpRetransSegs **OBJECT−TYPE**
      SYNTAX Counter
      ACCESS read−only
      STATUS mandatory
      ::= { tcp 12 }

950

−− *the TCP connections table*

tcpConnTable **OBJECT−TYPE**
      SYNTAX SEQUENCE OF TcpConnEntry
      ACCESS read−only
      STATUS mandatory
      ::= { tcp 13 }

960

tcpConnEntry **OBJECT−TYPE**
      SYNTAX TcpConnEntry
      ACCESS read−only
      STATUS mandatory
      ::= { tcpConnTable 1 }

TcpConnEntry ::=
  SEQUENCE {
      tcpConnState
        INTEGER,
      tcpConnLocalAddress
        IpAddress,
      tcpConnLocalPort
        INTEGER (0..65535),
      tcpConnRemAddress
        IpAddress,
      tcpConnRemPort
        INTEGER (0..65535)
  }

970

980

```
tcpConnState OBJECT–TYPE
        SYNTAX INTEGER {
                    closed(1),
                    listen(2),
                    synSent(3),
                    synReceived(4),
                    established(5),
                    finWait1(6),
                    finWait2(7),
                    closeWait(8),
                    lastAck(9),
                    closing(10),
                    timeWait(11)
                }
        ACCESS read–only
        STATUS mandatory
        ::= { tcpConnEntry 1 }

tcpConnLocalAddress OBJECT–TYPE
        SYNTAX IpAddress
        ACCESS read–only
        STATUS mandatory
        ::= { tcpConnEntry 2 }

tcpConnLocalPort OBJECT–TYPE
        SYNTAX INTEGER (0..65535)
        ACCESS read–only
        STATUS mandatory
        ::= { tcpConnEntry 3 }

tcpConnRemAddress OBJECT–TYPE
        SYNTAX IpAddress
        ACCESS read–only
        STATUS mandatory
        ::= { tcpConnEntry 4 }

tcpConnRemPort OBJECT–TYPE
        SYNTAX INTEGER (0..65535)
        ACCESS read–only
        STATUS mandatory
        ::= { tcpConnEntry 5 }

–– additional TCP variables

tcpInErrs OBJECT–TYPE
        SYNTAX Counter
        ACCESS read–only
        STATUS mandatory
        ::= { tcp 14 }

tcpOutRsts OBJECT–TYPE
        SYNTAX Counter
        ACCESS read–only
        STATUS mandatory
        ::= { tcp 15 }
```

990

1000

1010

1020

1030

-- the UDP group

udpInDatagrams **OBJECT-TYPE**
      SYNTAX Counter
      ACCESS read-only
      STATUS mandatory
      ::= { udp 1 }

udpNoPorts **OBJECT-TYPE**
      SYNTAX Counter
      ACCESS read-only
      STATUS mandatory
      ::= { udp 2 }

udpInErrors **OBJECT-TYPE**
      SYNTAX Counter
      ACCESS read-only
      STATUS mandatory
      ::= { udp 3 }

udpOutDatagrams **OBJECT-TYPE**
      SYNTAX Counter
      ACCESS read-only
      STATUS mandatory
      ::= { udp 4 }

-- the UDP listener table

udpTable **OBJECT-TYPE**
      SYNTAX **SEQUENCE OF** UdpEntry
      ACCESS read-only
      STATUS mandatory
      ::= { udp 5 }

udpEntry **OBJECT-TYPE**
      SYNTAX UdpEntry
      ACCESS read-only
      STATUS mandatory
      ::= { udpTable 1 }

UdpEntry ::=
  SEQUENCE {
      udpLocalAddress
        IpAddress,
      udpLocalPort
        INTEGER (0..65535)
  }

udpLocalAddress **OBJECT-TYPE**
      SYNTAX IpAddress
      ACCESS read-only
      STATUS mandatory
      ::= { udpEntry 1 }

udpLocalPort **OBJECT-TYPE**
      SYNTAX INTEGER (0..65535)

1040

1050

1060

1070

1080

1090

ACCESS read−only
STATUS mandatory
::= { udpEntry 2 }

−− the EGP group

egpInMsgs **OBJECT−TYPE**   1100
    SYNTAX Counter
    ACCESS read−only
    STATUS mandatory
    ::= { egp 1 }

egpInErrors **OBJECT−TYPE**
    SYNTAX Counter
    ACCESS read−only
    STATUS mandatory
    ::= { egp 2 }   1110

egpOutMsgs **OBJECT−TYPE**
    SYNTAX Counter
    ACCESS read−only
    STATUS mandatory
    ::= { egp 3 }

egpOutErrors **OBJECT−TYPE**
    SYNTAX Counter
    ACCESS read−only   1120
    STATUS mandatory
    ::= { egp 4 }

−− the EGP Neighbor table

egpNeighTable **OBJECT−TYPE**
    SYNTAX **SEQUENCE OF** EgpNeighEntry
    ACCESS read−only
    STATUS mandatory
    ::= { egp 5 }   1130

egpNeighEntry **OBJECT−TYPE**
    SYNTAX EgpNeighEntry
    ACCESS read−only
    STATUS mandatory
    ::= { egpNeighTable 1 }

EgpNeighEntry ::=
  SEQUENCE {
    egpNeighState   1140
      INTEGER,
    egpNeighAddr
      IpAddress,
    egpNeighAs
      INTEGER,
    egpNeighInMsgs
      Counter,
    egpNeighInErrs

```
                    Counter,
            egpNeighOutMsgs                                                 1150
                    Counter,
            egpNeighOutErrs
                    Counter,
            egpNeighInErrMsgs
                    Counter,
            egpNeighOutErrMsgs
                    Counter,
            egpNeighStateUps
                    Counter,
            egpNeighStateDowns                                              1160
                    Counter,
            egpNeighIntervalHello
                    INTEGER,
            egpNeighIntervalPoll
                    INTEGER,
            egpNeighMode
                    INTEGER,
            egpNeighEventTrigger
                    INTEGER
    }                                                                      1170

egpNeighState OBJECT-TYPE
        SYNTAX INTEGER {
                    idle(1),
                    acquisition(2),
                    down(3),
                    up(4),
                    cease(5)
                }
        ACCESS read-only                                                   1180
        STATUS mandatory
        ::= { egpNeighEntry 1 }

egpNeighAddr OBJECT-TYPE
        SYNTAX IpAddress
        ACCESS read-only
        STATUS mandatory
        ::= { egpNeighEntry 2 }

egpNeighAs OBJECT-TYPE                                                     1190
        SYNTAX INTEGER
        ACCESS read-only
        STATUS mandatory
        ::= { egpNeighEntry 3 }

egpNeighInMsgs OBJECT-TYPE
        SYNTAX Counter
        ACCESS read-only
        STATUS mandatory
        ::= { egpNeighEntry 4 }                                           1200

egpNeighInErrs OBJECT-TYPE
        SYNTAX Counter
        ACCESS read-only
```

```
        STATUS mandatory
        ::= { egpNeighEntry 5 }

egpNeighOutMsgs OBJECT-TYPE
        SYNTAX Counter
        ACCESS read-only                                    1210
        STATUS mandatory
        ::= { egpNeighEntry 6 }

egpNeighOutErrs OBJECT-TYPE
        SYNTAX Counter
        ACCESS read-only
        STATUS mandatory
        ::= { egpNeighEntry 7 }

egpNeighInErrMsgs OBJECT-TYPE                                1220
        SYNTAX Counter
        ACCESS read-only
        STATUS mandatory
        ::= { egpNeighEntry 8 }

egpNeighOutErrMsgs OBJECT-TYPE
        SYNTAX Counter
        ACCESS read-only
        STATUS mandatory
        ::= { egpNeighEntry 9 }                             1230

egpNeighStateUps OBJECT-TYPE
        SYNTAX Counter
        ACCESS read-only
        STATUS mandatory
        ::= { egpNeighEntry 10 }

egpNeighStateDowns OBJECT-TYPE
        SYNTAX Counter
        ACCESS read-only                                    1240
        STATUS mandatory
        ::= { egpNeighEntry 11 }

egpNeighIntervalHello OBJECT-TYPE
        SYNTAX INTEGER
        ACCESS read-only
        STATUS mandatory
        ::= { egpNeighEntry 12 }

egpNeighIntervalPoll OBJECT-TYPE                            1250
        SYNTAX INTEGER
        ACCESS read-only
        STATUS mandatory
        ::= { egpNeighEntry 13 }

egpNeighMode OBJECT-TYPE
        SYNTAX INTEGER {
                active(1),
                passive(2)
                }                                           1260
```

```
        ACCESS read−only
        STATUS mandatory
        ::= { egpNeighEntry 14 }

egpNeighEventTrigger OBJECT−TYPE
        SYNTAX INTEGER {
                start(1),
                stop(2)
            }
        ACCESS read−write
        STATUS mandatory
        ::= { egpNeighEntry 15 }

−− additional EGP variables

egpAs OBJECT−TYPE
        SYNTAX INTEGER
        ACCESS read−only
        STATUS mandatory
        ::= { egp 6 }


−− the Transmission group (empty at present)


−− the SNMP group

snmpInPkts OBJECT−TYPE
        SYNTAX Counter
        ACCESS read−only
        STATUS mandatory
        ::= { snmp 1 }

snmpOutPkts OBJECT−TYPE
        SYNTAX Counter
        ACCESS read−only
        STATUS mandatory
        ::= { snmp 2 }

snmpInBadVersions OBJECT−TYPE
        SYNTAX Counter
        ACCESS read−only
        STATUS mandatory
        ::= { snmp 3 }

snmpInBadCommunityNames OBJECT−TYPE
        SYNTAX Counter
        ACCESS read−only
        STATUS mandatory
        ::= { snmp 4 }

snmpInBadCommunityUses OBJECT−TYPE
        SYNTAX Counter
        ACCESS read−only
        STATUS mandatory
        ::= { snmp 5 }
```

1270

1280

1290

1300

1310

snmpInASNParseErrs **OBJECT − TYPE**
      SYNTAX Counter
      ACCESS read−only   1320
      STATUS mandatory
      ::= { snmp 6 }

snmpInBadTypes **OBJECT − TYPE**
      SYNTAX Counter
      ACCESS read−only
      STATUS mandatory
      ::= { snmp 7 }

snmpInTooBigs **OBJECT − TYPE**   1330
      SYNTAX Counter
      ACCESS read−only
      STATUS mandatory
      ::= { snmp 8 }

snmpInNoSuchNames **OBJECT − TYPE**
      SYNTAX Counter
      ACCESS read−only
      STATUS mandatory
      ::= { snmp 9 }   1340

snmpInBadValues **OBJECT − TYPE**
      SYNTAX Counter
      ACCESS rcad−only
      STATUS mandatory
      ::= { snmp 10 }

snmpInReadOnlys **OBJECT − TYPE**
      SYNTAX Counter
      ACCESS read−only   1350
      STATUS mandatory
      ::= { snmp 11 }

snmpInGenErrs **OBJECT − TYPE**
      SYNTAX Counter
      ACCESS read−only
      STATUS mandatory
      ::= { snmp 12 }

snmpInTotalReqVars **OBJECT − TYPE**   1360
      SYNTAX Counter
      ACCESS read−only
      STATUS mandatory
      ::= { snmp 13 }

snmpInTotalSetVars **OBJECT − TYPE**
      SYNTAX Counter
      ACCESS read−only
      STATUS mandatory
      ::= { snmp 14 }   1370

snmpInGetRequests **OBJECT − TYPE**

SYNTAX Counter
ACCESS read−only
STATUS mandatory
::= { snmp 15 }

snmpInGetNexts **OBJECT−TYPE**
SYNTAX Counter
ACCESS read−only   1380
STATUS mandatory
::= { snmp 16 }

snmpInSetRequests **OBJECT−TYPE**
SYNTAX Counter
ACCESS read−only
STATUS mandatory
::= { snmp 17 }

snmpInGetResponses **OBJECT−TYPE**   1390
SYNTAX Counter
ACCESS read−only
STATUS mandatory
::= { snmp 18 }

snmpInTraps **OBJECT−TYPE**
SYNTAX Counter
ACCESS read−only
STATUS mandatory
::= { snmp 19 }   1400

snmpOutTooBigs **OBJECT−TYPE**
SYNTAX Counter
ACCESS read−only
STATUS mandatory
::= { snmp 20 }

snmpOutNoSuchNames **OBJECT−TYPE**
SYNTAX Counter
ACCESS read−only   1410
STATUS mandatory
::= { snmp 21 }

snmpOutBadValues **OBJECT−TYPE**
SYNTAX Counter
ACCESS read−only
STATUS mandatory
::= { snmp 22 }

snmpOutReadOnlys **OBJECT−TYPE**   1420
SYNTAX Counter
ACCESS read−only
STATUS mandatory
::= { snmp 23 }

snmpOutGenErrs **OBJECT−TYPE**
SYNTAX Counter
ACCESS read−only

```
        STATUS mandatory
        ::= { snmp 24 }                                          1430

snmpOutGetRequests OBJECT−TYPE
        SYNTAX Counter
        ACCESS read−only
        STATUS mandatory
        ::= { snmp 25 }

snmpOutGetNexts OBJECT−TYPE
        SYNTAX Counter
        ACCESS read−only                                          1440
        STATUS mandatory
        ::= { snmp 26 }

snmpOutSetRequests OBJECT−TYPE
        SYNTAX Counter
        ACCESS read−only
        STATUS mandatory
        ::= { snmp 27 }

snmpOutGetResponses OBJECT−TYPE                                   1450
        SYNTAX Counter
        ACCESS read−only
        STATUS mandatory
        ::= { snmp 28 }

snmpOutTraps OBJECT−TYPE
        SYNTAX Counter
        ACCESS read−only
        STATUS mandatory
        ::= { snmp 29 }                                          1460

snmpEnableAuthTraps OBJECT−TYPE
        SYNTAX INTEGER {
                    enabled(1),
                    disabled(2)
               }
        ACCESS read−write
        STATUS mandatory
        ::= { snmp 30 }
                                                                  1470
END
```

Appendix D

Ordering ISODE

The *4BSD/ISODE SNMP* package is a part of ISODE. Reproduced here is the announcement for the ISODE 6.0 release. Note that information such as this is always out of date. It is best to call one of the phone numbers listed below to determine current ordering information:

ANNOUNCEMENT

The next release of *The ISO Development Environment* will be available on 24 January 1990. This release is called

ISODE 6.0

This software supports the development of certain kinds of OSI protocols and applications. Here are the details:

- ISODE is not proprietary, but it is not in the public domain. This was necessary to include a "hold harmless" clause in the release. The upshot of all this is that anyone can get a copy of the release and do anything they want with it, but no one takes any responsibility whatsoever for any (mis)use.

- ISODE runs on native Berkeley (BSD4.2 and later) and AT&T (SVR2, SVR3) systems, in addition to various other UNIX-like operating systems. No kernel modifications are required.

- Current modules include:

    - OSI transport service (TP0 on top of TCP and X.25; TP4 for SunLink OSI)
    - OSI session, presentation, and association control services
    - ASN.1 abstract syntax/transfer notation tools, including:
        * remote operations stub-generator
        * structure-generator (ASN.1 to C)
        * element-parser (basic encoding rules)
    - OSI reliable transfer and remote operations services
    - OSI file transfer, access and management
    - FTAM/FTP gateway
    - OSI directory services
    - OSI virtual terminal (basic class, TELNET profile)

- ISODE 6.0 consists of final "IS" level implementations with a few exceptions: ROSE and RTSE are current to the last circulated drafts (March, 1988); VT is a DIS implementation. ISODE also contains implementations of the 1984 X.400 versions of ROS and RTS. ISODE is aligned with the U.S. Government OSI Profile (GOSIP).

- Modules planned for future releases include:

    - OSI message handling system
    - MHS/SMTP gateway

- Although the ISODE is not "supported" per se, it does have an address to which problems may be reported:

    `Bug-ISODE@NISC.NYSER.NET`

    Bug reports (and fixes) are welcome, by the way.

- The discussion group `ISODE@NIC.DDN.MIL` is used as an open forum on ISODE. Contact `ISODE-Request@NIC.DDN.MIL` to be added to this list.

- The primary documentation for this release consists of a five volume User's Manual (approx. 1000 pages) and a set of UNIX manual pages. The sources to the User's Manual are in LaTeX format. In addition, there are a number of notes, papers, and presentations included in the documentation set, again in either LaTeX or SliTeX format.

For more information, contact:

> PSI, Inc.
> PSI California Office
> Attn: Marshall T. Rose
> POB 391776
> Mountain View, CA 94039
> US
>
> +1 415–961–3380

Information on getting a distribution follows on the next page.

DISTRIBUTION SITES

- NORTH AMERICA
  For mailings in NORTH AMERICA, send a check for 375 US
  Dollars to:

  Postal: University of Pennsylvania
                   Department of Computer and Information Science
                   Moore School
                   Attn: David J. Farber (ISODE Distribution)
                   200 South 33rd Street
                   Philadelphia, PA 19104-6314
                   US

  Telephone: +1 215–898–8560

  Specify one of:

  1. 1600bpi 1/2–inch tape, or

  2. Sun 1/4–inch cartridge tape.

  The tape will be written in *tar* format and returned with a documentation set. Do not send tapes or envelopes. Documentation
  only is the same price.

- EUROPE
  For mailings in EUROPE, send a cheque or bankers draft and
  a purchase order for 200 Pounds Sterling to:

  Postal address: Department of Computer Science
                    Attn: Natalie May/Dawn Bailey
                    University College London
                    Gower Street
                    London, WC1E 6BT
                    UK

  For information only:

  Telephone: +44 1–380–7214
  Fax: +44 1–387–1397
  Telex: 28722
  Internet: natalie@cs.ucl.ac.uk
               dawn@cs.ucl.ac.uk

Specify one of:

1. 1600bpi 1/2–inch tape, or

2. Sun 1/4–inch cartridge tape.

The tape will be written in *tar* format and returned with a documentation set. Do not send tapes or envelopes. Documentation only is the same price.

- EUROPE (tape only)
  Tapes without hardcopy documentation can be obtained via the European UNIX User Group (EUUG). The ISODE 6.0 distribution is called EUUGD14.

  Postal: EUUG Distributions
  c/o Frank Kuiper
  Centrum voor Wiskunde en Informatica
  Kruislann 413
  1098 SJ Amsterdam
  The Netherlands

For information only:

  Telephone: +31 20–5924121
  (or +31 20–5929333)
  Telex: 12571 mactr nl
  Telefax: +31 20–5924199
  Internet: `euug-tapes@cwi.nl`

Specify one of:

1. 1600bpi 1/2–inch tape: 130 Dutch Guilders

2. 800bpi 1/2–inch tape: 130 Dutch Guilders

3. Sun 1/4–inch cartridge tape (QIC-24 format): 190 Dutch Guilders

4. 1600 1/2–inch tape (QIC-11 format): 190 Dutch Guilders

If you require DHL, this is possible and will be billed through. Note that if you are not a member of EUUG, then there is an additional handling fee of 300 Dutch Guilders (please enclose a copy of your membership or contribution payment form when ordering). Do not send money, cheques, tapes or envelopes; you will be invoiced.

- AUSTRALIA and NEW ZEALAND
  For mailings in AUSTRALIA and NEW ZEALAND, send a cheque for 250 Dollars Australian to:

    Postal: CSIRO DIT
              Attn: Andrew Waugh (ISODE Distribution)
              55 Barry Street
              Carlton, 3053
              Australia

  For information only:

              Telephone: +61 3–347–8644
              Fax: +61 3–347–8987
              Internet: ajw@ditmela.oz.au

  Specify one of:

    1. 1600/3200/6250bpi 1/2–inch tape, or
    2. Sun 1/4—inch cartridge tape in either QIC-11 or QIC-24 format.

  The tape will be written in tar format and returned with a documentation set. Do not send tapes or envelopes. Documentation only is the same price.

- Internet
  If you can FTP to the Internet, then use anonymous FTP to the host nisc.nyser.net residing at [192.33.4.10] to retrieve isode-6.tar.Z in BINARY mode from the pub/isode/ directory. This file is the *tar* image after being run through the compress program and is approximately 4.5MB in size.

- NIFTP
  If you run NIFTP over the public X.25 or over JANET, and

are registered in the NRS at Salford, you can use NIFTP with username "guest" and your own name as password, to access `UK.AC.UCL.CS` to retrieve the file `<SRC>isode-6.tar`. This is a 14MB *tar* image. The file `<SRC>isode-6.tar.Z` is the *tar* image after being run through the compress program (4.5MB).

- FTAM on the JANET or PSS
  The source code is available by FTAM at the University College London over X.25 using JANET (DTE 00000511160013) or PSS (DTE 23421920030013) with TSEL 259 (ASCII encoding). Use the "anon" user-identity and retrieve the `<SRC>isode-6.tar`. This is a 14MB *tar* image. The file `<SRC>isode-6.tar.Z` is the *tar* image after being run through the compress program (4.5MB).

- FTAM on the Internet
  The source code is available by FTAM over the Internet at host `osi.nyser.net` residing at [192.33.4.10] (TCP port 102 selects the OSI transport service) with TSEL 259 (numeric encoding). Use the "anon" user-identity, supply any password, and retrieve `isode-6.tar.Z` from the `pub/isode/` directory. This file is the *tar* image after being run through the compress program and is approximately 4.5MB in size.

For distributions via FTAM, the file service is provided by the FTAM implementation in ISODE 5.0 or later (IS FTAM).

For distributions via either FTAM or FTP, there is an additional file available for retrieval, called `isode-ps.tar.Z` which is a compressed tar image (7MB) containing the entire documentation set in PostScript format.

SUPPORT

A UK company has been set up to provide support for ISODE and associated packages - X-Tel Services Ltd. This company provides an update service, general assistance and site specific support. Although inclusion of this information should not be considered an endorsement,

it should be noted that one of the primary ISODE developers now
works at X-Tel Services Ltd.

Postal address:	ISODE Distribution
	X-Tel Services Ltd.
	13–03 Tower Block
	Nottingham University
	Nottingham, NG7 2RD
	UK

Telephone:	+44 602–412648
Fax:	+44 602–588138
Telex:	37346
Internet:	`xtel@cs.nott.ac.uk`

If other organizations offering formal support for ISODE wish to be
included in future announcements, a suitable index will be organized.

Glossary

abstract syntax: a description of a data type that is independent of machine-oriented structures and restrictions.

Abstract Syntax Notation One: the OSI language for describing abstract syntax.

access mode: the level of authorization implied by an SNMP community.

ACK: the *acknowledgement* bit in a TCP segment.

active open: the sequence events of occurring when an application entity directs the TCP to establish a connection.

address class: a method used to determine the boundary between the network and host portions of an IP address.

address mask: a 32–bit quantity indicating which bits in an IP address refer to the network portion.

address resolution: a means for mapping network-layer addresses onto media-specific addresses.

Address Resolution Protocol: the protocol in the Internet suite of protocols used to map IP addresses onto Ethernet (and other media) addresses.

administrative framework: a scheme for defining a policy of authentication and authorization.

agent: see *network management agent.*

American National Standards Institute: the U.S. national standardization body. ANSI is a member of ISO.

ANSI: see *American National Standards Institute.*

AP: see *application process.*

API: see *Application Programmer's Interface.*

application layer: that portion of an OSI system ultimately responsible for managing communication between application processes (APs).

Applications Programmer's Interface: a set of calling conventions defining how a service is invoked through a software package.

ARP: see *Address Resolution Protocol.*

authentication entity: that portion of an SNMP agent responsible for verifying that an SNMP entity is a member of the community it claims to be in. This entity is also responsible for encoding/decoding SNMP messages according to the authentication algorithm of a given community.

ARPA: see *Defense Advanced Research Projects Agency.*

ASN.1: see *Abstract Syntax Notation One.*

Basic Encoding Rules: the OSI language for describing transfer syntax.

BER: see *Basic Encoding Rules.*

broadcast address: a media-specific or IP address referring to all stations on a media.

broadcasting: the act of sending to the broadcast address.

C: the *C programming language.*

Case Diagram: a pictorial representation of the relationship between counter objects in a MIB.

CCITT: see *International Telephone and Telegraph Consultative Committee.*

checksum: an arithmetic sum used to verify data integrity.

CL-mode: see *connection-less mode.*

CLNS: *connectionless-mode network service*

CLTS: *connectionless-mode transport service*

CMIP: see *Common Management Information Protocol.* Sometimes confused with the *(overly) Complex Management Information Protocol.* Of course, it doesn't exist.

CMIP over TCP: a mapping of the OSI network management framework to management of networks based on the Internet suite of protocols. Commonly thought of as "an idea whose time has come and gone."

CMIS: see *Common Mangement Information Service.*

CMISE: see *Common Management Information Service Element.*

CMOT: see *CMIP over TCP.*

CO-mode: see *connection-oriented mode.*

Common Management Information Protocol: the OSI protocol for network management.

Common Management Information Service: the service offered by CMIP.

Common Management Information Service Element: the application service element responsible for exchanging network management information.

community: an administrative relationship between SNMP entities.

community name: an opaque string of octets identifying a community.

community profile: that portion of the managed objects on an agent that a member of the community is allowed to manipulate.

connection: a logical binding between two or more users of a service.

connection-less mode: a service that has a single phase involving control mechanisms such as addressing in addition to data transfer.

connection-oriented mode: a service that has three distinct phases: *establishment,* in which two or more users are bound to a connection; *data transfer,* in which data is exchanged between the users; and, *release,* in which the binding is terminated.

CONS: *connection-oriented network service*

COTS: *connection-oriented transport service*

DARPA: see *Defense Advanced Research Projects Agency.*

DARPA Internet: see *Internet.*

data: (imprecise usage) see *user-data.*

data link layer: that portion of an OSI system responsible for transmission, framing, and error control over a single communications link.

datagram: a self-contained unit of data transmitted independently of other datagrams.

default route: when sending an IP datagram, an entry in the routing table which will be used if no other route is appropriate.

Defense Advanced Research Projects Agency: an agency of the U.S. Department of Defense that sponsors high-risk, high-payoff research. The Internet suite of protocols was developed under DARPA auspices. DARPA was previously known as ARPA, the Advanced Research Projects Agency, when the ARPANET was built.

device: a network element of some kind.

direct routing: the process of sending an IP datagram when the destination resides on the same IP network (or IP subnet) as the sender.

dotted quad notation: a convention for writing IP addresses in textual format.

EGP: see *Exterior Gateway Protocol.*

end-system: a network device performing functions from all layers of the OSI model. End-systems are commonly thought of as hosting applications.

End-System to Intermediate-System Protocol: the ISO protocol used for gateway detection and address resolution.

end-to-end services: the services collectively offered by the lower three layers of the OSI model.

ES: see *end-system.*

ES-IS: see *End-System to Intermediate-System Protocol.*

experimental MIB: a MIB module defined in the experimental portion of the Internet management space.

Exterior Gateway Protocol: a reachability protocol used by gateways in a two-level internet.

External Data Representation: a transfer syntax defined by Sun Microsystems, Inc.

Federal Research Internet: see *Internet.*

File Transfer Protocol: the application protocol offering file service in the Internet suite of protocols.

FIN: the *finish* bit in a TCP segment.

flow control: the mechanism whereby a receiver informs a sender how much data it is willing to accept.

fragment: an IP datagram containing only a portion of the user-data from a larger IP datagram.

fragmentation: the process of breaking an IP datagram into smaller parts, such that each fragment can be transmitted in whole on a given physical medium.

FTP: see *File Transfer Protocol.*

gateway: (Internet usage) a router; also, (imprecise usage) an entity responsible for complex mappings, usually at the application layer.

hardware address: see *media address.*

header: (imprecise usage) see *protocol control information.*

HEMS: see the *High-level Entity Management System.*

High-level Entity Management System: an early internetwork management experiment.

host: (Internet usage) an end-system.

host-identifier: that portion of an IP address corresponding to the host on the IP network.

host-number: that portion of a subnetted IP address corresponding to the host-number on the subnet.

IAB: see *Internet Activities Board.*

IANA: see *Internet Assigned Numbers Authority.*

ICMP: see *Internet Control Message Protocol.*

IEEE: see *Institute of Electrical and Electronics Engineers.*

IESG: see *Internet Engineering Steering Group.*

IETF: see *Internet Engineering Task Force.*

indirect routing: the process of sending an IP datagram to a gateway for (ultimate) forwarding to the destination.

instance: see *object instance.*

instance-identifier: a means of identifying an instance of a particular object type.

Institute of Electrical and Electronics Engineers: a professional organization, which, as a part of its services to the community, performs some pre-standardization work for OSI.

interface layer: the layer in the Internet suite of protocols responsible for transmission on a single physical network.

intermediate-system: a network device performing functions from the three lower-layers of the OSI model. Intermediate-systems are commonly thought of as routing data for end-systems.

International Organization for Standardization: the organization that produces many of the world's standards. OSI is only one of many areas standardized by the ISO/IEC.

International Standards Organization: there is no such thing. See the *International Organization for Standardization.*

International Telephone and Telegraph Consultative Committee: a body comprising the national Post, Telephone, and Telegraph (PTT) administrations.

Internet: a large collection of connected networks, primarily in the United States, running the Internet suite of protocols. Sometimes referred to as the *DARPA Internet*, *NSF/DARPA Internet*, or the *Federal Research Internet*.

Internet Activities Board: the technical body overseeing the development of the Internet suite of protocols.

Internet Assigned Numbers Authority: the entity responsible for assigning numbers in the Internet suite of protocols.

Internet Community: anyone, anywhere, who uses the Internet suite of protocols.

Internet Control Message Protocol: a simple reporting protocol for IP.

Internet Drafts: a means of documenting the work in progress of the IETF.

Internet Engineering Steering Group: the group coordinating the activities of the IETF.

Internet Engineering Task Force: a task force of the Internet Activities Board charged with resolving the short-term needs of the Internet.

internet layer: the layer in the Internet suite of protocols responsible for providing transparency over both the topology of the internet and the transmission media used in each physical network.

Internet Protocol: the network protocol offering a connectionless-mode network service in the Internet suite of protocols.

Internet suite of protocols: a collection of computer-communication protocols originally developed under DARPA sponsorship. The Internet suite of protocols is currently the de facto solution for open networking.

internet: (Internet usage) a network in the OSI sense; historically termed a *catenet*. The Internet is the largest internet in existence.

Internet-standard Network Management Framework: RFCs 1155, 1156, and 1157.

Internet-standard MIB: RFC 1156.

Internet-standard SMI: RFC 1155.

IP address: a 32–bit quantity used to represent a point of attachment in an internet.

ISO Development Environment: a research tool developed to study the upper-layers of OSI. It is an unfortunate historical coincidence that the first three letters of ISODE are "ISO." This is not an acronym for the International Organization for Standardization, but rather three letters which, when pronounced in English, produce a pleasing sound.

ISO/IEC: see *International Organization for Standardization.*

ISODE: see *ISO Development Environment.*

kernel dive: the process of reading data structures out of the UNIX kernel to determine the state of its protocol entities.

LAN: see *local area network.*

layer management entity: in OSI, the instrumentation within a layer which talks to the SMAE.

leaf object: an object type defined in a MIB module which has no child nodes. In particular, tables and rows are not leaf objects.

lexicographic ordering: a collation scheme.

lightweight presentation protocol: a protocol implementing a minimal OSI presentation service, but doing so using a special-purpose protocol.

LME: see *layer management entity.*

local area network: any one of a number of technologies providing high-speed, low-latency transfer and being limited in geographic size.

LPP: see *lightweight presentation protocol.*

managed node: a network device containing a network management agent implementation.

management framework: see *Internet-standard Network Management Framework.*

Management Information Base: a collection of objects that can be accessed via a network management protocol. See *Structure of Management Information.*

management protocol: see *network management protocol.*

management station: see *network management station.*

maximum transmission unit: the largest amount of user-data (e.g., the largest size of an IP datagram) that can be sent in a single frame on a particular medium.

media address: the address of a physical interface.

media device: a low-level device which does not use a protocol at the internet layer as its primary function.

MIB: see *Management Information Base.*

MIB module: a collection of managed objects.

MIB view: see *view.*

MIB-I: see the *Internet-standard MIB.*

MIB-II: currently RFC 1158; (someday) the successor to MIB-I.

MTU: see *maximum transmission unit.*

multi-homed: a host or gateway with more than one attachment to an IP network.

National Bureau of Standards: see *National Institute of Standards and Technology.*

National Institute of Standards and Technology: the branch of the U.S Department of Commerce charged with keeping track of standardization. Previously known as the *National Bureau of Standards.*

NBS: see *National Bureau of Standards.*

network: a collection of subnetworks connected by intermediate-systems and populated by end-systems; also, (Internet usage) a single subnetwork or a related set of subnetworks in the OSI sense.

network byte order: the Internet-standard ordering of the bytes corresponding to numeric values.

network layer: that portion of an OSI system responsible for data transfer across the network, independent of both the media comprising the underlying subnetworks and the topology of those subnetworks.

network management: the technology used to manage an internet.

network management agent: the implementation of a network management protocol which exchanges network management information with a network management station.

network management protocol: the protocol used to convey management information.

network mangement station: the system responsible for managing the network.

network-identifier: that portion of an IP address corresponding to a network in an Internet.

NIST: see *National Institute of Standards and Technology.*

NMS: see *network management station.*

NSF: *National Science Foundation*

NSF/DARPA Internet: see *Internet.*

OSI: see *Open Systems Interconnection.*

Open Systems Interconnection: an international effort to facilitate communications among computers of different manufacture and technology.

passive open: the sequence of events occurring when an application entity informs the TCP that it is willing to accept connections.

PDU: see *protocol data unit.*

PE: see *presentation element.*

physical layer: that portion of an OSI system responsible for the electro-mechanical interface to the communications media.

ping: a program used to test IP-level connectivity from one IP address to another.

port number: identifies an application entity to a transport service in the Internet suite of protocols.

powerful get-next operator: what more need be said?

presentation element: in the ISODE, a *C* data structure capable of representing any ASN.1 object in a machine-independent form.

presentation layer: that portion of an OSI system responsible for adding structure to the units of data that are exchanged.

presentation stream: in the ISODE, a set of routines providing an abstraction to provide transformations on presentation elements.

protocol control information: (conceptually) the initial part of a protocol data unit used by a protocol machine to communicate information to its peer.

protocol data unit: a data object exchanged by protocol machines, usually containing both protocol control information and user data.

protocol machine: a finite state machine (FSM) that implements a particular protocol. When a particular input (e.g., user request or network activity) occurs in a particular state, the FSM potentially generates a particular output (e.g., user indication or network activity) and possibly moves to another state.

prototype: (management usage) the object type corresponding to an instance.

pseudo-header: a 96–bit quantity used by a transport protocol in the Internet suite to guard against misbehaving implementations of IP.

PTT: a *post, telephone, and telegraph* authority.

reassembly: the process of recombining fragments, at the final destination, into the original IP datagram.

Request for Comments: the document series describing the Internet suite of protocols and related experiments.

retransmission: the process of repeatedly sending a unit of data while waiting for an acknowledgement.

RFC: see *Request for Comments*.

RFC Editor: the entity responsible for publishing RFCs in the Internet suite of protocols.

router: a level-3 (network layer) relay.

segment: the unit of exchange in the TCP.

selector: a portion of an address identifying a particular entity at an address (e.g., a session selector identifies a user of the session service residing at a particular session address).

service primitive: an artifact modeling how a service is requested or accepted by a user.

session layer: that portion of an OSI system responsible for adding control mechanisms to the data exchange.

SGMP: see *Simple Gateway Monitoring Protocol*.

Simple Gateway Monitoring Protocol: the predecessor of the Simple Network Management Protocol.

Simple Mail Transfer Protocol: the application protocol offering message handling service in the Internet suite of protocols.

Simple Network Management Protocol: the application protocol offering network management service in the Internet suite of Protocols.

SMAE: see *System Management Application-Entity*

SMI: see *Structure of Management Information*.

SMTP: see *Simple Mail Transfer Protocol*.

SMUX: see *SNMP Multiplexing Protocol*.

SMUX peer: an application entity which has formed a SMUX association with an SNMP agent.

SNMP: see *Simple Network Management Protocol.*

SNMP Multiplexing Protocol: a local-mechanism used for communication between an SNMP agent and arbitrary user-processes which export MIB modules to that agent.

SNMP Working Group: the working group of the IETF which standardized the technology used to manage TCP/IP-based internets, and which is ultimately responsible for providing *workable* solutions to the problems of network management for the Internet community.

SNPA: *subnetwork point of attachment*

socket: a pairing of an IP address and a port number.

Structure of Management Information: the rules used to define the objects that can be accessed via a network mangement protocol. See *Management Information Base.*

subnet: (most unfortunate Internet usage) a physical network within an IP network.

subnet mask: a 32–bit quantity indicating which bits in an IP address that identify the physical network.

subnet-number: that portion of an IP host-identifier which identifies a particular physical network within an IP network.

subnetting: the process of using IP subnetting procedures.

subnetwork: a single network connecting several nodes on a single (virtual) transmission medium.

SYN: the synchronize bit in a TCP segment.

system management: the OSI name for network management.

system management application-entity: in an OSI system, the process responsible for coordinating between the LMEs and the management protocol.

TCP: see *Transmission Control Protocol.*

TCP/IP: see *Internet suite of protocols.*

TELNET: the application protocol offering virtual terminal service in the Internet suite of protocols.

three-way handshake: a process whereby two protocol entities synchronize during connection establishment.

TLV: *tag, length, and value*

traceroute: a program used to determine the route from one IP address to another.

transfer syntax: a description of an instance of a data type that is expressed as string of bits.

Transmission Control Protocol: the transport protocol offering a connection-oriented transport service in the Internet suite of protocols.

transport layer: that portion of an OSI system responsible for reliability and multiplexing of data transfer across the network (over and above that provided by the network layer) to the level required by the application.

transport-stack: the combination of protocols, at the transport layer and below, used in a given context.

trivial authentication: password-based.

UDP: see *User Datagram Protocol.*

upper-layer protocol number: identifies a transport entity to the IP.

URG: the urgent bit in a TCP segment.

urgent data: user-data delivered in sequence but somehow more interesting to the receiving application entity.

User Datagram Protocol: the transport protocol offering a connectionless-mode transport service in the Internet suite of protocols.

user-data: conceptually, the part of a protocol data unit used to transparently communicate information between the users of the protocol.

variable: (SNMP usage) a pairing of an object instance name and associated value.

view: the collection of managed objects realized by an agent which is visible to a community.

WAN: see *wide area network*.

well-known port: a transport endpoint which is documented by the IANA.

wide area network: any one of a number of technologies providing geographically distant transfer.

X.121: the addressing format used by X.25–based networks.

X.25: a connection-oriented network facility.

X.409: the predecessor to Abstract Syntax Notation One.

XDR: see *External Data Representation*.

yacc: *yet another compiler compiler*, a UNIX-based compiler generation tool.

Bibliography

[1] DDN Protocol Implementations and Vendors Guide. DDN Network Information Center, August, 1989.

[2] John S. Quarterman. *The Matrix: Computer Networks and Conferencing Systems Worldwide.* Digital Press, 1989. ISBN 1–55558–033–5.

[3] Paul V. Mockapetris. *Domain Names — Concepts and Facilities.* Request for Comments 1033, DDN Network Information Center, SRI International, November, 1987.

[4] Bill Croft and John Gilmore. *Bootstrap Protocol (BOOTP).* Request for Comments 951, DDN Network Information Center, SRI International, September, 1985.

[5] Joyce K. Reynolds. *BOOTP vendor information extensions.* Request for Comments 1084, DDN Network Information Center, SRI International, December, 1988.

[6] Marshall T. Rose. *The Open Book: A Practical Perspective on Open Systems Interconnection.* Prentice-Hall, Englewood Cliffs, New Jersey, 1989. ISBN 0–13–643016–3.

[7] Information Processing Systems — Open Systems Interconnection: Service Conventions. International Organization for Standardization and International Electrotechnical Committee, 1987. Technical Report 8509.

[8] Information Processing Systems — Open Systems Interconnection: Basic Reference Model. International Organization for

Standardization and International Electrotechnical Committee, 1984. International Standard 7498.

[9] Danny Cohen and Jon B. Postel. The ISO Reference Model and Other Protocol Architectures. In *Proceedings of the IFIP Congress*, 1983. Paris, France.

[10] Information Processing Systems — Open Systems Interconnection: Basic Reference Model — Addendum 1: Connectionless-mode Transmission. International Organization for Standardization and International Electrotechnical Committee, 1987. International Standard 7498/AD 1.

[11] Jon B. Postel. *Simple Mail Transfer Protocol*. Request for Comments 821, DDN Network Information Center, SRI International, August, 1982. See also MIL-STD 1781.

[12] Craig Partridge. *Mail Routing and the Domain System*. Request for Comments 974, DDN Network Information Center, SRI International, January, 1986.

[13] David H. Crocker. *Standard for the Format of ARPA Internet Text Messages*. Request for Comments 822, DDN Network Information Center, SRI International, August, 1982.

[14] Jon B. Postel. *File Transfer Protocol*. Request for Comments 959, DDN Network Information Center, SRI International, October, 1985. See also MIL-STD 1780.

[15] Jon B. Postel. *TELNET Protocol Specification*. Request for Comments 854, DDN Network Information Center, SRI International, May, 1983. See also MIL-STD 1782.

[16] *Network File System Protocol Specification*. Sun Microsystems, Inc., Mountain View, California, February, 1986. Part Number 800-1324-03.

[17] Robert W. Scheifler and Jim Gettys. The X Window System. *ACM Transactions on Graphics*, 5(2):79–109, April, 1986. Special Issue on User Interface Software.

[18] Joyce K. Reynolds and Jon B. Postel. *Assigned Numbers*. Request for Comments 1060, DDN Network Information Center, SRI International, March, 1990.

[19] Joyce K. Reynolds and Jon B. Postel. *Official Internet Protocols*. Request for Comments 1011, DDN Network Information Center, SRI International, May, 1987.

[20] Robert T. Braden and Jon B. Postel. *Requirements for Internet gateways*. Request for Comments 1009, DDN Network Information Center, SRI International, June, 1987.

[21] Robert T. Braden. *Requirements for Internet hosts — Application and Support*. Request for Comments 1123, DDN Network Information Center, SRI International, October, 1989.

[22] Robert T. Braden. *Requirements for Internet hosts — Communication Layers*. Request for Comments 1122, DDN Network Information Center, SRI International, October, 1989.

[23] IAB. *IAB Official Protocol Standards*. Request for Comments 1140, DDN Network Information Center, SRI International, May, 1990. Internet Activities Board.

[24] Vinton G. Cerf and Edward A. Cain. The DoD Internet Architecture Model. *Computer Networks and ISDN Systems*, 7(10):307–318, October, 1983.

[25] Andrew S. Tanenbaum. *Computer Networks. Prentice Hall Software Series*, Prentice-Hall, Englewood Cliffs, New Jersey, 1988. ISBN 0–13–162959–X.

[26] The Ethernet — A Local Area Network. Digital Equipment Corporation, Intel Corporation, Xerox Corporation, September, 1980.

[27] Samuel J. Leffler and Mike J. Karels. *Trailer encapsulations*. Request for Comments 893, DDN Network Information Center, SRI International, April, 1984.

[28] David C. Plummer. *Ethernet Address Resolution Protocol.* Request for Comments 826, DDN Network Information Center, SRI International, November, 1982.

[29] J.H. Saltzer, D.P. Reed, and D.D. Clark. End-to-End Arguments in System Design. *Transactions on Computer Systems,* 2(4):277–288, November, 84.

[30] Ed Krol. *The Hitchhikers Guide to the Internet.* Request for Comments 1118, DDN Network Information Center, SRI International, September, 1989.

[31] David L. Mills. *Exterior Gateway Protocol formal specification.* Request for Comments 904, DDN Network Information Center, SRI International, April, 1984.

[32] Kirk Lougheed and Yakov Rekhter. *Border Gateway Protocol.* Request for Comments 1105, DDN Network Information Center, SRI International, June, 1989.

[33] Jeff Mogul and Jon B. Postel. *Internet Standard Subnetting Procedure.* Request for Comments 877, DDN Network Information Center, SRI International, September, 1983.

[34] Jon B. Postel. *Internet Protocol.* Request for Comments 791, DDN Network Information Center, SRI International, September, 1981. See also MIL-STD 1777.

[35] Jon B. Postel. *Internet Control Message Protocol.* Request for Comments 792, DDN Network Information Center, SRI International, September, 1981. See also MIL-STD 1777.

[36] Jon B. Postel. *User Datagram Protocol.* Request for Comments 768, DDN Network Information Center, SRI International, August, 1980.

[37] Jon B. Postel. *Transmission Control Protocol.* Request for Comments 793, DDN Network Information Center, SRI International, September, 1981. See also MIL-STD 1778.

[38] Van Jacobson. Congestion Avoidance and Control. In *Proceedings, SIGCOMM '88 Workshop*, pages 314–329, ACM SIGCOMM, ACM Press, August, 1988. Stanford, CA.

[39] Phil Karn and Craig Partridge. Improving Round-Trip Time Estimates in Reliable Transport Protocols. In *Proceedings, SIGCOMM '87 Workshop*, pages 2–7, ACM SIGCOMM, ACM Press, August, 1987. Stowe, Vermont.

[40] Jeffrey D. Case, James R. Davin, Mark S. Fedor, and Martin L. Schoffstall. Network Management and the Design of SNMP. *ConneXions—The Interoperability Report*, 3(3):22–26, March, 1989. ISSN 0894-5926.

[41] Information Processing — Open Systems Interconnection — Specification of Abstract Syntax Notation One (ASN.1). International Organization for Standardization and International Electrotechnical Committee, 1987. International Standard 8824.

[42] Information Processing — Open Systems Interconnection — Abstract Syntax Notation One (ASN.1) — Draft Addendum 1: Extensions to ASN.1. International Organization for Standardization and International Electrotechnical Committee, 1987. Draft Addendum 8824/DAD 1.

[43] Vinton G. Cerf. *IAB Recommendations for the Development of Internet Network Management Standards*. Request for Comments 1052, DDN Network Information Center, SRI International, April, 1988.

[44] Marshall T. Rose and Keith McCloghrie. *Structure and Identification of Management Information for TCP/IP based internets*. Request for Comments 1155, DDN Network Information Center, SRI International, May, 1990.

[45] Keith McCloghrie and Marshall T. Rose. *Management Information Base Network Management of TCP/IP based internets*. Request for Comments 1156, DDN Network Information Center, SRI International, May, 1990.

[46] Vinton G. Cerf. *Report of the Second Ad Hoc Network Manage-ment Review Group*. Request for Comments 1109, DDN Network Information Center, SRI International, August, 1989.

[47] Marshall T. Rose (editor). *Management Information Base Net-work Management of TCP/IP based internets: MIB-II*. Request for Comments 1158, DDN Network Information Center, SRI In-ternational, May, 1990.

[48] Jeffrey D. Case and Craig Partridge. Case Diagrams: A First Step to Diagrammed Management Information Bases. *Computer Communication Review*, 19(1):13–16, January, 1989.

[49] James R. Davin, Jeffrey D. Case, Mark S. Fedor, and Martin L. Schoffstall. *A Simple Gateway Monitoring Protocol*. Request for Comments 1028, DDN Network Information Center, SRI Inter-national, November, 1987.

[50] Jeffrey D. Case, Mark S. Fedor, Martin L. Schoffstall, and James R. Davin. *A Simple Network Management Protocol*. Re-quest for Comments 1157, DDN Network Information Center, SRI International, May, 1990.

[51] Martin L. Schoffstall, James R. Davin, Mark S. Fedor, and Jef-frey D. Case. *SNMP over Ethernet*. Request for Comments 1089, DDN Network Information Center, SRI International, February, 1989.

[52] Marshall T. Rose (editor). *SNMP over OSI*. Request for Com-ments 1161, DDN Network Information Center, SRI Interna-tional, June, 1990.

[53] Information Processing — Open Systems Interconnection — Specification of Basic Encoding Rules for Abstract Syntax No-tation One (ASN.1). International Organization for Standard-ization and International Electrotechnical Committee, 1987. In-ternational Standard 8825.

[54] Samual P. Leffler, Marshall Kirk McKusick, Michael J. Karels, and John S. Quarterman. *The Design and Implementation of the*

4.3BSD UNIX Operating System. Addison-Wesley Publishing Company, Reading, Massachussettes, 1989. ISBN 0–201–06196–1.

[55] Wengyik Yeong. *SNMP Query Language.* Technical Report 90-03-31-1, Performance Systems International, March, 1990.

Index